Ways of Knowing in Science and Mathematics Series

RICHARD DUSCHL, SERIES EDITOR

ADVISORY BOARD: Charles W. Anderson, Nancy Brickhouse, Rosalind Driver, Eleanor Duckworth, Peter Fensham, William Kyle, Roy Pea, Edward Silver, Russell Yeany

INVESTIGATING REAL DATA IN THE CLASSROOM

expanding children's understanding of math and science

RICHARD LEHRER
LEONA SCHAUBLE

Editors

Teachers College
Columbia University
New York and London

The following figures appeared in previous publications and are used by permission of Lawrence Erlbaum Associates:

Figures 9.2, 9.3, and 9.6 from Lehrer, R., & Schauble, L. (2000). Inventing data structures for representational purposes: Elementary grade students' classification models. *Mathematical Thinking and Learning, 2*(1&2), 51–74.

Figures 1.15, 2.3, 5.6, and 6.2 from Lehrer, R., & Schauble, L. (2000). Model-based reasoning in mathematics and science. In R. Glaser (Ed.), *Advances in instructional psychology, Vol. 5*. Mahwah, NJ: Lawrence Erlbaum Associates.

Published by Teachers College Press, 1234 Amsterdam Avenue, New York, NY 10027

Copyright © 2002 by Teachers College, Columbia University

All rights reserved. No part of this publication may be reproduced or transmitted in any form or by any means, electronic or mechanical, including photocopy, or any information storage and retrieval system, without permission from the publisher.

Library of Congress Cataloging-in-Publication Data

Investigating real data in the classroom : expanding children's understanding of math and science / Richard Lehrer, Leona Schauble, editors.
    p. cm. — (Ways of knowing in science and mathematics series)
  Includes bibliographical references and index.
  ISBN 0-8077-4141-8 (pbk. : acid-free paper)
    1. Mathematical statistics—Study and teaching (Elementary) 2. Mathematical statistics—Graphic methods—Study and teaching (Elementary) I. Lehrer, Richard. II. Schauble, Leona. III. Series.
  QA276.18 .I58 2002
  372.7—dc21   2001048001

ISBN 0-8077-4141-8 (paper)

Printed on acid-free paper
Manufactured in the United States of America

09 08 07 06 05 04 03 02   8 7 6 5 4 3 2 1

Contents

Contents

Acknowledgments

We gratefully thank all teachers and students who participated in the Modeling in Mathematics and Science Program—including those represented in this volume and those who are not authors here. Because we work in a community, many more individuals contributed to this work than the list of authors might lead one to believe. We also thank the staff and students who have participated in the university research project that supported our participation in this work, especially Annie Allen, Pam Asquith, Susan Carpenter, Fay Dremock, Cathlin Foy, Nancy Giles, Cathy Jacobson, Jeff Horvath, Matt Koehler, Lynn Levy, Tracy Madison, Tony Petrosino, Enrique Rueda, and Cassie Shultz. Finally, we are grateful for the encouragement and support that we have consistently received from Robert Gilpatrick, Superintendent; Linda Christensen, Director of Curriculum; Heidi Carvin; and all the building principals in the Verona Area School District.

This work was supported by the National Center for the Improvement of Student Learning and Achievement in Mathematics and Science (R305A600007-98), as administered by the Office of Educational Research and Improvement, U.S. Department of Education; the National Science Foundation; and the James S. McDonnell Foundation. The opinions expressed do not necessarily reflect the position, policy, or endorsement of the supporting agencies.

Introduction

As the complexity of the social and physical worlds escalates, we increasingly rely upon data and data modeling to "see" through the noise and identify the patterns that signal important relationships. Every day brings a flurry of newspapers, advertisements, and magazines, all filled with data-based arguments and positions—many disagreeing, or even competing. Without the ability to understand and evaluate data-based arguments, we are ill equipped to critically weigh the claims of "nine out of ten doctors"; to decide if we should be satisfied with the quality of teaching and learning in our local schools; to vote for or against conservation policies that constrain business development; or to determine whether we think the nation should make economic sacrifices to slow global warming.

And let's be clear, understanding and evaluating the arguments of others, although critical, is hardly enough. We also expect citizens in a participatory democracy to develop and defend their own arguments, to appeal to appropriate reasons and evidence, and to explain their perspectives clearly. Democracy depends upon mutual education and persuasion, so these arguments must both communicate and convince. Because of the ubiquity and importance of data-based arguments, students need repeated opportunities over the course of their schooling to learn to ask and investigate important questions; to construct and structure appropriate data; and to represent, analyze, and marshal data to develop and support claims and chains of reasoning. And if we want students to be able to reason critically and flexibly with data, these activities should be firmly anchored in the everyday practice of school subject-matter study, not relegated to an isolated mathematics or social sciences unit in "data and statistics." Integrating data into genuine investigations is consistent with the professional practice of historians, mathematicians, economists, and scientists, many of whom carry out their everyday work by developing, evaluating, revising, and elaborating increasingly powerful models of theoretically interesting aspects of the world. Many of these models are data models. Accordingly, the Na-

tional Standards promoted by professional organizations such as the National Research Council and the National Council of Teachers of Mathematics prescribe that data and statistics be included early in every student's education, and often thereafter.

But, you may be wondering, shouldn't data and statistics be reserved for higher grades, maybe secondary school and beyond? The teachers who wrote the chapters in this book don't think so, and the chapters constitute the data-based arguments that they are presenting to support this view.[1] The authors are elementary school teachers in Verona, Wisconsin, and partners in the nearby city of Madison, who have been working for several years in a cross-grade forum for the improvement and study of student learning in mathematics and science. This professional community was generated in collaboration between teachers and researchers at the University of Wisconsin and has subsequently been sustained through teacher governance. The purpose of the research collaboration is to improve teaching and learning by developing a public and sharable field of knowledge about the long-term development of student thinking in important ideas in mathematics and science—ideas such as data modeling. In their classrooms and out, in small groups, in cross-grade and within-grade teams, and in district-wide meetings, participating teachers work to construct, test, and finally share a growing base of information about how student knowledge develops across grades. This information includes typical patterns of change, common barriers to change, and instructional repertoires that support student learning. Teachers in the group have found that having a solid understanding of student thinking can provide a foundation for making the myriad on-line decisions entailed in daily instruction. Readers will find that these chapters, which share what the teachers learned in their investigations about student data modeling, provide compelling illustrations that help answer such questions as: (a) What do the standards mean when they say students should be acquiring foundational ideas in data and statistics? (b) What ideas about data are possible and worthwhile to pursue in elementary grades? (c) What varieties of student thinking am I likely to observe in the course of data investigations? (d) What can I do to help these forms of thinking evolve in mathematically and scientifically fruitful ways?

The focus of this volume is on a particular corner of the modeling universe, data modeling. A modeling perspective on data—one in which objects and phenomenona in the world are progressively "mathematized" in data—emphasizes that work with data should always be embedded in contexts of genuine inquiry. Children start by developing their initial familiarity with the target phenomena via direct observation, reading, and conversation. Once interest is engaged, they begin to pose questions, and teachers encourage children to collect, categorize, and evaluate the questions posed by the group. To investigate their questions, students must consider how to "carve up" intact objects and events by describing them as attributes, and then must come to agreement about appropriate ways of measuring attributes and recording the measurements. For example, when second-graders agreed to decide whose Halloween pumpkin was "biggest," they needed first to decide what counted as "big." Was it the tallest? The "biggest around?" The heaviest? How would they measure these attributes, and how could they resolve the disagreement if varying criteria resulted in different answers?

Once constructed, data need to be structured and represented. After recording the colors of all the mittens in their mitten box, a class of first-graders puzzled about the best ways to arrange the information so that they could describe the variety that they observed. Someone proposed making a table with columns headed, "green," "striped," and "other." This led another student to wonder aloud where on the table they would record the mittens that were green *and* striped. And, he asked, wouldn't the "other" column be way too big? The classification system was eventually revised and then re-revised, to support the distinctions that children considered useful and to eliminate those that were considered uninformative. It is important that from the beginning, representations—lists, tables, charts, graphs, and so on—be generated to support disciplinary-based argument, not as mere exercises in "learning to make a table" or "how to do a pie graph." Standards of communication and evidence-based persuasion need to be emphasized throughout. Students propose, justify, and evaluate alternative interpretations that bear on the original questions. Invariably, new questions emerge, often provoked by qualities of the data displays. For example, in the first grade, students studying "rot" decided at one point to map the dispersion of fruit flies from their classroom throughout the school. In chapter 2, Angie Putz explains the discussions that ensued

in the process of settling disagreements about how to count. Children eventually decided to classify classrooms as having "no fruit flies," "a few," "some," or "lots," and a map of the school was color-coded to show classrooms that fit these categories. When they inspected the map, children wondered why the fruit flies had clustered in many classrooms that were distant from the original source, and subsequently initiated a new series of investigations to answer this question. As you might expect, the new investigation about "what fruit flies need to live" motivated the collection and representation of additional data. It is common for one or more new cycles of inquiry to spiral up from the initial one in this manner. This emphasis on the construction and revision of models communicates to students that science is an ongoing pursuit of knowledge, rather than the attainment of a static, final "truth." This view of science contrasts sharply with the one conveyed by "canned" units on data collection or interpretation that are frequently provided by curriculum writers.

It is essential that activities remain anchored in the inquiry cycles that motivate and guide them, rather than being presented in instruction as disembodied activities or "skills." Algorithmic approaches to data are misguided, because in a data modeling context, selection of the best next thing to do can only be decided in light of the overall purpose of the investigation, one's current understanding of the phenomenon, and the standards of argument and evidence at play in the domain under investigation. If students are to use data to think with, they must come to understand how and why data are created and structured. The most effective way to do that is to participate in the process, ideally in the whole process, rather than a truncated part.

As this account suggests, the process of data modeling involves orchestrating a number of components. Each entails significant challenges for children, but as the chapters in this volume illustrate, an effective way for a teacher to begin is to evoke the conceptual and experiential resources that students have at hand. These include a propensity to ask questions about the world; to use language to describe; to make meaning by drawing on previous knowledge and experiences; and to draw, write, and make physical models, such as replicas or copies on a smaller scale. Teachers can then begin to work with students to stretch these initial performances so they become progressively more focused on the issues under investigation and more mathematical. For example, in the course of an investigation about "what helps insects grow better," a class of fifth-graders measured the length of 22 tobacco hornworms on each day of the worms' life cycle. However, once the data were collected, students were unsure how best to assemble and represent them. Debates ensued about the information that should be included on the class chart. Many insisted on including the name of the data collector for each piece of data, and whether that individual was a girl or a boy. (It is common for children to want to include all available information, whether or not it is relevant to the question under investigation.) Over the course of a half-hour debate, however, students eventually concluded that this information was not needed and, moreover, would simply "clutter up" the chart, making it impossible to see the shape of the data.

Given appropriate classroom norms, students can become quite incisive reviewers of their own questions and the questions of others. Similarly, opportunities to experience variation of representations, along with "critique sessions" in which students compare the effectiveness of representations for the purposes at hand, result in the evolution of their beginning representations and inscriptions. Over repeated cycles of revision, these inscriptions become more and more model-like—students come to appreciate their role in describing part of the world rather than copying it and come to understand the approximate nature of these descriptions. The emphasis on modeling serves to anchor instruction in ways of knowing and doing that are more authentic to science and mathematics; to spotlight disciplinary forms of argument, justification, and evidence; and to ensure that student thinking remains central in teachers' decision-making.

Chapter 1, written by university researchers, lays out an overall framework for organizing *Investigating Real Data in the Classroom* and concretely proposes the "big ideas" that are at the heart of teaching and learning about data modeling. This chapter also summarizes some of the important lessons that researchers and teachers have learned together about both the resources and capabilities that students typically have and the difficulties that they encounter in conducting data-based investigations.

The four chapters that immediately follow illustrate how even young students can construct data displays to support argument in ongoing programs of inquiry. Frequently, the data representations are initially developed to support "answers" to questions, but they invariably provoke new questions that were not in mind when the investigation began. In chapter 2, for example, Angie Putz explains how an investigation of decomposition in her second-grade classroom eventually evolved into the study of fruit fly dispersion briefly summarized above.

Jean Gavin recounts in chapter 3 how first- and second-graders documented changes in the traffic patterns on local roadways. These students carefully counted the number of cars passing a target corner, decided how to interpret the resulting distributions of counts, and drew conclusions about whether in fact there had been changes in the traffic flow after the opening of a new highway bypass. Later, students extended the investigation to conduct interviews with local merchants about whether customer visits were declining as traffic was being diverted away from the center of town.

The third-graders in Carmen Curtis's classroom also invented and evaluated alternative data displays for interpreting distributions—in this case, the typical number of items left weekly in each family's recycling bin. In chapter 4 Curtis explains how these students developed and critiqued conventions of frequency graphs.

Sue Wainwright's second-graders investigated a number of ways of modeling changes in their shadows over the course of a day. These representational forms, described in chapter 5, included bar graphs of shadow lengths, drawings, and physical models to explore how the projection of shadows changes with shifts in the position of a light source.

Chapters 6 and 7 share a common focus on displays of relationship and change, in the rather atypical context of exploring appreciation of literature and film. In chapter 6, Jennie Clement summarizes how primary grade students' thinking about representation provides the foundations for coming to understand the design and functions of conventional displays, like bar and line graphs. Deb Lucas, in chapter 7, explains how her sixth-graders constructed data displays that formed an evidence base for sophisticated explanations about the devices that authors use to create interesting text. Rather than imposing conventions for graphing, both teachers encouraged students to invent displays of data. The logic of traditional displays of data becomes more apparent to students once they have tried to solve representational problems for themselves.

In Chapters 8 and 9, the focus shifts to data classification. How can we assign members reliably to a class? Can a classification system be a good way of organizing data to support further inquiry? This is a question that biologists address when they develop or adapt taxonomies and that behavioral researchers confront when they decide which of several behaviors can be considered to be of a common kind. In chapter 8, Erin DiPerna describes how her third-grade students needed to resolve similar problems as they reviewed student portraits and tried to make reliable decisions about the age of the artist. As their ideas were represented in a model that was then tested on new data, students struggled with the possibility that a model might be very effective, yet still fail to preserve some of the details of the original phenomena. The chapter is especially valuable in unpacking the forms of knowledge that needed to be developed along the way—everything from how to section a circle (to create a pie chart) to reasoning about probability. Chapter 9 features an abbreviated and adapted version of the portrait modeling task; here the emphasis is on a cross-grade comparison. Eric James, Sally Hanner, and Mark Rohlfing posed a variant of the portrait model task to their first-, fourth-, and fifth-grade students, respectively. Like the chapters by Clement and Lucas, this chapter provides insight about the limitations and strengths observed in children of different ages working on "the same" project.

Cumulatively, these chapters provide important insights about how children think and reason as they work on data modeling investigations. The primary spotlight is on student understanding and its development. In this Introduction, however, we seek to call readers' attention to a secondary spotlight, as well, one that highlights teachers' professional development of a unique form of knowledge. Most teachers will probably never master as much mathematics or science as the professionals in these disciplines, but why should teachers compete on these grounds? Instead, the expertise that undergirds teaching is a body of knowledge about teaching and its interactions with the long-term development of student thinking about mathematics and science. The development of this knowledge into a field requires professional participation in the activities of representing it, critiquing it, and holding it up to standards of evidence that are public and consensual in the profession. When teachers craft their identities as inquirers and as members of a community of inquirers, they cultivate the conditions for generative and innovative teaching and learning.

This book provides an opportunity to look over the shoulders of teachers who have taken on this challenge. Becoming a virtual "observer" as teachers orchestrate these data modeling activities in their classrooms can help in a number of ways if you are planning to launch your own data modeling investigations with students. First, you may be surprised at what even young students can do if they are given the chance to ask questions, consider how best to pursue them, and generate and revise alternative data representations. Seeing what is possible may raise your confidence level about letting young students take a crack at inventing their own way of representing data to investigate a question of interest to them. Second, you will be able to identify many useful starting points for investigations that you might borrow or adapt for your own students. Equally valuable are the insights about the places where children's thinking is liable to "hang up" on character-

istic misunderstandings or difficulties. Finally, because the authors reflect about how the process of data generation and modeling played out, it is possible for a reader to see how children's interim representations and models helped teachers decide on the next instructional steps to take. In this way, the book serves as a test of one of our premises—that practice-generated models of student thinking can serve as a contribution to the wider teaching profession, especially if we can help others understand their utility in informing teacher decision-making.

Educational researchers will find in these chapters a number of themes that deserve further attention from the research community. One such theme is the close coordination in which inscriptions and conceptual change develop, so that representational change both reflects and inspires cognitive growth. Similarly, the chapters demonstrate new ways of thinking about the collective activity of the group (that is, a classroom of students) and the activity of an individual in the group—a particular student. Traditionally, researchers have focused on one or the other of these levels of analysis, with little consideration of how they intersect. What clearly emerges in the work of the teachers is how collective and individual activity constitute each other, so that individual students both contribute to and are shaped by the forms of epistemology and argument that emerge as norms in the classroom community. Finally, the volume provides a vision about how a set of big ideas (in this case, in data and data modeling) develops across a substantial slice of time—from Grades 1 through 6. The assumption is that development is not some form of spontaneous growth or maturation, but rather, is sensitive to the specific culture and histories of teaching and learning in which an individual participates.

We hope that this information will inspire your own activity, whether teaching, administration, research, or the development of theory—and that, like the teacher-authors in the volume, you also find a way to pass along to others what you learn.

NOTE

1. Neither does the National Council of Teachers of Mathematics, which advocates in its *Principles and Standards for School Mathematics* (2000) that an emphasis on data span *all* grades rather than being reserved for upper grades.

INVESTIGATING REAL DATA IN THE CLASSROOM

Chapter 1

Children's Work with Data

RICHARD LEHRER, NANCY D. GILES, AND LEONA SCHAUBLE

Wisconsin Center for Education Research, School of Education
University of Wisconsin-Madison

When the first-graders in Angie Putz's class wanted to convince the cafeteria cooks that a soup other than tomato should be offered as a lunch selection, they collected data on the soup preferences of students and teachers throughout their elementary school. The activities of these students included discussing how to pose a productive question, collect and record responses, summarize their data, and present it to the cooks in a convincing display. The first-graders' simple question, "What's your favorite soup?" provided experience with some of the same data-handling issues faced by researchers in marketing, agriculture, and the sciences.

When we think about data, images of charts, graphs, and relationships spring to mind. Data, as presented to us in textbooks, newspapers, and magazines, are in formats so familiar that we rarely stop to think about the process of creating data. But creating data is far different from working with the interpreted forms we commonly see in project reports or on television news programs. As we introduce students to working with data, allowing them to experience and resolve the problems associated with collecting, analyzing, and modeling data, we need to explicitly address a number of issues. These issues range from the purposes, methods, and characteristics of data creation and collection to the construction, use, and revision of models that describe or predict patterns in the data. Standards from the National Council of Teachers of Mathematics (2000) and the National Research Council (1996) concur on the

need for an increased emphasis in all grades on working directly with data to formulate and pursue questions of interest. This work should include gathering and organizing data, generating and interpreting data displays, analyzing data, and developing and defending data-based explanations and arguments.

In this chapter, we use the experiences of participating teachers to illustrate some of the opportunities and problems that can arise as students work with data. We begin with a discussion of the role of questions in research and some of the issues that students face in this initial stage of data modeling.

USING RESEARCH QUESTIONS TO GUIDE DATA COLLECTION AND ANALYSIS

Data Are Constructed to Answer Questions

The National Council of Teachers of Mathematics (2000) emphasizes that the study of data and statistics should be firmly anchored in students' inquiry. As explained in their *Standards*, "The Data Analysis and Probability Standard recommends that students formulate questions that can be answered using data and address what is involved in gathering and using the data wisely" (p. 48). Questions are important because they motivate the collection of certain types of information and not others.

Investigating Real Data in the Classroom: Expanding Children's Understanding of Math and Science. Copyright © 2002 by Teachers College, Columbia University. All rights reserved. ISBN 0-8077-4141-8 (pbk.). Prior to photocopying items for classroom use, please contact the Copyright Clearance Center, Customer Service, 222 Rosewood Dr., Danvers, MA 01923, USA, tel. (508) 750-8400.

For example, Jean Gavin wanted her first/second-grade students to explore whether the new highway bypass would affect the traffic flowing through the town of Verona. To answer their research question, the students counted the number of cars, passing a checkpoint at a particular time of day. They did not record the color or make of the cars, because these issues were irrelevant to their guiding question. Similarly, unless we have a question about whether boys and girls differ in their soup preferences, for instance, it is unlikely that we would include the gender of the respondents when collecting data about soup preferences.

Many aspects of data coding (i.e., setting up categories of responses) also depend on the question we want to answer. Why, for example, should it make any difference whether there are 2, 20, or 2,000 data categories? This issue came up in the third-grade, when Erin's students were categorizing self-portraits made by other classes. Because they had no guiding questions to constrain their analysis, the students generated 23 different categories to describe eye shape—a category, as Erin recounted, for "every eyeball shape they could possibly find."

Developing Good Research Questions Can Be a Challenge for Students (and Researchers)

However, there are some basic "ingredients" in research questions that can guide their composition. All research questions (a) must specify the persons or objects of study and (b) focus on issues such as attributes of persons and objects and how they vary. Although Angie Putz's students asked individuals to name their favorite soup, that question was not the overall research question for their project. Rather, the broader question they addressed was, "What are the favorite soups of people at Country View Elementary School?" Because the first-graders used an open-ended question and allowed each respondent to name a favorite soup, they had data that described the variation in soup preferences and the most preferred soup among their target population. (By the way, chicken noodle was named by more people than any other soup and won out over tomato by a long shot.)

Defining the Variables Named in a Research Question Can Take Time

When Angie's students discussed their survey, they realized that they had to define the population they would survey. Eventually, they decided to ask both teachers and students, because the "cafeteria lunch" population comprised both groups. During the discussion of procedures for surveying that population, one student foresaw a problem: "What if they say they have two favorite soups?" After some discussion, the same student proposed the solution: "Just ask them which soup they would want right now." In effect, the student defined the variable of interest—favorite soup—as the one an individual would prefer to eat "right now."

Students benefit from developing explicit research questions and discussing issues concerning which data to collect and the methods and timing they will use to collect it. *Giving students explicit instructions on what to do cuts off this process.* Moreover, discussions of how students plan to record their data can be beneficial. For instance, when a class of first/second-graders prepared for their end-of-the-year archeological dig, some of their most productive discussions involved developing a method for recording the locations of their finds. Thinking ahead about how to record information and exploring various formats on paper and the chalkboard also helped students consider what information they needed to record.

The development of research questions, and their use in creating and collecting data, is the initial phase of data modeling. Good research questions suggest fruitful courses of action and contain the seeds of the genesis of new ones, so this initial phase is often revisited throughout a cycle of inquiry. Once students have collected their data, they must then try to understand what they have recorded.

MAKING SENSE OF DATA

Data interpretation begins with the basic acts of constructing, collecting, and recording data, but making sense of raw data also requires us to abstract, structure, and objectify the data collected. Although we often think of data as "out there," data result from a constructive process. What follows is a discussion of that process.

Defining and Measuring Attributes

Constructing data involves a progressive selection and abstraction of perception. Something spoken is replaced by something written, an event is replaced by a video of that event (what you see depends on camera angle and leaves out smell, taste, texture, etc.), a sensation of heat is replaced by a pointer reading on a thermometer, and so on. Just deciding *what to observe* is a major accomplishment, and one that takes time and effort. Observation is grounded in beliefs about what is important to notice (and why). But beyond that, at all grades, deciding *how to measure* variables of interest also presents an intellectual challenge. We can, of course, "pre-solve" these issues for students by telling them what and how to measure, but students can learn a lot about phenomena and their measurement if they participate in those decisions, explaining and justifying their choices to one another. In Angie Putz's first-grade class, for example, students explored whether there was a relationship between the size of a pumpkin and the number of its seeds. Answering this question required students to come to an agreement about what they meant by *size*. Some children focused on the width of their pumpkins ("I have a really fat pumpkin"); others talked about height or weight. Having made decisions about which attribute to measure, they had to decide how to measure. The discussion that arose not only clarified their conception of size, but also deepened their understanding of measure. Later on, when the children counted the seeds, they realized that they had to come to an agreement about whether or not they should include seeds that were not "full-grown." Similarly, in Deb Lucas's sixth-grade class, students wondered if an idea such as interest could even be measured, and if so, what form such a measure might take. Quantification of interest on a scale took place only after due consideration of other possibilities

After the initial data collection, researchers often find that their data require further abstraction. Categories of an attribute such as "favorite sport" may need to be developed further (e.g., winter sports, summer sports) in order to answer research questions. Conversely, students might find, as did Erin DiPerna's third-graders, that their original number of categories was too precise. After agreeing that 23 categories of eye shape were unwieldy, Erin's students held an extended discussion about the most informative ways to regroup these shapes. Describing items at a fine-grained detail is a natural first step for students who are carefully inspecting items and trying to figure out how they differ. For this reason, it often takes teacher assistance to remind them that this level of detail may not be helpful in identifying categories that can summarize the variability in the entire collection.

Structuring Data

Data do not come with an inherent structure: Structure must be imposed. By this, we mean that the only structure for a set of data comes from an inquirer's prior and developing understanding of the phenomenon being studied. The researcher imposes structure by deciding the focus of the original research question and selecting categories around which to describe and organize the collected data.

Every research question should lead to a data set that contains at least two basic types of information: a name or number identifying who or what was studied and terms that describe the qualities studied. For instance, when some of Mark Rohlfing's fifth-graders gathered data about trees, their data set contained the species of trees studied as well as the circumference and height of each tree. Their focus on tree species, circumference, and height provided a framework for structuring the data.

One format commonly used to structure data is the data table, or *spreadsheet*. The two essential parts of a data table are (a) rows, or *records*, consisting of *cases* (e.g., the individual trees observed); and (b) columns, or *fields*, consisting of the *variables*—the characteristics or measurements of attributes of each case. Each field is given a variable name. These *field labels* provide the means for physically organizing data and aid data summarization. Tables can be constructed using educational software programs such as Tabletop (TERC, 1994) or their commercial counterparts. Table 1.1 shows the table one group of Mark's fifth-graders organized from the data they collected concerning trees growing in the school wood lot. The students organized their *records* on nine trees into three *fields*.

Students often find the concept of field creation tricky to master. Fields are "flat" structures. Because there are no hierarchy or set-subset relationships in the fields other than those the data analyst builds into the structure, field designation requires preplanning in order that questions can be answered about these relationships. When designating fields, students occasionally omit certain information that is obvious to them but that might have a bearing on other fields. For example, the fact that arborvitae trees have needles and that sugar maples have broad leaves is not noted in Table 1.1, even though this information may be related to the information in the other fields.

Sometimes students (even college students) err in the opposite direction, creating fields that are redun-

Table 1.1. Table created by fifth graders based on data they collected on trees in the school woodlot.

Tree Species	Circumference (cm)	Height (cm)
Aborvitae	58	1080
Abrovitae	42	1300
Arborvitae	51	1000
Sugar Maple	140	2000
Sugar Maple	161	1840
Sugar Maple	97	1300
Box Elder	150	2107
Blue Spruce	169	2500
Norway Maple	84	818

dant. We "borrowed" some of the fifth-graders' tree data and created Table 1.2 to illustrate this problem. The two columns in Table 1.2A, labeled "Needle" and "Broad Leaf," provide information that can be combined into one column, as we have done in Table 1.2B. Combining two related fields can make it much easier to compare, for example, tree differences that might relate to leaf type. Class discussion about which fields might have a bearing on the research question and about how to merge or separate attributes into more general or more specific fields can prove to be beneficial to the data collection and less frustrating to the students as they collect and interpret their data.

Objectifying Data

Objectifying data means treating data as objects in their own right: counting them, manipulating data to discover relationships, and asking new questions of already collected data rather than collecting new data. This is a large step for students, who often assume that exploring relationships among different fields (variables) requires a new data collection. In this case, the teacher might consider suggesting that the data students already have may be sufficient for answering a new question.

Often, exploring relationships among different variables leads to new questions. For example, as part of their study of change, Angie's first-graders studied the relationship between the amount of sunlight and the rate of ripening in green tomatos. They noticed, however, that the tomatos placed in sunnier locations were also generally exposed to warmer temperatures. This observation led them to explore whether changes in the

Table 1.2a. A table that contains redundant data.

Tree Species	Circumference (cm)	Height	Needle	Broad Leaf
Aborvitae	58	1080	Yes	No
Sugar Maple	97	1300	No	Yes
Box Elder	150	2107	No	Yes
Blue Spruce	169	2500	Yes	No
Norway Maple	84	818	No	Yes

(Continued)

Table 1.2b. A version that combines the two related fields.

Tree Species	Circumference (cm)	Height	Leaf Type
Aborvitae	58	1080	Needle
Sugar Maple	97	1300	Broad
Box Elder	150	2107	Broad
Blue Spruce	169	2500	Needle
Norway Maple	84	818	Broad

Note: Sometimes students err by creating tables that contain redundant data. The last two columns of data in A are more informative when reduced into one field for leaf type as shown as in B. The tables shown here, although based on student data, were created by authors to illustrate a common student error.

tomatos were primarily due to the amount of sunlight, the temperature, or the effect of both.

Representing selected information in a concrete form, whether in drawings such as those made by Angie's students, in a data table such as those made by Mark's students, or by some other means, is an act that seems simple, but it allows students to separate observations from the original experience and to begin abstracting, objectifying, and structuring the data derived from those observations, measurements, and so on. One way to start this process is to ask students to record their data in ways that make it physically manageable and comprehensible both to themselves and others and to remind them that the original form of data does not have to be maintained. When the students in Angie's class surveyed classmates about their favorite play activities, they originally recorded each response next to the individual's name on a class roll sheet. On the roll sheet, they had data in raw form, with no informative structure. In order to impose structure, the students needed to think about the properties they saw, based upon their knowledge of the data. A few students noted that some of their peers had given the same or similar answers, which they could lump together, forming categories of responses. For instance, one student merged the individual responses of "cat," "dog," and "kitten" into a category she labeled "animals." Learning how to alter the original form of data appropriately into categories that facilitate handling data is an important step in interpreting data.

When students begin to engage in authentic work with data, we want them to consider and plan how they will record their data in addition to thinking about and discussing the question(s) they will address, the information they will collect, and the ways they will collect it. The form and format in which data are recorded should be thought of as tools that allow researchers (whether elementary students or university professors) to concentrate on making sense of their data. Unless students are working with a small data set, however, their first recording of the raw data will not be very revealing, and they may benefit from a renewed discussion of ways to look at/record their data in light of their research question.

In addition to developing an understanding of a data set, the usual objective of working with data is to present a convincing argument to others about what the data shows. In the following sections, we discuss visual displays and statistical summarizations of data—forms for data that can aid understanding and make children's interpretation of the data obvious to their intended audience.

REPRESENTING AND VISUALIZING DATA

We usually need to look at representations of data in order to see or understand general trends. Different displays can tell us different things (e.g., frequencies, proportions, distributions, relationships), but the purpose of every display is to give us a sense of the parts as well as the whole. In this section, we provide classroom examples of some of the data representations students used and some that we think teachers might like to try with their elementary students.

Frequency Tables and Bar Graphs

Frequency tables and bar graphs provide two kinds of information: the categories of data and the frequencies of occurrence within those categories. They are used for data that vary categorically (e.g., by color, name, leaf type) as opposed to data that vary along a continuum (e.g., height, weight, age, temperature).

Because frequency tables and bar graphs reduce the number of data points that have to be considered simultaneously, they help the viewer think about the characteristics of the data. For instance, when Angie Putz's first-graders asked individuals to name their favorite soups, they found that they were collecting data about the types of soups preferred (categorical data) and the number of individuals preferring each type (the frequency with which each type of soup was chosen). Rather than representing the individual responses given by every person surveyed, frequency tables and bar graphs collapse across similar responses. The frequency table in Figure 1.1 lists the categories and frequency of responses Angie's students received and provides a good summarization of the data.

Frequency tables may be preferable when students need to carry out operations on the data (e.g., totaling

Figure 1.1. Students' representations of soup survey (adapted for this example). (a) is a frequency table; (b) is a bar graph. Although frequency tables can aid students' efforts to carry out mathematical operations on the data, bar graphs have greater visual impact.

(a)

Favorite Soup	Frequency
Potato	4
Squid	1
No Soup	9
Noodle	19
Vegetable Beef	20
Tomato	31
Cream of Mushroom	6
Beef Stew	8
Cream of Broccoli	6
Clam Chowder	30
Chicken Noodle	175

(b)

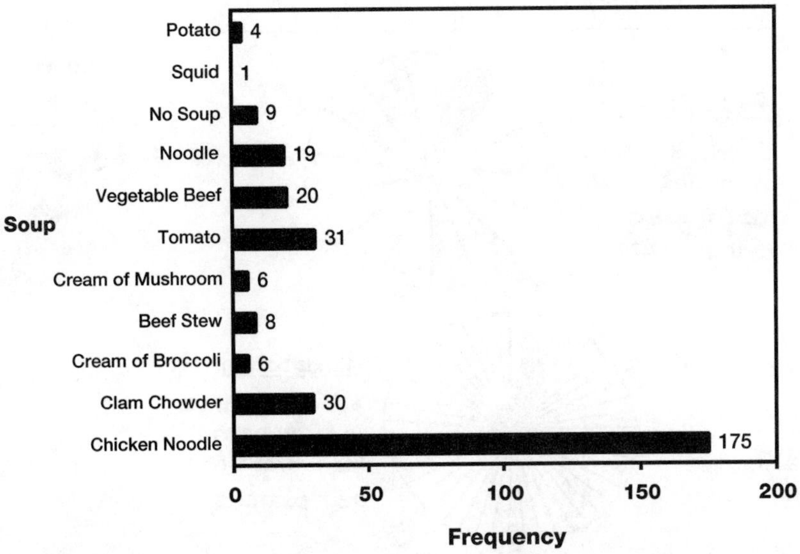

or sorting responses), but the visual impact of a bar graph can often make characteristics of the data easier for students to understand and can help students communicate their interpretations in ways a table cannot. Compare the frequency table in Figure 1.1a with the bar graph in Figure 1.1b. Moving data from one type of display to another can sometimes change the way data is perceived.

Pie Charts

Bar graphs are generally used to compare frequencies. But what if we wanted to look at proportions? We could position the bars end to end: Such a representation would show one long bar of responses, with the length of each section (category) seen in proportion to the whole (total number of responses). Another common way of showing proportions of the whole is with a pie chart (circle graph). Pie charts help us to see relative proportions of categorical data at a glance. They are useful for comparisons in which the base rates are not equal. For example, the third-graders in Erin DiPerna's class used pie charts to study and describe their data. The pie charts in Figure 1.2 show the proportion of prekindergarten and kindergarten students in their study whose self-portraits depicted hands with five fingers. According to the charts, although only one child in prekindergarten versus three children in kindergarten included all five fingers, the proportions of the total students in each class who did so are very similar.

Frequency Distributions

Whereas frequency tables, bar graphs, and pie charts provide information on variables that are in the form of categories, frequency distributions show the frequency and magnitude of cases within a single, continuous variable such as height or circumference. Because they display both the frequency and magnitude of cases within a two-dimensional field, frequency distributions also provide a visual representation of characteristics such as the general shape, center (typicality) and variability (range, clustering) of a data set.

Frequency Graphs. A frequency graph of a data set can be formed easily by using a number line as a base on which to stack individual cases of the same magnitude. For example, the frequency graph in Figure 1.3 shows the variation in the heights of a batch of Wisconsin Fast Plants (Wisconsin Alumni Research Foundation, 1989) grown in a fourth-grade classroom.

Notice that by looking at the frequency graph, we get a sense of center, spread, and clustering. We also can see that at least one plant stands out from the crowd. Outliers, such as this one, can sometimes result from measurement error but should not be dismissed without consideration just because they are unusual. For example, one team of Jean Gavin's first/second-graders counted approximately twice as many cars passing through Verona as did the other three teams. Their count was an extreme outlier on the frequency graph. After an interesting discussion, the students decided that, unlike the other teams, that group probably had counted cars traveling in both directions. Because of the discussion and their decision, they discarded the value.

Figure 1.2. Pie charts comparing the proportions of prekindergarten and kindergarten students who drew five fingered self portraits.

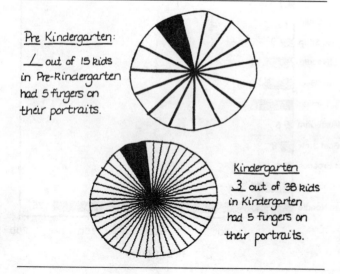

Pre Kindergarten:

_1_ out of 15 kids in Pre-Kindergarten had 5 fingers on their portraits.

Kindergarten

_3_ out of 38 kids in Kindergarten had 5 fingers on their portraits.

Figure 1.3. Frequency graph of the final heights of fourth graders' Fast Plants.

```
                              X
                              X
                              X
                         X  X
                         X  X
                         X X X
              X      X X X              X
  0   5   10  15  20  25  30  35  40
```

Height in Centimeters

Stem-and-Leaf Displays. Stem-and-leaf displays also illustrate the frequency and magnitudes of cases within a single continuous variable. Like the frequency graph, a stem-and-leaf plot shows every case in a data set. A stem-and-leaf is easily made by lining up common values, using the numbers in the tens places, for example, as the "stems," and hanging the "leaf," the first (rightmost) digit in each number from the stems. For example, in Figure 1.4, the leftmost digits on the display, or the "stems" (1, 2, 3, and 4), categorize the measurements between 10 and 19, 20 and 29, 30 and 39, 40 and 49, respectively. Following these stems are the "leaves," the digits representing each of the measurements. Constructing these displays helps students think about convenient partitions of the data (the stem) and also helps them see "clumps" and "holes." The fact that each case is represented helps students reason simultaneously about the individual cases and the aggregate (the shape of the display).

The stem-and-leaf displays in Figure 1.4 show the final heights of Fast Plants, measured in centimeters, that were grown in two different classrooms. The set of data in Figure 1.4a is the same data set displayed in the frequency graph in Figure 1.3. The second set of data (see Figure 1.4b) was provided by the third-graders in the classroom of Carmen Curtis. Compare the two displays. Most of the Fast Plants grew within the same range for height, between 9 and 40 cm. However, the heights of the plants represented in Figure 1.4a were more clustered than those represented in Figure 1.4b.

Histograms. Histograms show the same type of information as frequency graphs and stem-and-leaf displays but do not represent each case or value individually. Instead, similar values are grouped into intervals (like the choice of stem for stem-and-leaf displays) and represented on the graph as a bar. Each bar shows the frequency of values within a specific interval (i.e., intervals of 5, 10, 100, etc.). In essence, when creating a histogram, we specify subgroups or categories within the continuous variable of interest. Histograms are particularly useful when one is working with a large data set. For example, a stem-and-leaf display to show distribution of the heights of individuals in a population the size of the United States would be enormous. A histogram, however, could summarize all that data in one display. Similarly, a histogram could summarize height data on Fast Plants grown in all classrooms over many years.

Our example of a histogram (Figure 1.5) depicts the width of Fast Plants (the span across the longest leaves

Figure 1.4. Stem-and-leaf displays of the final heights (cm) of students' Fast Plants: (a) data collected by fourth-grade class, (b) data collected by third-grade class.

(a)

Data Set: **15, 20, 20, 20, 20, 22, 22, 22, 23, 23, 23, 23, 23, 23, 23, 40**
Stem-and-Leaf:

    1|5

    2|00002223333333

    3|

    4|0

(b)

Data Set: **9, 14, 17, 22, 23, 25, 25, 26, 27, 27, 27, 28, 29, 29, 30, 31, 31, 31, 32, 33, 33, 35, 39, 40**
Stem-and-Leaf:

    0|9

    1|47

    2|23556777899

    3|0123359

    4|0

Figure 1.5. Histogram of the final widths of the third graders' Fast Plants. The width of each bar represents an interval of 25 millimeters.

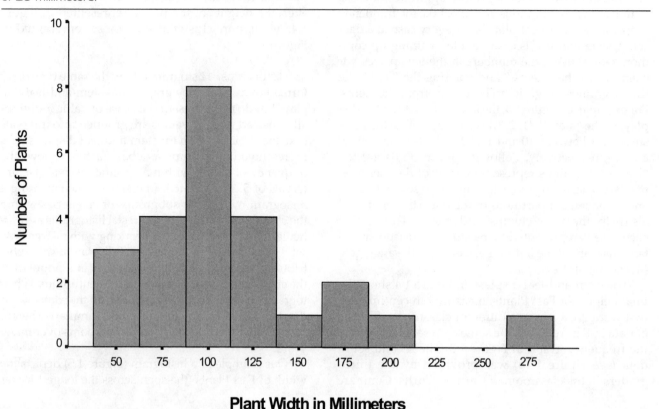

and stems) grown by Carmen's third-graders. Note that most of the bars in this histogram are placed side by side, whereas the individual bars in a bar graph (see again Figure 1.1) are separated. A histogram depicts the frequency of one continuous variable, so the bars touch unless an interval contains no data. In comparison, a bar graph is used for two or more variables that differ categorically rather than continuously, so the bars do not touch.

Although construction of a histogram seems relatively straightforward, the idea of grouping data by intervals (what students often call *bins*) is somewhat challenging. Efforts to reconcile individual cases with the aggregates defined by intervals take many forms. For example, third-grade children in Carmen's class first "binned" some of their data about the number of recyclable materials collected by each family, but then treated other cases as simply "attached" without regard for interval (see Figure 1.6. Note the juxtaposition of 80s and 100s. Note also that the values are explicitly represented, as they are in a stem-and-leaf display.)

Mark's fifth-graders handled the challenge of representing the heights of Fast Plants on Day 19 in a manner like that invented by the third-graders. They, too, were reluctant to lose information about individual

cases, but they represented intervals that did not have data (Figure 1.7). Mark found it productive for students to compare Figure 1.7 with a corresponding stem-and-leaf display. Conversations about the comparative representational "work" and functions of different displays of distributions often help students develop understandings of both distribution and display.

Investigating Relationships

When students' research questions have to do with the relationships between variables (e.g., circumference and strength, time and height, number of fingers, and the shape of eyes in children's drawings), the relationships can be made visual by plotting them in displays such as line graphs, scatter plots, and Venn diagrams. Scatter plots and line graphs use a two-dimensional coordinate system to illustrate the relationship between two continuous variables. Venn diagrams, in contrast, use circles to display shared attributes of cases.

Line Graphs. Line graphs, like that displayed in Figure 1.8, illustrate change in one variable over time. Figure 1.8 depicts changes in a Wisconsin Fast Plant's

Figure 1.6. Third-graders' display of bins and values of the number of recyclables.

			39						
			38						
			38	47					
		28	38	47					
	18	28	37	46					
	18	27	37	46					
	17	24	36	44					
	17	24	35	44					
	16	22	35	43					
	15	21	33	43					
	15	21	33	43					
	15	21	32	42		66			
	14	21	32	42	56	64			
8	12	20	31	41	52	62			
6	12	20	30	40	52	61			119
0	10	20	30	40	51	61	72	80	106

height over time. It was constructed by a third-grade student to investigate changes in rate of growth. Because we cannot continuously collect data on plant growth, we concentrate on selected occasions, plot those points on a graph, draw lines connecting our known data points, and assume that the resulting line represents the locations of intermediate points. One weakness of such line graphs is that if data are collected on too few occasions, information about the pattern of growth can go undetected. Therefore, the timing of data collection is an important issue for students investigating growth to discuss.

Line graphs can also provide opportunities to reason about trends in light of variation. The students in Deb Lucas's sixth-grade found that ratings of their interest in *The Charge of the Light Brigade* varied within each stanza and also between stanzas. Students decided to rely on modal interest ratings for each stanza to track change over time, as displayed in Figure 1.9.

Scatter Plots. A scatter plot represents the joint variation between two continuous variables. For example, the students in a first/second-grade class were asked to predict the relationship between the circumference of a paper tower and its ability to support the weight of pennies. Some of the students believed that as circumference increased, so would strength. In other words, they predicted a positive relationship or correlation between circumference and strength (see Figure 1.10a). The first/second-graders also speculated about the possibility that as circumference increased, strength would decrease (see Figure 1.10b), suggesting a negative relationship. As is often the case, neither predicted model provided a close fit to the actual data (see Figure 1.10c), although one did provide a better fit than the other.

To discover what the relationship would actually be, the students designed an experiment. They held constant the height of paper towers while they varied circumference and number of pennies (the weight). Their data suggests a less-linear positive relationship than the students had proposed with the first model. The configuration of the data points in Figure 1.10c, however, suggests that although the circumference of a tower does appear to affect the amount of weight it can sup-

Figure 1.7. Data display created by fifth-grade students to show the "shape" of the data representing plant heights.

30	40	50	60	70	80	90	100	110	120	130	140	150	160	170	180	190	200	210	220	230	240	250	260	270	280	290	300	310	320	330	340
													169																		
													166																		
													165																		
													165																		
													163																		
								116					163	178																	
								115				159	160	176		199															
				79			105	114	125			156	160	175		195															
				75	86		103	112	122		147	153	160	173		193															
		55		71	84	96	102	111	121	130	140	150	160	170		190	205														
30	45	50		70	80	96	100	110	120	130	140	150	160	170		190	200	212				255									

Figure 1.8. Line graph showing the changes in the height of a Wisconsin Fast Plant™ over its life cycle.

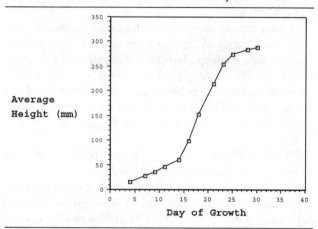

dents may find the effects of the fertilizer on growth easier to see by creating two different Venn diagrams, one for each amount of fertilizer.

Despite a "missing" point problem (Tabletop sometimes places the data points for two or more cases on top of one another, making it appear as if one or more points are missing), there are several advantages to using database programs such as Tabletop for recording and organizing data. These programs force students to specify what their study is about—what their cases and variables of interest are. By specifying these properties, students add structure to their data. In addition, because the tables created with database programs help students keep records of the attributes of individual cases, students can use them to summarize and display their results in other ways.

port, other factors might also be involved. Seeing their data in the scatter plot led the students to discuss other factors, such as experimenter effects or tower defects, that may have contributed to their test results. However, a full appreciation of scatter plots is difficult for many, partly because one has to imagine variation in two dimensions simultaneously.

Venn Diagrams. In contrast to scatter plots and line graphs, Venn diagrams illustrate the attributes of categorical variables. To display shared and unshared attributes in the categorical data collected on self-portraits, Erin's third-grade students could have created a Venn diagram similar to the one shown in Figure 1.11 (created with Tabletop [TERC, 1994]). The Venn diagram shows that of our 10 fictitious students, (a) only 2 drew oval-shaped eyes, five fingers, and hair on their self-portraits; (b) no child drew a self-portrait consisting only of oval-shaped eyes or of five fingers; and (c) more than half the children (6) drew in hair.

Venn diagrams also can be used to display attributes of continuous data. To do so, however, we need to specify ways to divide the continuous properties of the data into defined groups. For instance, to create the Venn diagram in Figure 1.12, we organized the Fast Plant data from Carmen's third-graders by the three variables of interest and specified two subgroups within each of those: (a) fertilizer amount, 6 or 18 pellets; (b) plant height, shorter than the median height or equal to/taller than the median height; (c) plant width, more narrow than the median width or equal to/wider than the median width. From this Venn diagram, we can see the effect of the higher amount of fertilizer on the growth of the plants: Of the 7 plants (out of 24) that grew both tall and wide, 6 received the larger amount of fertilizer, and only 1 received the smaller amount. Although this Venn diagram contains information from all 24 plants in the study, stu-

Figure 1.9. Sixth-graders' modal interest ratings by stanza: *The Charge of the Light Brigade.*

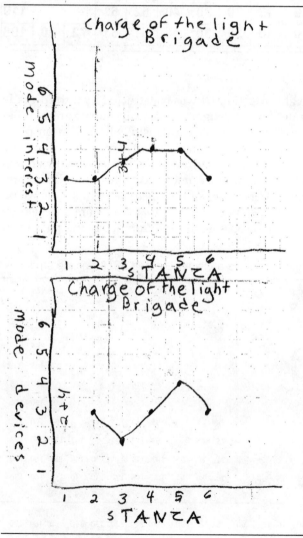

Figure 1.10. Scatter plot illustrating the relationship between paper towel circumference and number of pennies (weight) supported: (a) students' prediction of positive relationship; (b) students' prediction of negative relationship; (c) observed relationship.

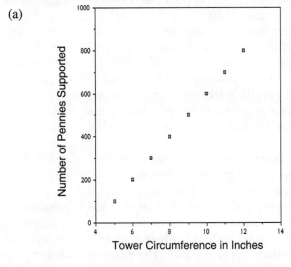

(a)

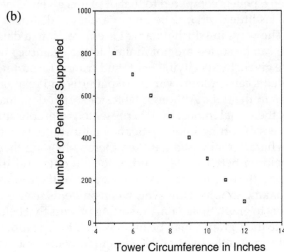

(b)

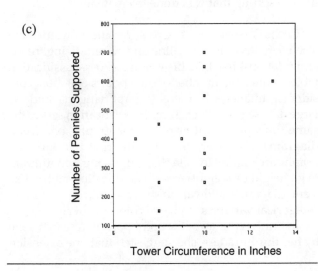

(c)

Figure 1.11. Venn diagram sorting our fictional self-portrait data by eye shape, finger, and hair attributes. When students use Tabletop™ (TERC, 1994) to create a Venn diagram, like this one, they will see the icon representing each case in their data set migrate to its appropriate location.

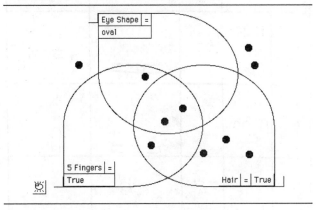

Data Tables

Graphs are powerful tools for getting acquainted with a set of data, but not all types of data lend themselves to a graph format. We noted previously that tables can be used as tools to structure data. Here we describe some of the ways students can use tables to study and display characteristics of data. A second-grader in an investigation supervised by Sue Wainwright recorded the pictorial data shown in Figure 1.13. The table summarizes how the position of the student's shadow changed in relation to the position of the sun. The table also may have helped the student notice that her shadow became shorter throughout the course of

Figure 1.12. Venn diagram sorting Fast Plants by fertilizer amount, plant height, and plant width. To represent the continuous height and width measures as categorical data, we specified that Tabletop™ use the median height of the plants (276 mm) as the minimal criterion for "tall" and the median width (113 mm) as the minimal criterion for "wide."

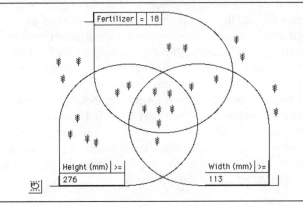

Figure 1.13. Student's data table showing shadow length and position in relation to the time of day and position of the sun.

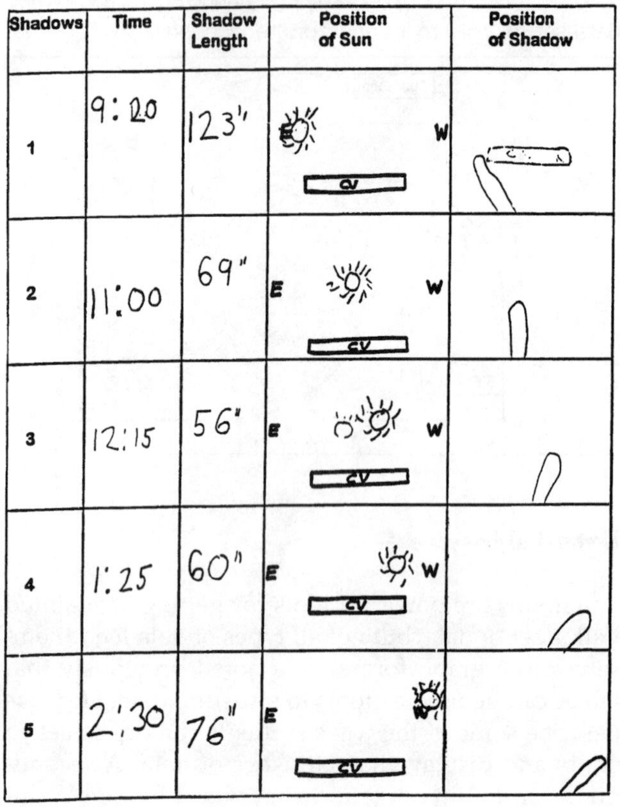

Shadows	Time	Shadow Length	Position of Sun	Position of Shadow
1	9:20	123"		
2	11:00	69"		
3	12:15	56"		
4	1:25	60"		
5	2:30	76"		

the morning and that, after noon, her shadow began to lengthen. The second-grader recorded her data over time, and her table preserves this organization. The orderly presentation of data enables us to more easily notice trends and relationships.

Sorting Data to Study Patterns and Relationships. Data often need to be organized or sorted in meaningful ways before we begin to notice relationships. Recall our discussion of data structure and the organization of data by cases (rows) and fields (columns). When we sort data, we want to preserve the association within cases (i.e., all the data within a row that describes a case) but also to be able to rearrange entries according to the changes (variation) within a variable. If we had our data organized in a table drawn on paper, we could sort by cutting our table apart and rearranging the rows. We also could record all the information about each case on separate cards and then sort the cards according to specified criteria (e.g., ascending or descending order for a continuous variable, shared attributes for a categorical variable). Or we can use computer software programs to do the sorting for us.

Using Tabletop (TERC, 1994), we recorded data on the final height of Fast Plants from Carmen's third-graders. The data had been arranged according to whether plants received a low (6 pellets) or high (18 pellets) amount of fertilizer. With Tabletop, we also sorted the data by height. Figure 1.14a shows the original order of the data: Plants are sorted only by the amount of fertilizer they received. Figure 1.14b shows our resorting of the data by both the amount of fertilizer received *and* the height of plants. We can easily see from this second table that the amount of fertilizer a plant received did not greatly affect its height. The range in height for plants given 6 pellets compared to that of plants given 18 pellets shows considerable overlap: There is no real separation of range.

Because we also were interested in whether the amount of fertilizer a plant received affected its width (measured across the broadest spread of stems and leaves on each plant), we constructed a third table, sorting the data by fertilizer amount and plant width. Figure 1.14c shows that fertilizer amount does seem to have an effect on plant width. The range in width in plants given 6 pellets compared to that of plants given 18 pellets has little overlap: The ranges are more distinct.

The ways in which data that is entered into a database can be sorted are not limited to the examples we have given. By specifying fields and criteria for sorting, students can explore a variety of patterns and relationships in the data. Although tables of sorted data may lack the visual impact of data presented in graphs, the process of sorting might better acquaint students with the characteristics of a data set, thereby helping them develop a better understanding of the data and the graphs. Sorting the data is, in fact, part of the process of making graphs. However, when students use computers to graph their data, the sorting process that helps create their graphs may be hidden. In effect, a student could create effective graphs without fully understanding the sorting that was done to create them.

Cross-Classifications. Cross-classification tables are also useful tools for revealing and summarizing trends and relationships. Like histograms, cross-classification tables reduce the number of data points one must consider simultaneously, thereby simplifying the study of large data sets. In effect, a cross-classification serves the same function as scatter plots, line graphs, and Venn diagrams. However, although the first two kinds of graphs are limited to data that vary along a continuum (e.g., height or weight), cross-classification tables, like Venn diagrams, allow us to study relationships among categorical variables (e.g., eye color, gender).

In Erin's write-up of the body-portrait research done by her third-graders, she suggested that one extension

Figure 1.14. Sorting data in tables to study relationships: (a) Data sorted by plant identification and fertilizer amount; (b) data sorted by fertilizer amount and plant height; (c) data sorted by fertilizer amount and plant width. Note that relationships (or lack of relationships) are difficult to notice in (a); that (b) shows no relationship between amount of fertilizer and plant height, and that (c) reveals a possible relationship between fertilizer amount and plant width.

(a)

Plant ID	Fertilizer amount (pellets)	Final height (mm)	Final width (mm)
1	6	310	130
2	6	290	60
3	6	270	90
4	6	305	40
5	6	270	94
6	6	310	90
7	6	170	98
8	6	245	99
9	6	261	55
10	6	252	80
11	6	390	100
12	6	270	105
13	18	325	
14	18	290	
15	18	280	
16	18	225	
17	18	350	
18	18	322	
19	18	92	
20	18	300	
21	18	223	
22	18	140	
23	18	327	
24	18	402	

(b)

Plant ID	Fertilizer amount (pellets)	Final height (mm)	Final width (mm)
7	6	170	98
8	6	245	99
10	6	252	80
9	6	261	55
3	6	270	90
5	6	270	94
12	6	270	105
	6	290	60
	6	305	40
	6	310	130
	6	310	90
	6	390	100
	18	92	65
	18	140	108
	18	223	130
	18	225	180
	18	280	130
	18	290	145
	18	300	131
	18	322	80
	18	325	165
	18	327	75
	18	350	270
	18	402	200

(c)

Plant ID	Fertilizer amount (pellets)	Final height (mm)	Final width (mm)
4	6	305	40
9	6	261	55
2	6	290	60
10	6	252	80
3	6	270	90
6	6	310	90
5	6	270	94
7	6	170	98
8	6	245	99
11	6	390	100
12	6	270	105
1	6	310	130
19	18	92	65
23	18	327	75
18	18	322	80
22	18	140	108
21	18	223	130
15	18	280	130
20	18	300	131
14	18	290	145
13	18	325	165
16	18	225	180
24	18	402	200
17	18	350	270

of their work could have been the study of relationships among the ways children drew different body parts. For instance, the third-graders could have asked whether children who tended to draw the appropriate number of fingers also tended to draw eyes more realistically. As Erin suggested, such a question could have been addressed by having students organize their data into a cross-classification table.

To make a cross-classification table similar to one that Erin's third-graders could have made, we again used our fictitious portrait data (the same data used to create the Venn diagram in Figure 1.11) and sorted it into the subcategories of eye shape and number of fingers (see Table 1.3). Had the third-graders made such a summarization, they would have had the information needed to consider such trends within and between their variables as the following: (a) Did more students draw a particular shape of eye? (b) Did more or fewer draw five-fingered hands? (c) Did the students who drew fewer than five fingers per hand also tend to draw eyes that were not oval? Finding the answer to the first question would require totaling frequencies within columns and then comparing across the columns. Referring to our small, fictitious data set, we find that three children drew oval-shaped eyes, four drew circles, and three drew eyes of other shapes. To answer the second question, we can total the frequencies within rows and then compare the total for the top row to that for the bottom row. Again using this data set, we find that four children drew hands with five fingers and six drew hands with fewer than five fingers. By looking at the pattern of frequencies recorded at the intersection points (cells) for fingers and eye shape, we can now answer our question about the relationship between the ways these children drew their fingers and eyes in their self-portraits. None of our fictitious students who included fewer than five fingers per hand drew oval-shaped eyes on their portraits, whereas three "students" who drew five-fingered hands also drew oval-shaped eyes. At least for our fictitious students, there seems to be an association between the shape of the eyes and the number of fingers they drew on their self-portraits.

Table 1.3. Cross-classification of finger and eye shape data from the fictitious self-portrait data set.

	Eye shape		
Number of Fingers	Oval	Circle	Other
Five	3	1	0
Fewer than five	0	3	3

Cross-classification tables are analogs to scatter plots: They display joint variation. Like scatter plots, they require tracking two dimensions of variation simultaneously, and so may be difficult for students to understand. Our impression is that this form of joint variation is probably an important precursor to the study of continuous variation in two or more variables.

Pictures, Maps, and Other Displays of Data

One of the most impressive displays we have seen depicting the concentration of the population of our country was a photograph taken at night from space. The abundance of city lights along the East Coast compared with their sparseness in the Midwest provided a dramatic depiction of the differences in population density between the two regions. Experimenting with displays of data other than tables and graphs can help students gain further understanding of their data and the ways representations of data can affect what we convey to the viewer.

When Angie's first-grade students wanted to investigate the infestation of fruit flies in their school building, Angie provided them with a diagram of the building floor plan. The students developed a coding scheme for recording on their diagram the number of fruit flies observed in each room. They used green to indicate rooms, such as their own, in which there were "a lot of" fruit flies (8 or more), red to indicate rooms with "some" fruit flies (5–7), blue to indicate rooms with "few" fruit flies (1–4), and purple to indicate rooms where there was no evidence of fruit fly infestation. (Figure 1.15 is a gray-tone adaptation of the students' diagram.) With their brightly colored diagram, the students could easily notice patterns of infestation in their building. The diagram also prompted a discussion of why the flies had taken up residence in some classrooms but not in others. Color—colored tacks, chalk, or marker pens—can make data (such as fruit fly infestations) remarkably vivid to children.

Representing Data: A Summary

In the preceding sections, we provided a sampling of ways to explore and display data through various types of graphs and tables. Deciding which type of display best brings out the characteristics of a particular set of data depends not only on the type of data (e.g., categorical or continuous) being studied, but also on the judgment and creativity of the researcher (in this case, the student). How we display data determines what we see. Nuances that would otherwise go unnoticed in one display might be quite visible in a different graph or table: The individual who chose squid soup is noticeable in the bar graph (see again Figure 1.1b) but would

Figure 1.15. First-grade students' diagram to show location and concentration of fruit flies (adapted). In the original, students used four different colors to code the different levels of fly infestation they observed.

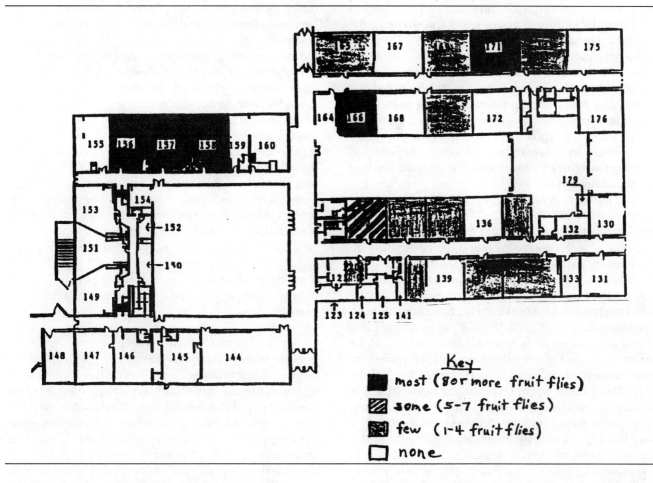

be nearly invisible in a pie chart, which shows proportions. Conversely, characteristics that may distract the viewer from what the researcher sees as important trends can be downplayed by changing representations of the data. If that same bar graph of soup choices were recategorized as "soups containing red meat" versus "soups without red meat," the frequency with which chicken noodle soup was chosen (175 out of 299 total data points) would be entirely hidden. Exploring the same set of data through a variety of displays and organizations, deciding what story needs to be told, and deciding how best to tell it can easily lead to interesting discussions—and a variety of meaningful data interpretations.

SUMMARIZING DATA

Statistics are numerical summaries of batches of data. Some common forms of summary include indicators of center and spread of distribution, and of relationships between two or more variables. Each pro-

vides a different kind of information about the data collected or the population that the data represent. Although data displays help us visualize characteristics of data such as the spread and clustering of cases (distribution), statistics numerically summarize those characteristics.

Representing Typicality: Indicators of Center

One of the questions most commonly asked about a set of data is "How can we summarize what is typical about our data?" Indicators of center are values that do just that: They represent what is typical of the data (and, under some circumstances, of the population from which they were drawn). Three well-established, conventional measures of center—the mean, median, and mode—each can serve as a model of the data it represents. Which is preferable for a particular set of data depends on three issues: (a) the kind of information on which the data are based (e.g., continuous or categorical data), (b) the distribution of the data, and (c) the research question being addressed.

Mean. The indicator of center most often used for modeling what is typical about a set of continuous data is the mean. The mean is the arithmetic average of a data set, found by summing across cases and dividing the sum by the number of cases (Mean = Sum/N). The mean is the only indicator of center that uses the numerical value of each case and thus provides a "per case" summary of the data. In contexts such as measurement, the mean has a ready interpretation as a "true score." For example, a group of fifth-graders measured the height of the school's flagpole with the expectation of a true height. Their measures of height formed a bell-shaped distribution, where the mean was interpreted as the best approximation to real height.

The mean, however might not always be the best way to summarize what is typical about a batch of data. The fact that the mean is derived from the exact numerical value of each case means that it can be strongly influenced by extreme values. For example, when students in Jean's class were collecting data on traffic flow, one group of students reported a car count that greatly stood out from those reported by the three other groups. The four counts of 120, 150, 185, 320 yield a mean of 194. In this case, the mean is greater than all but one of the original counts. The one extreme value (320) pulled the measurement of the mean away from the other values. In addition, as this example shows, the mean often does not coincide with any observed value. This feature can be troublesome for students, because even though they may be able to calculate the mean, they might find it strange to end up with a "typical value" that fails to correspond to any case in the data. (Students often rely on individual cases to guide their interpretation of data, an issue discussed again in the section on data modeling later in the chapter.) More important, reasoning about the mean relies on a firm grasp of ratio, because the mean represents amount per case.

Median. The second indicator of center, the median, can be found by placing cases from the data set in ascending or descending order and finding the middle value—the one with the same number of cases above it and below it. If the count of a batch of data points is an odd number, the median will be the single middle value (e.g., the median of 2, 4, and 9 is 4). If the count of the batch is even, the median is the mean of the two middle values. For example, the median of 2, 4, 8, and 9 is 6, calculated by $(4 + 8)/2$. Half of the data cases lie above the median, and half lie below it (again note that this is not necessarily true for the mean). Although the median uses information about the order of cases in the data set, it does not use their exact values. In other words, the median treats all cases as if distance did not matter, whereas the mean uses the information about relative distance (variation) among cases.

Despite the fact that the median ignores some information, it has several advantages. For one, it is not affected by extreme values. Therefore, in data sets that contain outliers, the median often provides a better representation of what is typical about the data than does the mean. Another advantage is that the median always corresponds to an actual value when the number of cases is odd (as noted above), and sometimes does so when the number of cases is even (e.g., for the batch 25, 35, 35, and 55, the median is 35). Students often find this a necessary first step for thinking about typicality. A third potential value of the median is that it helps students begin to think about partitions of data: half above and half below. Related partitions, such as quartiles, then follow as medians of each half. For example, the lower quartile is marked by the median value of the lower half of the distribution. Mark's fifth-graders compared each quartile to a "hinge" and the corresponding width of the partitions to "doors." This kind of thinking marks a transition toward considering distributions as aggregates, rather than simply as a collection of cases.

Mode. The mode is the value that occurs most frequently in the data. In the frequency graph shown in Figure 1.3, the mode is 23 cm. The mode of a data set is a good summary statistic when your question involves the most popular outcomes (e.g., What are the most frequently ordered foods in the school cafeteria?) or when the distribution is markedly asymmetric. The mode is an indicator of center frequently preferred by students, and it is the only one that can be used to describe both quantitative and categorical data (e.g., What was the most common final height for Fast Plants? Which type of soup was named by the most people?)

Midrange. Another characteristic of data that students will sometimes use as an indicator of center, especially when working with frequency graphs, is the midrange or midpoint (the halfway point between the lowest and highest values in the data set). The midrange can indicate the spread of the data and sometimes provides the same or nearly the same value as the median (e.g., for the data set 10, 14, 17, 21, 24, both the midrange $[(10 + 24)/2]$ and the median are 17). The midrange, however, ignores the clustering and frequency of values and is highly sensitive (even more so than the mean) to the "pull" of extreme values. For instance, for the Fast Plant data set shown in the frequency graph in Figure 1.3, the mean, median, and mode all fall around 23 cm, whereas the midrange is about 27 cm. Although the midrange may not be a conventional indicator of center, students' use and misuse of this feature of a data set can provide a beginning point for thinking about different senses of "middle" or center.

Placing Center in Context: Distributions of Data

Interpreting summaries of center without having some idea of the distribution or general shape of a batch of data is often misleading. We find that even very young students can readily reason about "clusters" of values in displays, showing that they tend to think about variation. Distributions capture the notions of data spread and clumpiness—the variability of the data. Displays of distributions help illustrate the variability among cases within a data set, and it is only within light of this variability that reasonable choices can be made about what is typical. For instance, some data tend to cluster around a central value and have symmetrical tails (e.g., the so-called "normal" distributions). The histogram in Figure 1.16 demonstrates the general shape of a normal distribution. We constructed this histogram by combining the Fast Plant data shown earlier in Figure 1.3. For the new set of 40 cases, the mean (25.6 cm), median (24 cm), and mode (23 cm) all fall within the large cluster of data located in the middle of the distribution. The fact that these measures are all centrally located in the largest cluster suggests that the distribution is normal. If this group of Fast Plants contained a couple of extreme outliers, the mean would be far less likely to fall in the middle largest cluster and might, in fact, drift to one of the "tails" of the graph; the mode would probably remain about where it now lies; and the median, depending on where the outliers fell,

could drift slightly left or slightly right or remain about where it is.

Some data distributions, although symmetrical, have a "hole" or "valley" between the "peaks" (large clumps) of data. The histogram in Figure 1.17 shows a bimodal (i.e., two-clump) distribution. Using only the mean or median (each of which would fall in the "valley") to describe this set of data would not provide a very accurate picture of the whole set. When one is working with a data set like this one, the immediate question is probably why the data fell into two such distinct clumps.

Data are not always symmetric around some central value. The histogram in Figure 1.18 demonstrates a data set that has a *skewed distribution*. Most of the distribution is located to one side rather than in the middle, as with a normal distribution, or balanced on either side, as with a bimodal distribution. The data shown in the distribution display the final width (the span across the longest leaves and stems) of a batch of Fast Plants grown by Carmen's third-graders. The large clump of data on the left side and the single outlier on the right indicate that it was typical for these plants to reach "widths" in the range of about 40 mm to 140 mm, and unusual for them to grown to around 275 mm wide.

Distributions and Processes. Shapes of distributions are often signatures of processes. There is often good reason for the shape observed. In Figure 1.19, fourth-graders compared the measurement errors in-

Figure 1.16. Histogram of a normal distribution. The fact that the combined data set falls into a normal distribution indicates that the plants can all be considered members of the same population.

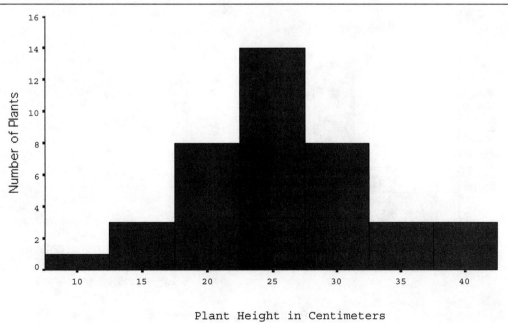

Figure 1.17. Histogram of a bimodal distribution. Such a distribution in a set of data could indicate an important difference within the sample or an error incurred by the use of two different measurement methods.

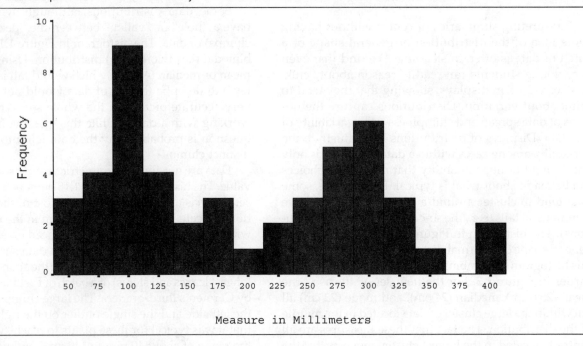

Figure 1.18. Histogram of a skewed distribution. This distribution is said to skew to the left because the largest clump of data is located to the lower end (the left side) of the range for the distribution.

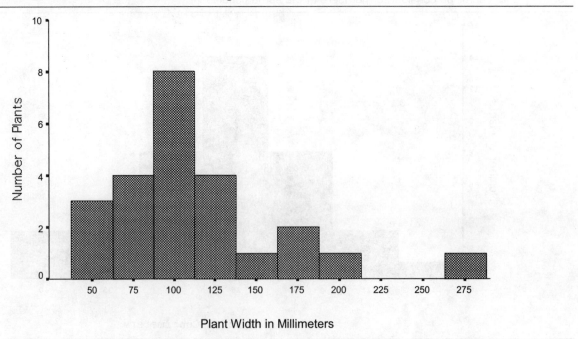

Figure 1.19. Distributions of measurements: (a) measured lengths of a pencil; (b) measured heights of the school's flagpole.

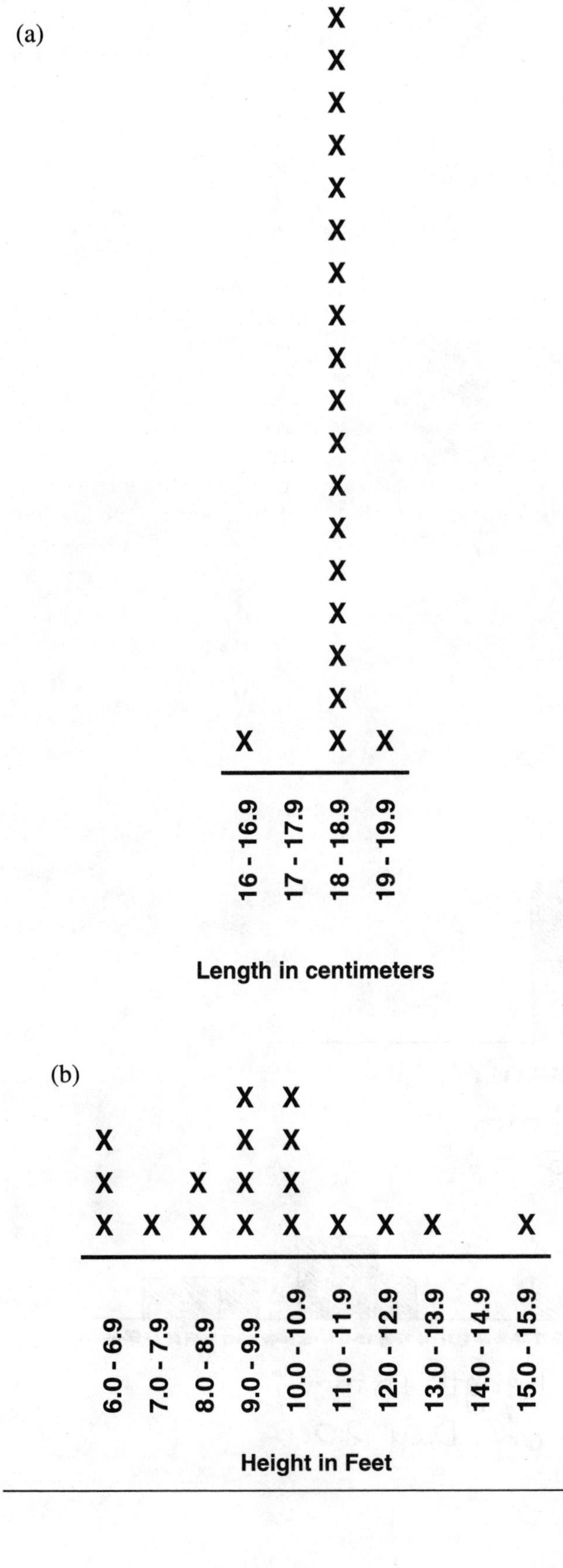

(a)

```
                              X
                              X
                              X
                              X
                              X
                              X
                              X
                              X
                              X
                              X
                              X
                              X
                              X
                              X
                              X
                              X
                     X        X    X
                  _____
                   16 - 16.9
                          17 - 17.9
                                 18 - 18.9
                                        19 - 19.9
```

Length in centimeters

(b)

```
                        X    X
         X              X    X
         X         X    X    X
         X    X    X    X    X    X    X    X              X
      _____
       6.0 - 6.9
            7.0 - 7.9
                 8.0 - 8.9
                      9.0 - 9.9
                           10.0 - 10.9
                                11.0 - 11.9
                                     12.0 - 12.9
                                          13.0 - 13.9
                                               14.0 - 14.9
                                                    15.0 - 15.9
```

Height in Feet

volved in determining the length of a pencil and the height of a flagpole. They decided that the shapes of the distributions might be similar because a person could "measure a little high or a little low," yet the spread of the distributions differed because of the relative precision of the measurement instruments and processes involved (using a ruler vs. a "height-o-meter").

Figure 1.20 suggested to a class of fifth-graders that hornworms fed green pepper and those fed "recipe" had similar-looking distributions early in the life cycle, but very different ones later on. They speculated about how differences in these foodstuffs might have contributed to such different outcomes. Distributions in these classrooms were used as tools for thinking.

Using distributions as signatures of processes relies on well-grounded ideas about core notions such as "shape." Consider, for example, two senses of shape generated by Mark's fifth-graders. In the top panel of Figure 1.21, a small group of students proposed that the shape of the heights of Fast Plants on Day 19 was best thought of as a set of ordered lengths, one for every plant. In the bottom panel, another small group decided that shape would better be displayed by "binning" the data "so we can see the gaps and chunks." By considering both of these senses of *shape*, the whole class came to understand shape as a way of aggregating cases, rather than an inherent quality of a distribution.

Comparing Distributions. Often, comparisons between data sets are made solely on the basis of their centers. It is almost meaningless, however, to interpret differences between centers without some idea about the distributions of the data involved. An apparently large difference between centers could be simply the effect of great variability in the data. If there is little variability in the data, apparent small differences could, in fact, prove quite meaningful.

Figure 1.22 shows a frequency graph of the final heights from the first round of Fast Plants grown by Carmen's third-graders. (We used these same data earlier in Figures 1.4b, 1.12, and 1.14.) To find out if the amount of fertilizer affects plant height, the third-graders gave half of their plants a low amount of fertilizer (6 pellets per plant) and the other half a higher amount (18 pellets each). Comparing centers would be one way to address this question. However, a better understanding of the differences (or lack thereof) related to amount of fertilizer would be provided by studying the spread and clumpiness of the data distributions for the two conditions. The students in Carmen's class eventually made such a comparison by using different colors to represent whether a plant received the low amount or high amount of fertilizer and then plotting the color-coded data on a frequency graph. We used Tabletop (TERC, 1994) to re-create

Figure 1.20. Frequency graphs of body lengths of hornworms by diet (green pepper, recipe).

Frequency graphs of hornworm length on Day 7, Day 15, and Day 20 (replicas of classroom graphs)

X = hornworms fed green pepper

■ = hornworms fed "recipe"

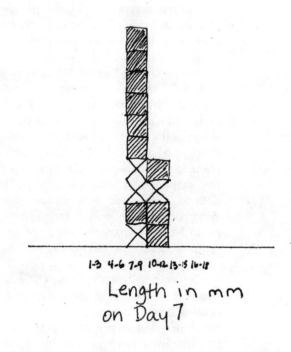

1-3 4-6 7-9 10-12 13-15 16-18

Length in mm
on Day 7

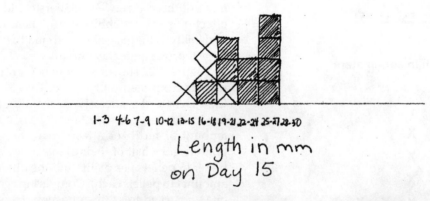

1-3 4-6 7-9 10-12 13-15 16-18 19-21 22-24 25-27 28-30

Length in mm
on Day 15

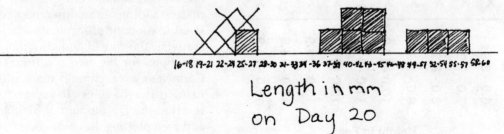

16-18 19-21 22-24 25-27 28-30 31-33 34-36 37-39 40-42 43-45 46-48 49-51 52-54 55-57 58-60

Length in mm
on Day 20

Figure 1.21. Ways fifth-graders invented to show the "shape" of the data: (a) case magnitude graph; (b) frequency-histogram hybrid display.

(a)

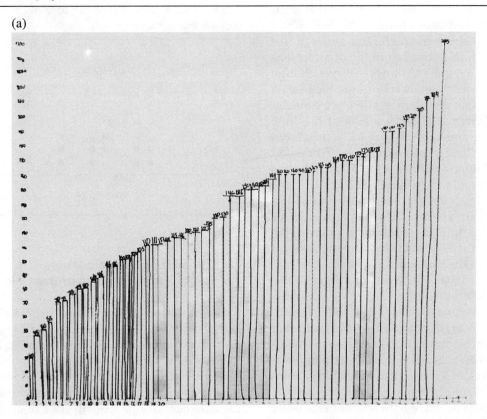

(b)

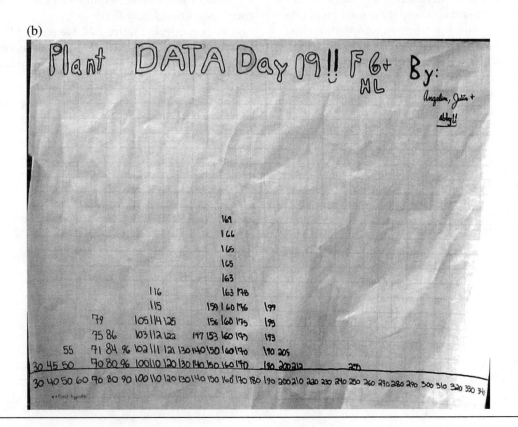

what Carmen and her students constructed on a marker board. The one-third-filled icons in Figure 1.22 represent the low-fertilizer plants and the filled icons represent the high-fertilizer plants.

As we noticed earlier in graphs and tables of this data set, there is a lot of overlap in the distributions for heights. In fact, Figure 1.22 shows that even though the plants grew under different conditions, they are all members of the same distribution when we consider final heights. However, when we look at the final widths of the same plants (see Figure 1.23), such is not the case. Low-fertilizer plants clump toward the left side of the distribution and have little spread, whereas the high-fertilizer plants clump more toward the middle of the distribution and show more variability (spread) in their final widths. The display indicates that when final width is the attribute of interest, the plants in the two different conditions are members of distinctly different distributions.

Students often develop a series of strategies for thinking about the extent of overlap between two distributions. One strategy is to define a *cut-point* or threshold value, and then to count the number of cases that exceed this value. This strategy often needs to be modified to *proportions* of cases when the distributions have unequal number of cases. Some students employ a summary statistic from one distribution, such as the median, and then locate this summary statistic within the other distribution to see how the distributions "fit." One strategy employed by students is to see if the median of one distribution falls within the "center clump" (the cluster of values around the median) of the other. If it does, then the reason is that the two distributions are alike. An alternative strategy is to see if the value of the summary statistic exceeds a cut-point. Such strategies are at the heart of statistical inference.

Figure 1.22. Frequency graph illustrating that the amount of fertilizer given to the Fast Plants did not affect their final height. (Filled icons = high-fertilizer plants; partially filled icons = low-fertilizer plants.)

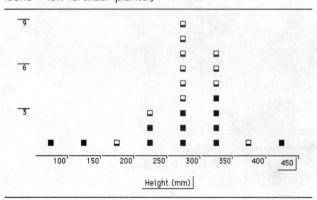

Figure 1.23. Frequency graph illustrating that the amount of fertilizer given to the Fast Plants did affect their final widths. (Filled icons = high-fertilizer plants; partially filled icons = low-fertilizer plants).

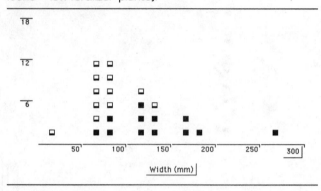

Mathematizing Relationships: Rules, Ratios, and Lines-of-Best-Fit

In the section on displays, we provided examples of how graphs and tables can be used to help students visualize relationships between variables. The next step in understanding and describing a relationship between variables is to have the students find a way to summarize the meaning of the relationship with a mathematical statement or rule (e.g., the rate of growth per day, the ratio of increasing height to increasing circumference), or a line-of-best-fit, or both.

For example, in Figure 1.24, we plotted the tree data provided by Mark's students, who were interested in finding out whether tree circumference related to tree

Figure 1.24. Scatter plot of the relationship between tree circumference and height.

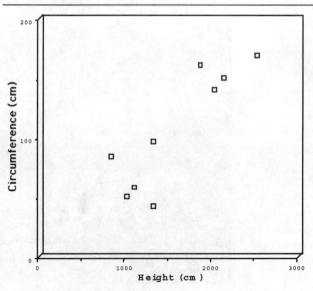

height. Because a line can represent the best mathematical summary of a relationship in the data, we might try fitting or summarizing this data into a line. Children, however, often have a problem with this way of describing relationships. Many believe that data fitting means that all the cases or data points must fit exactly on the line. Because of children's tendency to want to "connect the dots," they often have difficulty seeing how a line that does not intersect all, or even the majority of, data points can be a useful summary of the data. This is especially difficult for children when the line-of-best-fit fails to intersect any of the data points. (Notice the similarity with children's discomfort with measures of central tendency that do not match any value in the distribution.)

Figure 1.25 shows multiple lines of growth (height vs. time) for several Fast Plants, as well as the most "typical" line, which does not exactly match any of the lines that it typifies. When children can generate and evaluate properties of such a typical line, they clearly have moved beyond considering individual plants and have begun to think about varieties of models for data. However, there are many issues involved in reasoning about two distributions jointly that we have not yet explored.

MODELING DATA

To complete our work with data, we now add prediction (based on summaries of data) and the development and "fitting" of data models. Children need to "test-run" different data models—exploring them, testing them by making predictions, and then finding a way to fit the models to their observations.

Making Predictions

In a third-grade classroom, children compared their birth heights (lengths) to their current heights. They used these data to plot their own rates of growth and then asked whether the resulting relation (between passage of time and amount of growth) could be used to predict their heights as adults. To their surprise, they found that if they continued to grow at the same rate, they could expect at age 25 to be several feet taller than their parents, their teacher, and any members of a comparison group of university undergraduates. Obviously, there was a mismatch between their model and the phenomenon being modeled.

In the fourth-grade classes, students measured the growth of their Fast Plants at regular intervals and plotted the resulting curves (time vs. height). The resulting graphs served as baseline (reference) models for making predictions about the growth of plants under other conditions (e.g., less or more fertilizer or light, crowdedness, etc.). Similarly, the third-grade's self-portrait classification data allowed them to make predictions about drawings they had not yet analyzed and to compare these new analyses with their predictions. In other words, they could examine how well their model fit their data.

Fifth-grade students used several weeks of data collected on the length and direction of their shadows (cast by the sun at various times of the day) to make a prediction about the length of the shadow cast by their shadow-stick at a new day and time. Working in pairs, the students drew a "predicted shadow" on a large piece of paper and, at the assigned time, went to the playground to compare their predicted shadow with the real one. Deborah's sixth-grade students used trends in interest ratings of movies and poems to make predictions about authors' use of text devices.

In all these cases, one essential attribute of data modeling is the idea of constructing relationships in the data and then using those relationships as a basis for making predictions about new cases. Yet when making predictions, children (and adults) tend to be very influenced by compelling cases and examples. Indeed, the power of memorable cases very easily swamps the logic of patterns and mathematical relations. Because data modeling often begins with children's own questions and familiar experiences, helping children to separate the data from the phenomenon being modeled requires that teachers negotiate a tricky balancing act between capitalizing on the familiar and deliberately stepping away from it. Along the way, this balancing act evolves into helping students consider the data themselves as objects of reflection—with the potential result that their familiar meanings and beliefs may be challenged.

Fitting the Model to the Data

Very rarely does a data model "fit" the data exactly: There is virtually always some degree of misfit. Deciding whether a model is the best one, generating and trying out alternative models, and discussing possible sources of misfit or error are very valuable activities. (They are also at the heart of what scientists and mathematicians do.)

In our work with teachers, we sometimes explore materials and scientific concepts that the teachers, in turn, explore with their students. In one exploration, we (teachers and university researchers) collected data on the operation of a first-class lever (with the fulcrum at the center). We placed a filled water bucket weighing 1,500 g at one end of the lever and, using a spring scale, measured the amount of force needed to balance the bucket at a range of fulcrum positions. Columns 1, 2, 4, and 5 of Table 1.4 summarize the data we collected. We

Figure 1.25. Modeling the growth of Fast Plants. Four of the lines in this graph represent the growth patterns of individual Fast Plants grown by third-graders. The fifth line illustrates the "typical" pattern of growth for the four plants. The data points for the "typical" growth line were found by calculating the median height of the plants on each day.

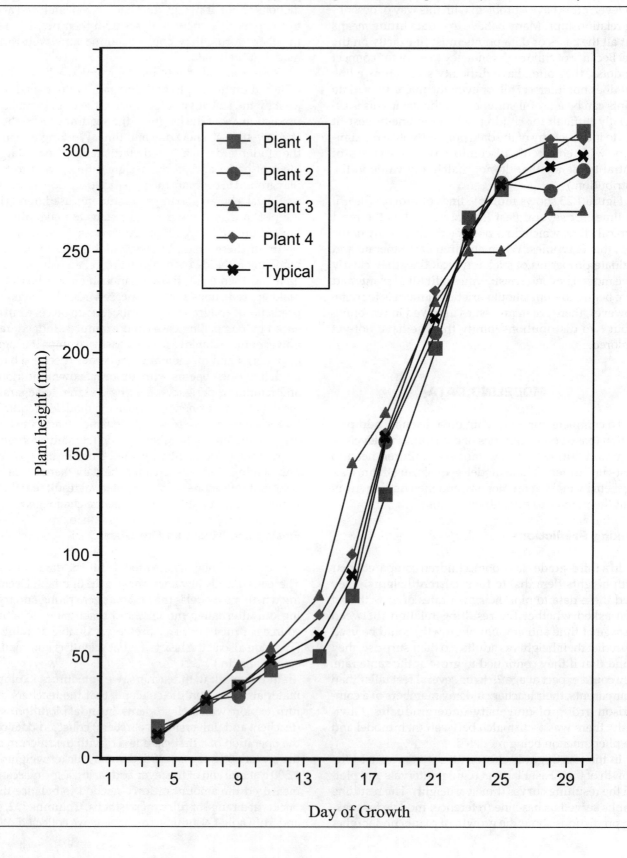

Table 1.4. Summarization of fulcrum load and effort data.

Load (gm)	Load Arm Distance (in)	Product (Load x Distance)	Effort Exerted (gm)	Effort Arm Distance (in)	Product (Effort x Distance)
1500	47	70,500	1500	47	70,500
1500	37	55,500	1000	57	57,000
1500	27	40,500	500	67	33,500
1500	17	25,500	250	77	19,250

Note that the product of load and fulcrum arm length is roughly equal to the product of effort and effort arm length.

used our recorded data to write number rules that described the relationships we observed.

The rule that best fit the data suggested that the load times the length of the load arm equaled the effort times the length of the effort arm. The third and sixth columns summarize this relationship. The relationship, however, was only approximate, and at some placements of the fulcrum there was more mismatch than at others. We had a lengthy discussion (one that our students could also profitably have) about whether and why we thought our data model was the best one and how we could account for the misfit. In the end we decided to retain this model provisionally. (The discussion, however, led to the generation and testing of alternative models, which we discarded because they did not account for the observed cases as well as the original model.)

Often we shy away from activities that do not result in clean-fitting models because we are concerned that if the relationships are not precise, our students may fail to perceive them. This might be a mistake. If students learn that math problems always have exact answers and that the numbers in science are supposed to "come out right," they develop misconceptions about the nature of science and mathematics and may also miss out on the chance to learn certain fundamental ideas about data and models.

Consider one source of model misfit—measurement variability. If one person measures the same variable repeatedly, or if several people measure the same variable once, the measures are not likely to be the same. For example, we observed fourth-graders who were using stopwatches to time cars as they "raced" a two-foot distance across a flat tabletop. After the first car finished the course, the three timers announced times of 2.02, 2.17, and 2.69 seconds, respectively. Although the children originally were concerned that some of the values were "wrong," the discussion soon turned to the amount of variability among the measures, possible

ways of reducing measurement variance, and ways of agreeing on the best "typical" measure for each car.

SUMMARY

Beginning at a very young age, children ask many questions about their world and informally generate (and interpret) the data needed to answer those questions. For children to understand the *idea* of data, however, requires that they learn to separate data from their experiences of that data (the cases the data represent). This is no mean feat: Humans are inherently predisposed to recall examples from their experience, not logical patterns and relations.

As children work with data, they learn that the ways they generate, structure, objectify, represent, and summarize data not only affect what they see in the data, but also enable them to recognize and explore promising relationships between attributes and variables. Developing ways of characterizing distribution by investigating "shape," "typical," "spread," and "clumpiness" helps children begin to reason about aggregates. All these ways of looking at data help children learn to interpret the data they collect, and the process itself very often gives rise to new questions that may entail further cycles of data gathering, structuring, and interpretation.

Key to students' working with data is the process of data modeling: developing data models, generating alternative models, evaluating those models for their degree of fit to the data, considering possible sources of misfit, and revising models accordingly. As children work with data, they learn to apply this *iterative* cycle of data modeling not only to describe cases that they have already observed, but also to make predictions about future events based on their data set or on related sets of cases that they have not yet had the opportunity to study.

Helping children work with data is not only about exploring mathematical concepts and developing scientific knowledge. Making the transition from experiencing data to interpreting data involves the use and development of many cognitive skills. For example, guided by questions that are generated by their own interests, students learn to view abstract objects, events, and experiences as clusters of attributes. A pumpkin is not just "big," but has width, height, and weight. Deciding how best to measure these attributes takes students through a range of decisions, often discussed with peers. (How children develop a sound theory of measure is fascinating in its own right, and several teachers have been exploring this issue and articulating what they find and what they question.) Early and frequent practice with data, learning to separate data from the cases they represent, and generating and evaluating data models are likely to encourage children to develop the habits of thought needed in a democratic society—

the predisposition to reflect critically about their own beliefs, to consider plausible alternatives, and to reason on the basis of evidence.

Acknowledgment: The authors thank Dr. Clifford Konold for his thoughtful comments and suggestions about the chapter and its contents.

REFERENCES

National Council of Teachers of Mathematics. (2000). *Principles and standards for school mathematics*. Reston, VA: NCTM.

National Research Council. (1996). *National science education standards*. Washington, DC: National Academy Press.

Tabletop™ [Computer software]. (1994). Cambridge, MA: TERC; Novato, CA: Broderbund.

Wisconsin Fast Plants™ [University of Wisconsin–Madison, Department of Plant Pathology Developers]. (1989). Madison, WI: Wisconsin Alumni Research Foundation; Burlington, NC: Carolina Biological Supply Company.

Chapter 2

How Children Organize and Understand Data

ANGIE PUTZ

Country View Elementary School, First Grade
Verona, Wisconsin

This chapter focuses on how first-graders can be involved in survey research and how they organize the data they find to share with others. First-graders can be introduced to core ideas in scientific work with data, including classification of objects and the making of models such as graphs. I was exploring how children can deepen their understanding of data by doing research meaningful to their own experiences. In past lessons, children in first grade had learned only to read and create graphs for which the data was already provided. I wanted to take this concept and extend it so that the children were actively involved with the collection of information and in the organization of that information into modes they felt would explain mathematically what they had learned. This was not just a new way to teach an old idea, but a process that involves new levels and types of understanding. The research I am reporting here focuses on classroom experimentation.

My purposes were to

1. Expose the children to a variety of data-collecting experiences related to a topic we were learning about.
2. Discover what was common across experiences, if anything.
3. Observe how students thought about and created the organization of their data. (Would the children be able to weigh the evidence, reason, and reach a conclusion from their findings?)

4. Observe how the children chose to model the information they wanted to share and how they revised their models, if necessary.

The research experiences my class participated in were "Fruit Flies," "How Do You Wake Up?" "What Do You Like to Play/Pretend?" and "What Is Your Favorite Soup?" The time spent collecting data and creating graphs for these research experiences varied from one day (Fruit Flies and How Do You Wake Up?) to several weeks, depending on the work involved. The research was done once or twice a week, averaging 2–3 hours for each research day. At the time of my writing, my class was continuing their soup research, described at the end of the chapter.

FRUIT FLIES

The data collection for the Fruit Fly experiment was thoroughly accidental. It was a wonderful experience because it was the children's idea to gather this information. In our classroom, where we were studying pumpkin rot, we already had four compost columns with decomposing food. The children noticed over a week's time that there were fruit flies everywhere in our room. About a week later, the rest of the school also began noticing fruit flies. My first-graders wanted to

Investigating Real Data in the Classroom: Expanding Children's Understanding of Math and Science. Copyright © 2002 by Teachers College, Columbia University. All rights reserved. ISBN 0-8077-4141-8 (pbk.). Prior to photocopying items for classroom use, please contact the Copyright Clearance Center, Customer Service, 222 Rosewood Dr., Danvers, MA 01923, USA, tel. (508) 750-8400.

find out where everyone was seeing fruit flies: Were our fruit flies flying all over the school?

I wanted first to find a baseline of the children's knowledge about data. First, we had a whole-class discussion and brainstormed together about what we thought data and data collection are. I was impressed that a third of my 18 children knew that collecting data means finding out information. Another third felt that it was finding out something in order to tell someone else what you found. The other third did not say anything at all. I was aware that in kindergarten, children make and interpret graphs, but I was not aware if the teachers had ever discussed data collecting with them. I was almost wondering if the way I had posed some statement could have led them to think that data was finding information. I remembered that I had told the children prior to our whole-group discussion that if we wanted to find out where all the fruit flies were, we would have to collect data. So whether the children really had any prior knowledge about data is unknown.

Preplanning

I asked the class, "How do you want to collect your information on where in our school the fruit flies are?" Most of the children wanted to go from room to room and ask. When I asked them, "How are we going to record our data?" I received a variety of answers. One child suggested that we write the teacher's name down and record a yes or no next to the name. A couple of students said that it would be too hard because they did not know how to spell the teachers' names. I admitted that could be a problem and asked how we could resolve it. A few children said that we could get a list from the office, and another child said they could just ask me. I brought out a floor plan of our school and had the children take a look at it. The floor plan showed every classroom with its number and the name of the appropriate teacher. I gave the children a choice of how and on what to record their information. It was interesting that the class decided to take the map. When I asked why, we had a nice conversation about why this map was efficient (see Figure 2.1).

What Categories?

I asked the children if they still wanted to record yes or no in the boxes. A few boys said they wanted to keep it that way, but one girl said that we could ask how many fruit flies the class saw in each room. When I asked her why we might do that, she replied that then we could see if there were a lot, some, or a few. One boy asked, "What if there were none?" The girl said we could have a group for none. It was interesting to me that she had said group. Was she already sorting the

fruit flies into groups by number? I wrote "a lot," "some," "few," and "0" on the board and asked, "If we want to find out how many are a few, some, and a lot, what numbers would you say for each?" The class pondered this for a while. One boy said, "A few means 3." I wrote 3 under "few." Another child said, " A lot would be 10." When I asked how he was able to say 10 was a lot, he responded that it was just a guess. I asked the class if they agreed that 10 fruit flies was enough. Most of them agreed. That left "some." One girl said that she felt we should say "some" is 5. She said that 5 is half of 10, and "some" was in the middle of "a lot" and "few." The class voted on the number of fruit flies for each group and agreed to adopt these suggestions.

How to Record?

I wanted to find out how the children were planning to record "a lot," "some," "few," and "0." I asked, "If I ask [another teacher's] class if they have seen fruit flies, and they say 'a few,' how will we record that on our map?" One boy suggested that we write "few" in the box with the teacher's name in it. There were no other suggestions, so I asked, "What would happen if we colored in each box to show how many?" There were a lot of "yeas." I asked the class if we should color each box the same color. Hands went up right away, and I heard a few "nos." When I asked why not, one child said, "Then you can't tell by the color how many there were." I asked them what they suggested. One boy said we could assign a different color to each group. The class agreed. Together we decided that if there were a lot of fruit flies, then we would color the room green. If there were some, we would color the room red. If there were a few fruit flies in the room, the room would be blue. If there were 0 fruit flies in the room, the room would be purple. I had the children flip over their maps and record what we had agreed on.

What If?

One boy raised his hand with a question: "What color are we going to color if they say they have seen 4 fruit flies?" The class looked at their color codes and numbers and realized we had a problem with our number system. Many other children noticed other numbers that were not included as well. I asked, "Is this color code going to help us?" Many of the children said no. I said that we were going to need to change or revise our number system. This was the first opportunity I had to teach the children what revising was. As a class we shared situations in which what we had made, we'd had to revise—either a part or the whole thing. We then got back to our problem with the number system. I asked, "Do we need to change '0?'" Many children said that 0

Figure 2.1. Preplanning data collection: Recording on paper or using floor plan.

Writing Teacher's Names on Paper
We don't know how to spell the teachers names.

It will take a long time.

Will we know if we asked every class in our school?

Using A Prepared Map
The teachers name is already on the paper.

We have a map of the school so we know where to go and ask.

It will not take as long since we do not have to write as much

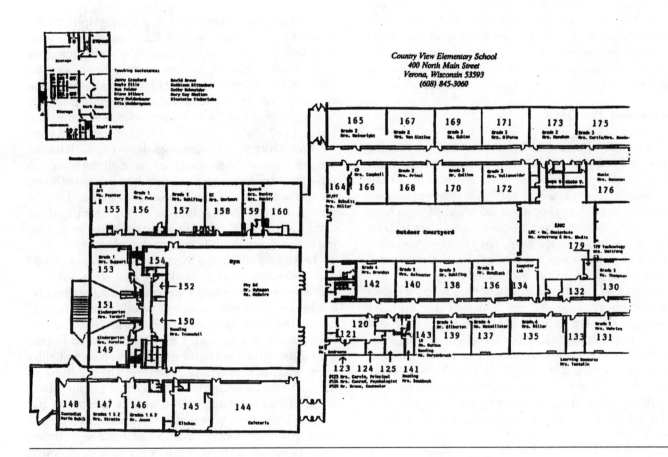

Country View Elementary School
400 North Main Street
Verona, Wisconsin 53593
(608) 845-3060

was 0, so we couldn't add additional numbers. One child noticed that because "some" was in the middle, and we had suggested 5, then "few" would have to be 4 or fewer. The children continued with "a lot" and "some." One boy, counting on his fingers, said, "When you start with 5 and count up to 7, that is three numbers. When you count 8, 9, 10 in a lot, that is three numbers, too." The children agreed that all of the numbers would now be taken care of. One child asked, "What will we do if there are more than 10 fruit flies?" The

children decided that it wouldn't make a difference because the number was still over 10, and 10 were "a lot," anyway. The child who had asked still felt it was important to write the number if it was over 10. I suggested that if we had 4–1 for "few," then we could place a + after the 10 representing more than 10. The class agreed that this solution would work. Now we had our table as follows: A Lot (8–10+), Some (5–7), Few (4–1), 0.

I suggested that as we went from classroom to classroom asking about fruit flies, we might also be interested in knowing where they had seen the fruit flies. We brainstormed about where we had seen them in our room. The children had noticed them by water, in the air, by food, by plants, and near our animal cages. For practice in recording data, I passed out an empty vertical graph. The children decided to label the groups at the bottom of the graph according to where we had seen them in our classroom. I wondered aloud if all other classrooms had pets in them as we did. The children responded that some did and some didn't. When I asked if we should have a column labeled "animals," some of the children replied yes, and one girl suggested that we could call it "other." I asked her why we should want an "other" group. She said that it might be for animals, but it might be for fruit flies some place in their room where we did not see them in ours. I asked her how she came up with the word *other*. She said that our class had used it before when we made graphs. I left this choice up to the children as they recorded where each class had seen fruit flies.

Collecting the Data

We traveled as a class from room to room, and the class decided that I would ask the survey questions: "Have you seen fruit flies in your classroom?" "About how many have you seen?" and "Where have you seen the fruit flies?" The people we interviewed from each class were either the teacher, students, or both. The children recorded as we went. They were very excited to take each classroom's information and see where it fit in their color code from the map as well as where they had seen fruit flies. In some classrooms, the respondents had seen the fruit flies in more than one place. My class discussed this and decided that on the graph we could mark more than one place per classroom.

When we got back to our classroom, I asked the class what they could tell me from their map. Because it was colored-coded, it was very easy for them to read. A couple of girls noticed that rooms 156, 157, and 158 had a lot of fruit flies and were right next to each other. I asked them why they thought these three rooms had a lot. Some of the children concluded that these rooms had a lot of fruit flies because we had a lot in our classroom (156). When I asked why two other rooms, both close to our room, didn't, one boy said that he remembered that respondents had seen flies around food and water. He also added that Ms. R. had said that the few there were flying around in the air. I asked why rooms 171 and 166 were the only rooms in the other hallway that had a lot. The children remembered that the teacher in room 166 had said they had a lot of food in the room. The teacher in room 171 had said that they had had a party—with a lot of food. The children concluded that

there were a lot of fruit flies in the green rooms because the fruit flies were looking for food. I asked if there was anything else they had noticed. The children made more-than and less-than comparisons from the map. They noticed there were more rooms with 0 fruit flies. There was only one room out of the whole school that had "some" fruit flies. One student noticed that the fourth-grade rooms all had fruit flies around plants. I asked him, "Why do you think the fruit flies were around the plants?" He didn't know, but another girl thought maybe it was because the flies had to have water, and the plants would have to be watered.

Displaying the Data

I asked the children to look at their graphs to find where they had seen the fruit flies. I asked them what they saw. The children said that there were more fruit flies seen flying in the air than in any other place. One child said that there were a lot of flies around food, but not as many as in the air. Another child said that "plant," "by water," and "other" were the same. One boy noticed that in "other," all four of the boxes were "by animal cages." He suggested that we could have left the title "animal" because "they were all the same." A few of the children noted that they had run out of boxes for "in the air" and "food." I asked how they had solved that problem. Their solutions varied from making extra boxes on top, to using some boxes twice, to adding boxes down the side next to the column.

I asked the children if their graphs were easy to read and understand. Some said yes, and some said no. Those who said yes said they knew what they had recorded so the graph was easy to read. Those who said no said that the graph looked messy and would be hard for someone else to read. I asked the children to take their information and make graphs, either using Unifix cubes or creating graphs on their own. The children had the rest of the class time to construct their graphs. Many children created Unifix cube graphs similar to bar graphs. There were both vertical and horizontal graphs (see Figure 2.2). Some of them were in the same order; many of the others were numerically correct, although arranged differently.

A few children created their own bar graphs by drawing boxes and coloring them in. The boxes were not of equal size or length, but the number of boxes equaled the number of places where fruit flies were found in each category. There were also a couple of graphs where the graphs did not have a starting point (0) horizontally or vertically. These children had the correct number of boxes representing their groups, but because there was no starting point, visual comparison of groups was difficult.

Figure 2.2. Unifix™ cube graphs.

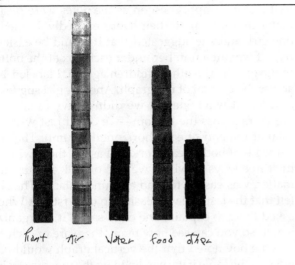

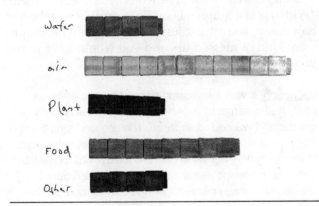

HOW DO YOU WAKE UP?

This data experience tied in with our reading a story about someone waking up. I asked the class, "How do you wake up in the morning?" I gave the children time to think, and hands went up in the air. I put a poster on the board with the question across the top. The children shared how they woke up in the morning: mom and dad, an alarm clock, the radio, and so on. I told them that although a lot of boys and girls woke up the same way, there was still a variety of ways mentioned by the students. I gave each child a yellow note and asked them to write their names on the notes and to draw a picture that showed how they woke up in the morning.

Displaying the Data

After the children had drawn their pictures, I asked them to place their notes on the poster. The notes were scattered all over the poster (see Figure 2.3a). I asked, "Is this easy to read? Can we tell easily how boys and girls in our classroom wake up?" The whole class replied, "No." I asked, "Why is this so difficult to read?" One of the children said that it was not organized enough, and the rest of the class agreed. When I asked how they could organize it to make it easier to read, one girl said that we could put the notes into groups. When I asked how, a couple of the children said that we had to find things that were the same. I asked them how they would like me to place our information on a new piece of paper. The children suggested that I put the names of the groups across the top of the paper. The children decided on the groups: "alarm clock," "mom/dad" "radio," and "other."

The children then instructed me to draw lines vertically between the groups to separate them (see Figure 2.3b). I asked the children to move their notes to the right group. It was interesting that they considered "radio"a group, especially when it only had one note in it (mine). I asked, "Why is my radio in a group and the

Figure 2.3. "How Do You Wake Up?" poster samples: (a) scattered, (b) vertical graph; (c) horizontal graph.

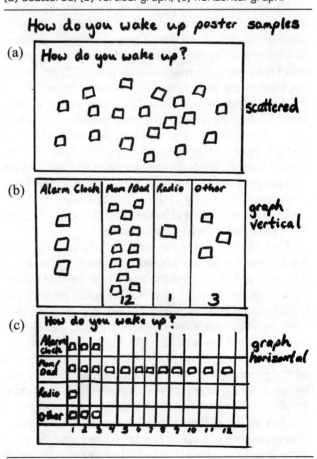

others are not in their own groups?" One child said that the radio is a common way for people to get up, but the other ways were not. The others consisted of waking up naturally, being woken by mom's shower running, and being woken by a sister. I asked, "Even though these are other ways to wake up, could we put each one of these into its own group?" The children replied, "Yes." One boy said that it would be silly to do that because there would only be one in each group. When I asked him, "Isn't there only one in the 'radio' group?" He said yes. When I then asked if we could make a group for each "other," he again said yes. I also asked, "Could I do something differently with the one radio?" One child said that I could put it in "other" because there was only one. Another child argued, "But people do wake up with the radio." I asked this same child, "So do people wake up in other ways besides the radio, mom/dad, and alarm clocks?" This same child said yes, but noted that most people did not wake up in other ways. For argument's sake, we left the poster as it was. I asked the children if it was easy to read and to understand how many children were woken up by mom/dad.

Revising the Graphs

Children started to point with their fingers, trying to count the number of notes. I said, "I notice some of you are counting with your finger. Is there something that we can do to the graph to make it easier to understand how many there are in each group? Then you do not need to use your finger each time to count?" Most children responded out loud, "Put numbers on the bottom." I labeled each group with a number at the bottom of the column. The children agreed that it was easier to read and understand, but a couple of children argued that we really would not need to put numbers next to the smaller groups, because their numbers were easily seen by looking at the notes. Two girls said that the labeling all needed to be the same. The class decided that either way would be acceptable.

I asked the children to look at the graph again to think if there was an even better way to organize our data. One girl came up to the board to show that we did not have to graph vertically, that we could go horizontally. I put up another piece of poster paper so the children could compare the two side by side. I asked the children to tell me how to make the graph horizontal. The children asked me to write the name of the group on the paper and draw a horizontal line under it (see Figure 2.3c). I gave them some time to look at the two graphs next to each other. One of the boys suggested that I draw boxes that were all the same, so each piece of paper could fit in a box. I complied and gave the class more time to compare. I asked, "Is there anything else I could do?" There was no response.

I had the groups come up and transfer their notes to the other graph. As soon as the notes were posted, many children raised their hands excitedly. I called on one girl, and she suggested that it would be easier to read if we put a number under each box at the bottom of the graph. The other children agreed. I labeled 1–12 across the bottom of the graph. Another girl suggested a different way: She felt we didn't have to label the numbers across the bottom—we could just write the total at the end of each horizontal column. The class agreed that both ideas worked. I asked them which of the three ways in which we had organized our information was easiest to read and understand. The class felt that the last one was easiest to understand. When I asked them to explain, one child said, "It is organized better, so you see how many there are of each."

One boy noted that the vertical graph would have worked the same if we had lined up the notes in straight lines like those in the horizontal graph. I asked him, "If you were to revise the graph, would you do it the way you suggested?" He said he would. Another child said, "With our last graph it is easier to read the numbers of how many. You can use just your eyes. The other graphs were kind of messed up, and you would have to use your fingers to count how many."

Reflection: It was interesting to me that the children really had a sense of organizing the information into groups and wanted to separate the groups using lines. The use of different lines created mathematical graphs. Numbering was not as important for the children's use. They did, however, see it as being helpful/efficient in reading the graph without having to finger-count.

WHAT DO YOU LIKE TO PLAY/PRETEND?

After reading a book, our class talked about what we liked to pretend. I then asked the children, "How can we collect data/information on what our class likes to pretend?" Most of the children said that we could just ask everyone in our room. I asked, "How would you keep track of what each person said?" Most said they would just write the name down and what the person liked to pretend next to it. A couple of the children said that I could document it on the board as we did for "How do you wake up?" I said that we could do it both ways and asked if anyone else had any ideas. There weren't any, so I explained that I would like each person to see what it was like to find his or her own information. I provided the class with a class list organized in columns. I explained to the class that we had to find our information by surveying the people in our class. I asked if anyone knew what I meant by surveying. There were no responses, so I asked one of the children to role-play making a survey with me. Together she and I asked each other what we liked to pretend. We then modeled how to record next to each other's name what we found out.

One boy asked, "Could we have a different question besides what you like to pretend? Sometimes you like to pretend by playing with something." I allowed the children to choose their survey question: "What do you like to pretend?" or "What do you like to play with?" I asked one more child to come up and help me model an interview. I told the children to watch and listen carefully. I had the boy ask me what my favorite thing was to pretend. This time I gave him a different answer than I had given the first child. There was immediate response, and many hands went up. One girl said, "You can't do that." When I asked her why, she said, "That's like a lie. You have to keep the same answer as you gave before." I asked, "Is that important to always give the same answer?" There were not too many who understood. I had a boy and girl who said that if that happened, everyone in the class would not have the same information. As a class we agreed that we had to give the same answer for each question.

One girl wanted to know if she could take her survey sheet home so that she could ask her friends. I asked the class what they felt. The children said it would be OK. I asked, "Are we collecting data from all of Verona, the whole school, or just our classroom?" The children responded, "Just our room." There were only a couple of children who understood that children outside our classroom were not part of the data. The rest did not understand that the outside data would bias our results. The children then asked if I should be in the data. I threw the question back to them. Most of the children said, "Yes." When I asked them why, one child said, "You are our teacher, and you are part of this classroom." It was then decided that I would be included in the survey.

Collecting the Data

The children grabbed slates and survey sheets and began collecting their data, walking around the room and asking one another their questions. I was concerned that having two different questions would confuse those being asked or those asking, but they did very well. There was only 1 child, out of 18 children, who mixed up his data. He had collected both "pretend" and "play" answers. He solved the problem by counting more play answers than pretend. I asked him what he planned to do with the answers that were pretend. He replied that he was going to go to those children again and ask them what they liked to play with. After the children had asked everyone in our classroom, I directed them to

organize their data in any way they wanted. I told them that when they were finished, they would share what they found with the class.

Organizing the Data

The way the children organized their data varied a lot from child to child. I had provided the children with tools to use to organize their data: large, blank sheets of poster paper; empty graphs; Unifix cube columns; the computers to create graphs; rulers, markers, and notes. My role was to make sure they had the tools they needed and to help as necessary. The majority of the children were able to organize their information independently. When there were problems, they were mostly mechanical in the making of the graph. A couple of boys had problems drawing vertical and horizontal lines. A couple of children looked at their data sheet and did not know how they were going to organize it. When we read it out loud together, I asked the children if they heard anything that was the same. "Oh, I get it!" was the usual response, and then there was no longer a problem. It was interesting to look around and see that the children were all working differently from one another and were able to stay actively involved. I noticed a lot of children using techniques to keep track of what they had already placed on their graph. Some were placing check marks next to each item recorded. Some were highlighting the names. There were children who highlighted or checked over their information more than one time. I found this to be very interesting because I had not asked them to do that.

The children created a variety of graphs. Two girls put boxes all across the poster paper in 3–4 rows. In each box was the name of the group, the names of the people who liked to pretend that item, and the total number of people in that box. One girl created a picture graph. She had the names of the groups in a horizontal graph. She made a picture on each note that represented one person and what it was he/she liked to play with (see Figure 2.4). Many children created Unifix cube graphs that were either vertical or horizontal. The children colored in the appropriate number of cubes for each group. The children then labeled the top or bottom of the column with the name of the group. Some of the children also included the number in each column; others did not. One child used the Unifix™ cube graph vertically. She labeled each group on the bottom and filled in each column cube with the appropriate child's initials.

It was interesting how many children chose to create their own graphs on large, empty sheets of poster paper. Only a few children were able to create a vertical or horizontal graph with the number of children labeled correctly. Other graphs had a number line, but the children did not correctly label the quantity in each

Figure 2.4. Horizontal picture graph (adapted student work).

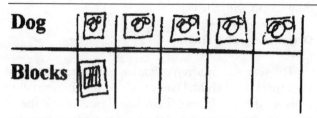

group. I wondered if these children used the numbers because they remembered past experiences reading graphs. Did they feel it was "the way" to model a vertical or horizontal graph? Did they really understand the use of the numbers in a graph, or was it just a mechanical problem in creating the graph?

Four children wanted to make graphs on the computer. The children discovered that the program restricted them to only seven category boxes, and they had more categories than the computer program was able to provide. Three of these children then decided not to make a graph on the computer. The one child who remained decided to make the graph even though there were only seven boxes available. This forced him to combine groups on his data sheet. He asked if he could do that on the computer. I asked him how he planned to group his information. He said that kids who like to pretend they are animals, hunting, or in a forest could be in a group called "forest things." He could not find any other similarities among the other groups, other than things that kids like to pretend that started with *T*. He still was not able to combine enough groups to get seven categories. I suggested that he try "other." He did not want to take my suggestion and decided to make a graph on poster paper.

Revising the Data

It was very interesting for me to watch the children create their graphs and see how they handled problems that arose. Most of the children started all over if they came across a problem that required moving lines or groups. Many children asked me for help if they felt it was a large enough problem to require adult guidance. Much of the time, what they needed was additional tools, such as extra paper to add to their existing graph or correction fluid to cover their mistakes. The children were very helpful to one another. There were many instances of suggestions between peers. Some of the suggestions were taken; some were not.

At times our class shared their graphs, and there was time for the class to ask questions, if there were any. These times were also used as revising sessions. Some

children created more than one graph for the same data, giving the class a wonderful opportunity to reflect on which graph was their favorite and why. When there were problems with a graph, the children shared ideas about how to improve it. The children learned that revising was very important in creating graphs.

Displaying the Data

When children finished creating one graph for their data, I challenged them to think of another way to show the same data. About three quarters of the class were able to come up with another way to show the same data. One girl came up with three different ways. She was one of few children who could identify similar groups and combine them into new groups.

In her first graph, she had five groups: "anmls" (animals), "prsen" (person), "steftanaos "(stuffed animals), "nentando" (Nintendo), and "staf" (stuff). She put numbers under the boxes at the bottom of her horizontal graph (see Figure 2.5a). When I asked her what the numbers meant, she said that she had messed up. Her purpose was to have a number under each box. She started with the numbers first, and the boxes were drawn on top of them. She then decided to write a number in each box next to the group it represented. When I challenged her to think of another way to show her data, she chose to make a horizontal graph using the Unifix cube sheets. It was interesting to see that she then took her information and broke it up into more specific groups than she had the first time (see Figure 2.5b). Her third graph came after our conversation together about her first graph. She said she wanted to make a graph with the numbers going across the bottom. I asked her if there was a tool in our classroom that would help her with that. She found the roll of empty graph paper, cut enough off, and went to work on her third graph (see Figure 2.5c). When she returned half an hour later, we compared all three of her graphs. I asked her, " Of all of your graphs, which one is the best way to show your information?" She chose her third graph. When I asked her why, she said that it was easier to read with the numbers on the bottom and the groups on the side: "Your eyes just slide across."

Reflection: It was interesting to me to see what children did when they ran out of a particular tool. For example, many of the children had only one piece of paper for their graph. It was interesting to see how they compensated for the lack of or for too much room on their paper. The changes they made to compensate often changed their understanding of the graphs. Many of the graphs were difficult to read because they were pieced together to get everything on one sheet. The children learned to use more than one resource to make a final product they were happy with.

Figure 2.5. One student's work showing data three different ways.

(a)

(b)

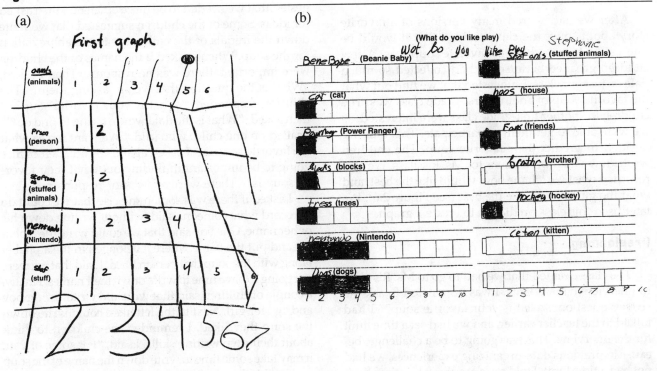

(c)

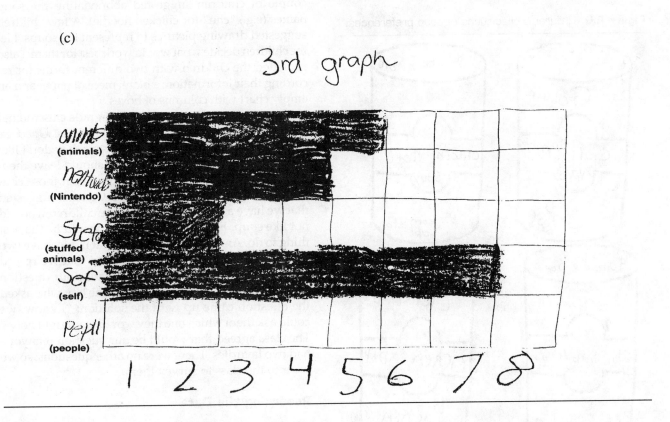

WHAT IS YOUR FAVORITE SOUP?

After we had shared many versions of a favorite story about soup, the class decided that it would be interesting to see what our favorite soup was. A few children groaned because we had collected so much data on just our class. I suggested that we find out what the favorite soup of another first-grade class was. The children in another first-grade class were interested, so we were able to get them to participate. This time we decided to predict their favorite soup. The children wrote down their predictions for Ms. R's class. We also recorded what we felt the boys would like the best, and what the girls would like the best (see Figure 2.6). We later used this class prediction to create a graph.

Preplanning

The class decided that we had to go to Ms. R's class to interview her students. I was nominated to ask the survey question "What is your favorite soup?" I had talked to the teacher earlier, and we had set a time limit for the interview. This was going to be a challenge, because in previous data-organizing experiences, we had not had a time limit. I told my class about this time limit

Figure 2.6. Children's predictions of soup preferences.

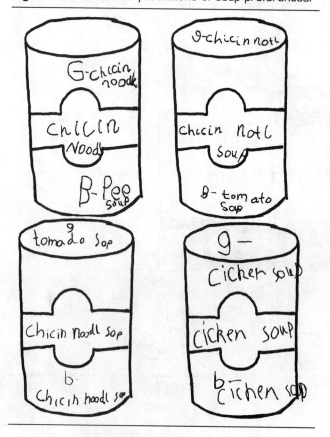

before we went to interview the other class and suggested that we needed to be more efficient. I then asked for ideas. Some of the children suggested that we write down the initials of the child next to the abbreviation for the soup. When I asked if the names of the children were important, there was no response. Then I asked, "What is the question that we are asking them?" The children responded, "What is your favorite soup?" I then asked, "What is the data we are trying to find out?" I called on one child, who said, "We want to see what the favorite soup is." I asked again, "So are their names going to be important in finding out what their favorite soup is?" There were a few "no" responses.

I asked if there was something else that we could do to record what someone said, without writing down his or her name. One boy said that we could write the alphabet and put the name where it belonged in the alphabet along with the soup that person liked. I said that we were not going to have time to write down their names. Finally, a couple of children said that we could write "b" for boy and "g" for girl. Next to the letter we could write down the soup they liked. I reminded the children to think about their own writing skills. I said, "For some of you, it may take some time to write down the name of the soup each child likes. Is there something else we could do to be more efficient when writing down soup names?" A couple of children suggested abbreviating the soup names (e.g., "chn" for chicken noodle). A few children suggested drawing pictures to represent the soups. I let the children decide what would work best for them. I also provided the children with two different forms for recording their information: a blank piece of paper and an empty chart with columns of boxes.

Before we went to the other first-grade classroom, I asked my class if they had any questions. One boy asked, "What do we do if someone says they don't like soup?" A couple of children felt we should leave them out of the data. Other children argued that those children were still part of Ms. R's class. One girl suggested that we have a "no" column for those children who did not like soup. Everyone agreed that would be the best thing to do. Another boy asked, "What if they have two favorite soups?" One child suggested that we record both. Many children disagreed because our question was "What is your favorite soup?" The boy who asked the question came up with the solution: "I know, we could ask them which one they would want right now." The class agreed that would be our question if anyone had two favorites. There were no other questions, so we went to the class to survey them.

Recording the Data

We first asked Ms. R's class to make the same predictions our class had made. Our class planned to take their predictions and compare them to our own. I then went to each student to ask our class survey question, "What is your favorite soup?" After recording the data, we returned to our own classroom. When I asked if anyone wanted to share how he or she recorded the data, many said they had written "b" or "g" (for *boy* or *girl*) for gender and showed their representations of the soups (see Figure 2.7). Some wrote abbreviations for both gender and soup names. One girl had created a "no soup" space ahead of time. She had also made areas on her paper for boy responses and girl responses. It was going to be interesting to see if the children would be able to remember later how they had recorded their information. After class, two girls came up to me with concerns. One

of the girls had drawn soup bowls, but she couldn't remember which soups were which. We discussed the problem and decided that because the data the class collected were all the same, the girl would be able to fill in the missing soup names from other class members.

Creating Graphs

The children seemed to have an easier time creating graphs from the information they recorded from Ms. R's class than they had had with the play/pretend data. It was not clear whether this was because there was less information to work with or because of the time we had already spent working with data. The graphs were simi-

Figure 2.7. Students' data sheets showing data on soup preferences.

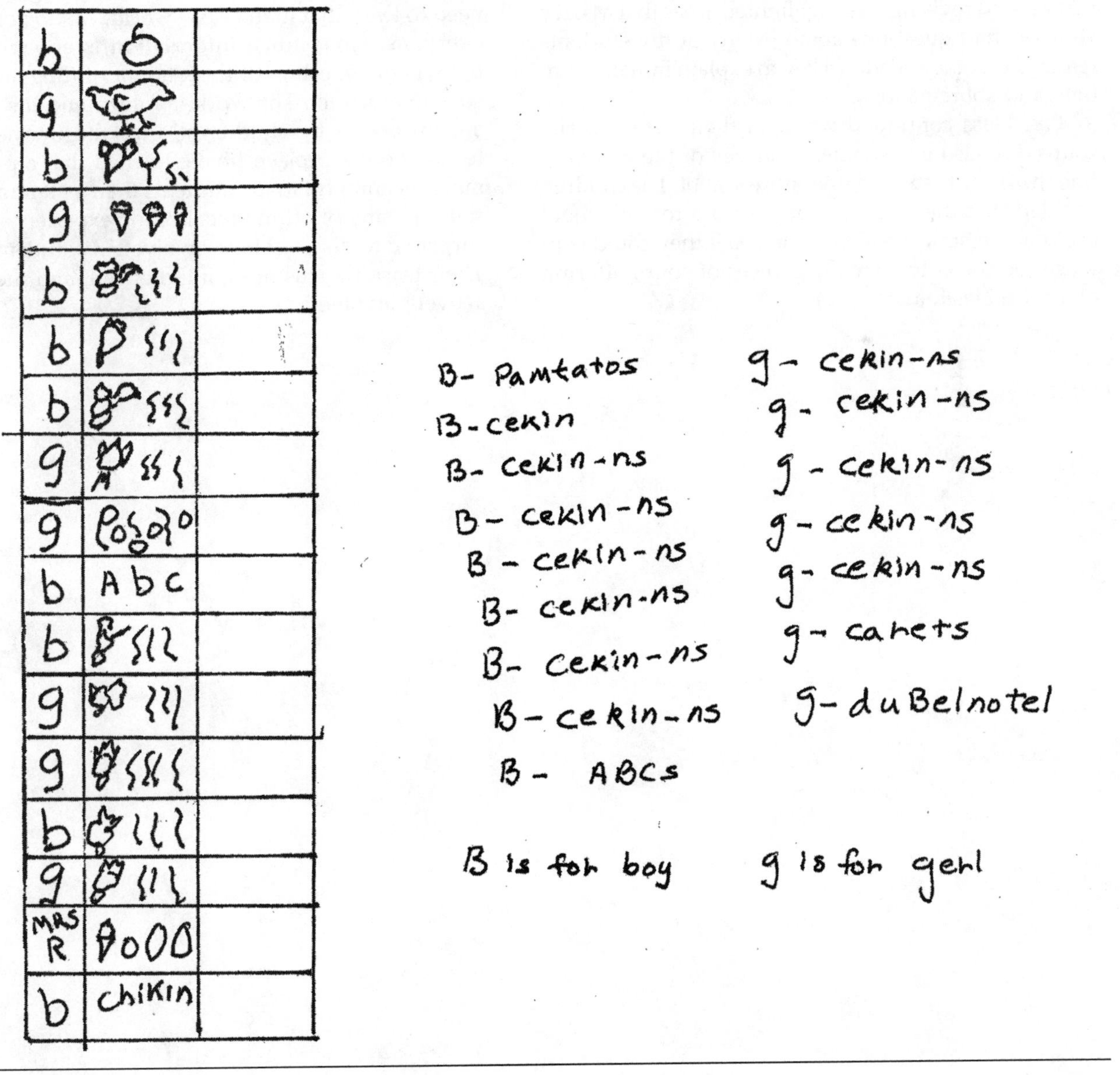

lar to those made before, but were more varied. There were bar graphs this time, and children also created successful graphs on the computer. I did not have the children create more than one graph this time. Instead, I wanted to revisit Ms. R's class with our information. When many of the children had finished their graphs, I had them share the graphs with the rest of the class to see if they were able to read and understand the graphs created. The children did an excellent job of revising, and there were many children who did not need to revise.

We then revisited Ms. R's class with our information. I told my class not to give the other class any additional information unless they asked for it. We wanted to see if a different class could read the graphs my students had created and could understand the information. There were no problems except for clarification on what "b" and "g" were for. My students had brought markers with them to highlight any area on their graphs that needed revising. We highlighted areas that Ms. R's students had questions about. Many of my students realized that they needed a key to explain initials, symbols, and abbreviations.

Our class continued work on their own favorite soups. We also investigated a survey of the school to find the favorite soup for the entire school. The children decided that they wanted to give data to our school cooks about soup preferences to see if they could convince the cooks to vary the choices of soup, offering others besides tomato.

SUMMARY

Through the experiences of my students, I noticed that children of this age seem to have a natural sense of organization. The more we collected data and organized them, the more efficient and better the students became. The next time I do this, I would like to start with a benchmark in mind and with an idea about how much the class knew about graphs before we started. Also, because it was difficult for the children to understand exactly what a survey is, it would be nice to provide them with an example of a real survey. It would, however, be difficult to find a survey appropriate for a first-grader.

It is difficult for students at this age to find similarities among groups and recombine those groups to make new groups. Only a few students in my classroom were able to combine groups with similarities. Children also need to learn that in the adult world, we do not survey everyone: How much information is enough? Then there is the question of the amount of time needed to sustain a project. The work involved and the interest and purpose of the children all affect the time necessary to carry out a project. I have learned that a project is more meaningful to my students than a 40-minute lesson. In many of our data-collecting experiences, I was surprised to discover how involved my students were. Their learning was more internalized, and they were actively involved.

Chapter 3

How Much Traffic?: Beep! Beep! Get That Car Off the Number Line!

JEAN GAVIN

Sugar Creek Elementary School, First and Second Grades
Verona, Wisconsin

How can the flow of traffic be represented by a collection of data? In order for the first- and second-grade students at Sugar Creek to work with, generate, interpret, and ask questions of data they collected as they tangled with this problem, they had to understand many underlying concepts. Moreover, these ideas popped up at varying times in the project, requiring that students grapple with them en route to pursuing their overall program of inquiry: namely, to find out whether the new highway bypass would have an affect on the amount of traffic passing through Verona. Here are some of the conceptual challenges students confronted along the way in their investigation of this question:

- Data can be a vehicle that carries a message. It is a way of keeping track of phenomena, as well as a means to communicate information about phenomena.
- Change can be indicated by patterns that appear in data. In that respect, data can also serve as a model for making predictions about a group of things by looking at a small sample from the group.
- In many ways, spatial sense is inherent to understanding a data structure. Measurement is necessary for collecting, representing, and understanding data modeling.
- Spatial patterns provide a visual picture of concentrations and extremes in a data sample. They can be used to identify shifts and distributions, which indicate stability or cycles of change.
- Because data can be represented by symbols, listed in tables, displayed in diagrams, or plotted on number lines, data can present a huge directionality problem for children—especially for students who are learning to use another notational system for reading and writing. The pattern for decoding our language moves from left to right and from top to bottom. In making sense of data represented on a number line or a quadrant with x and y axes, it is necessary to locate zero and use that point as the point of reference for orientating information. Some of the first graphing experiences my students had this year indicated that although most of them could build a graph along the x axis with numbers moving from left to right, many had problems building a similar graph along the y axis moving from the bottom to the top. Locating zero as the point of origin presented a challenge.
- Charts and spreadsheets use a matrix for organization, so information is found by intersecting vertical and horizontal columns of data. Venn diagrams offer yet another spatial format that represents included or excluded elements of a set.
- Number sense, relations, and operations are also important for manipulating and summarizing data to find the mean, median, and range of a sample.

Investigating Real Data in the Classroom: Expanding Children's Understanding of Math and Science. Copyright © 2002 by Teachers College, Columbia University. All rights reserved. ISBN 0-8077-4141-8 (pbk.). Prior to photocopying items for classroom use, please contact the Copyright Clearance Center, Customer Service, 222 Rosewood Dr., Danvers, MA 01923, USA, tel. (508) 750-8400.

THE PROJECT: BACK TO THE ROAD

The timing of this project corresponded to completion of the construction of a highway bypass around the city of Verona. I did not inform students about the new road or a possible change in traffic patterns. They were asked to count the number of cars that traveled through Verona, and thereby, past their school. So on Friday mornings from 10:30 to 10:45, the students counted traffic for two weeks before the new road opened and for two weeks afterward.

October 6

Students conducted a survey in which they counted the cars going through Verona on Highways 18 and 151. They worked with the same partner all 4 weeks, in hopes of achieving a more reliable or consistent process for collecting data. It was raining on the first day, so we counted traffic from the window of a second-story classroom overlooking the highway.

Because we would be working with large numbers, I anticipated that many students would have difficulty keeping track of them. Tallies were suggested as a method for recording, and we shared an example of how they could be used. Because tallies are used to represent information, they force a separation from the real world to symbolic notation. We had never worked with tallies in the classroom before, so I wanted to find out how students might use them to represent the traffic and what they would do to total them. I didn't expect that many children would have an organized way of grouping or counting their numbers.

Each group determined whether they would count by 1s, 2s, 5s, or 10s. They indicated their decision at the bottom of their tally sheet, for example: 1 tally = 5 cars. Four groups counted traffic going west toward Mount Horeb, and five partners counted traffic moving east toward Madison. After counting, each group worked together to find the total number of cars. It was difficult for some partners to come to an agreement. Most groups had used a tally to represent five cars, then skip-counted by 5s to find a total. One group that had difficulty with sequence and place value counted 5, 10, 15 . . . 100, 200, 300 . . . and on into millions. This group also indicated that each tally equaled five cars, then proceeded to count ++++ as 5 rather than as 25. Two other groups that counted by 1s organized their tallies into groups of 5, as the previous group had. They had no difficulty, then, counting by 5s to get a total. The last two groups had marked a tally for every 10 cars and counted by 10s.

Because we didn't have time to plot our numbers before going to lunch, I had a chance to look at the tallies and totals. After lunch I marked several tallies on the board, explained that each tally was equal to one car, and asked students to total them. They tried counting by ones, but had difficulty in tracking the tallies and keeping their place:

T: Is it easy or hard to count the tallies like this [see Figure 3.1a]?
S1: It's hard because everyone else is counting.
S2: I'm getting mixed up.
T: Is there anything we could do to make it easier?
S3: We could count them together.
S4: We can put a line through the tallies
T: How would we do that? Tell me more.
S4: Count 5 tallies and put a line across them [see Figure 3.1b].
T: Why would that be easier?
S4: Then we can count them by 5s.
T: Should we count the line that we put through the tallies?
S4: No, because that wasn't a car, and then we'd have too many.
TI: I noticed that some people did put a line through their tallies when they were counting the traffic. Would someone be willing to tell us how you did that?

Figure 3.1. Counting tallies: The difficulty of keeping track. (a) Tallies without grouping; (b) tallies grouped by 5 (crossbar not counted); (c) tallies grouped by 5 (crossbar is fifth member of group); (d) tallies circled in groups of 10.

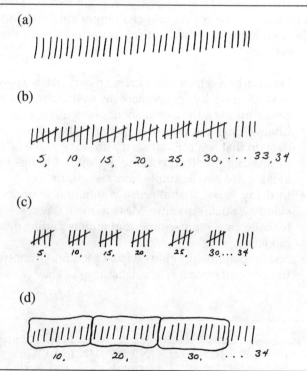

S5: I put four tallies down, and then when we saw another car, I put a line across [see Figure 3.1c].

T: Did you count the line across as a car then?

S5: Yeah.

T: How did you count the tallies, then?

S5: We went by 5s.

T: So, if we group them [the tallies] together, does that make it easier to count? Could we also count by 10s and circle the groups that way? Let's try that with our tallies here on the board [see Figure 3.1d].

Students told me their total count, and the information was organized as a table on the chalkboard, as shown in Figure 3.2. (Even though some groups had written numbers like 3009, they recognized the value as 309.) From the table, we found the lowest and the highest number of cars counted, in other words, the range.

The data were then plotted on a number line, as represented in the bottom portion of Figure 3.2. The following exchange took place:

T: Why do you think we got so many different answers?

S1: Sometimes it was hard to count with a partner.

S2: Some people counted by 1s and some counted by 2s.

T: What do you think was happening over here? [points to 310 on the number line of traffic to Madison] Why did some people get a number that is much bigger than what other people counted? Looking at the information, what would you think is the most valid or the most likely number for the traffic going to Madison?

S3: Maybe about 140, because two people got that number.

October 13

It was a beautiful fall day, and students were anxious to get outside, sit in the warm sun, and collect more information about the traffic. I expected the counting and tallying to go much more smoothly this week and

Figure 3.2. Traffic counts on October 6, plotted on number lines (class work).

To Madison	To Mount Horeb	Range:	130 - 300
130	210		(lowest to highest)
140	220		
140	290		
185	300		
310			

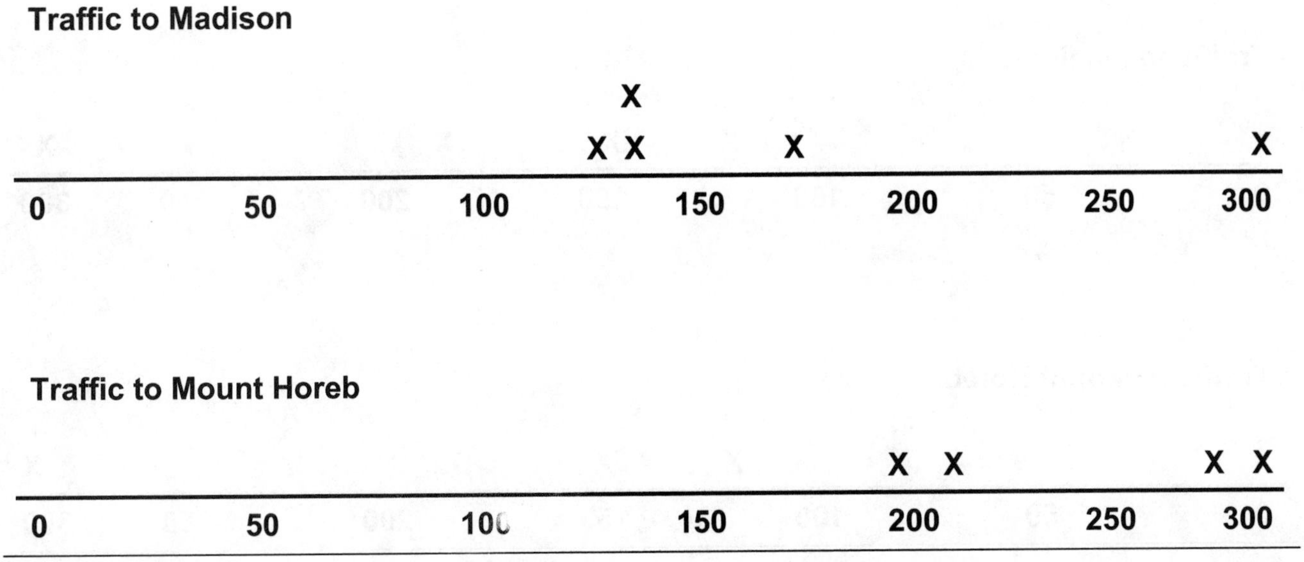

Traffic to Madison

Traffic to Mount Horeb

the traffic totals to be more consistent between groups. Because there was one group that had had several difficulties using tallies the previous week, I worked with them more closely. After we plotted our totals, as displayed in Figure 3.3, the following conversation occurred:

T: Look at our count for this week. What can you tell me about the traffic?
S1: Some people got really big numbers.
T: They did. How do you think that might have happened?
S2: Maybe they counted both ways.
T: What should we do with those numbers?
S3: X them out.
T: Can we do that? Do they seem unreasonable because all of the other groups got totals that were fairly close to one another and quite a bit smaller?

After looking at the tally sheets, I questioned one person in each of the groups that had counted 320 cars. Neither could count their tallies for me and come up with the number they had given. In fact, one of them

was the student who had said, "Maybe they counted [traffic] both ways."

October 20

By October 20, the highway bypass was open. Because the weather was rainy and cold, we again counted traffic from the second-floor classroom in the old school building. Aside from the two groups who had counted traffic going both ways the previous week, there was another group who had problems working together. The two students in that group each kept an individual count this time. Other students worked with the same partner and recorded their information on their clipboards.

By this time, I expected students to be fairly proficient in using tallies and working together to record information. I also expected the traffic flow to be reduced, which would make the count more manageable. I was curious about whether anyone would notice that the road did not seem as busy. Would it occur to them that their numbers were smaller than in previous weeks? Would they notice a drop when we plot-

Figure 3.3. Traffic counts on October 13, plotted on number lines (class work).

To Madison	To Mount Horeb
190	185
145	120
320	150
120	320
140	

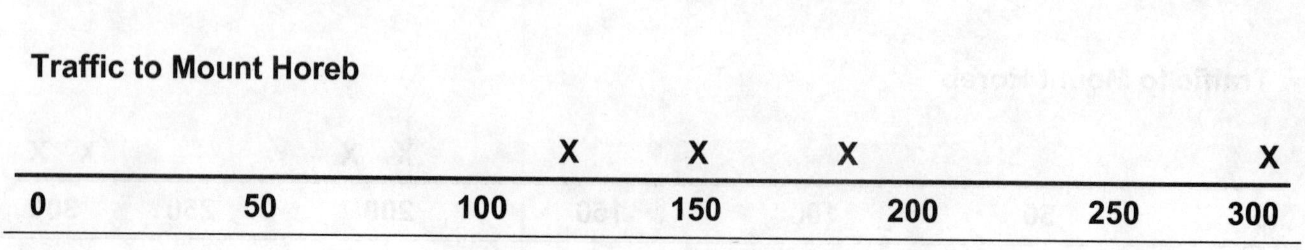

Traffic to Madison

				X	XX		X			X
0	50	100	150	200	250	300

Traffic to Mount Horeb

			X	X	X		X
0	50	100	150	200	250	300

ted the count on the number line, or would they need an extra nudge to look at trends? Would we be able to use this as a model to predict a change in the flow of traffic?

One student did comment about the traffic count being boring. I couldn't determine, however, whether that reflection was based on student attitude, weather, or the reduced traffic flow.

That week, even though the numbers were smaller, some students still had difficulties reading their own numbers after the tallies were totaled. One group read 105 as 150, and another group had written a 5 backward and then read it as a 2 (50 became 20). In both cases, the partners did not catch the mistake. This provided a good opportunity to revisit the data and double-check the information. It gave us new insights into variability as well as a very important reason for using standard notations in recording numbers. We plotted our data as shown in Figure 3.4. As we looked at the display, we had the following conversation:

T: What do you notice about the amount of traffic today, as compared to the last two weeks that we counted?

S1: The numbers are smaller.

T: What do you think that might tell us?

S2: Maybe the people didn't have to go to work today or the grocery store, so they just stayed home.

S3: There's a new intersection that just opened up. Maybe the cars went that way.

T: Is there anything we could do to find out whether traffic is taking a different route? How could we prove it?

S4: We could go count the cars on the other road.

T: We'd have to hike for about a mile on the bike trail just to get to the bypass.

All: Yeah! Yeah! Let's do it!

T: If we did go to the new highway to count traffic, how would that help us? What would that tell us?

S5: Then we'd know how many cars are going on the new road.

Figure 3.4. Traffic counts on October 20, plotted on number lines (class work).

To Madison	To Mount Horeb
50	55
80	40
50	40
50	122
105	

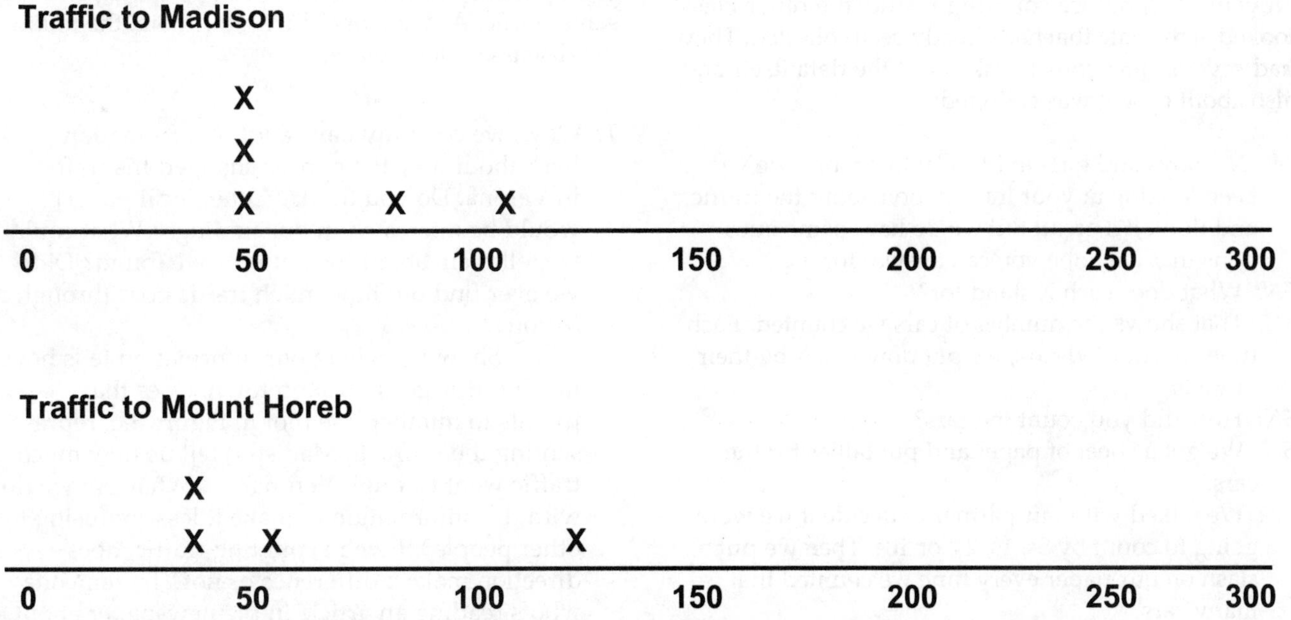

Traffic to Madison

Traffic to Mount Horeb

T: You're right. That would tell us how many cars are traveling on the new highway. But what information do we want to know? What have we been collecting for the past few weeks? If there are two different ways for the traffic to go now, instead of just one, what will we need to do in order to count how much traffic goes through Verona?

S6: Well, some of us could stay here and count while the rest of us go on the bike trail to count.

November 2

To prove that the change in traffic flow was caused by the opening of a new road, my students enlisted the help of another class. Between 10:30 and 10:45 on Friday, Ms. N.'s class was to count the traffic that passed by the school on what had become Business 18 and 151, or Verona Road. My students hiked a mile out along the bike trail to a point where they could count the traffic on the new bypass during the same period of time.

I wondered how my students would describe to the other class what we were doing. I expected that they could explain our number line plot, indicate the different counts, and explain the ways they had taken them. But I doubted that anyone would point out the pattern or trend in the traffic flow, or why this time we were going out on the bike trail to count.

I also wondered if students would be confused by the direction of traffic, once we were on the bike trail. We wouldn't have landmarks to help identify which cars were going to Mount Horeb and which to Madison, and we would be facing south on the bike trail instead of north on Verona Road. The traffic would also be much farther away and perhaps more difficult to see. I was really curious about what students would do. On November 2, before counting traffic, the other class looked at the data that had already been collected. They had several questions to ask about the data itself and also about how it was collected:

Ms. N: Boys and girls in Ms. Gavin's room, we've been looking at your information about the traffic and think it's great! But we do have some questions that we hope you can answer for us.

SN: What does each X stand for?

SG: That shows the number of cars we counted. Each time we counted cars, we put down an X by their number.

SN: How did you count the cars?

SG: We got a sheet of paper and put tallies for the cars.

SG: We talked with our partner to decide if we were going to count by 5s, 1s, 2s, or 10s. Then we put a slash on our paper every time we counted that many cars.

Ms. G: Should we try it together on the board, so you can see an example of how we counted? [draws tallies and counts]

SN: Why did you put a compass rose on the bottom?

SG: Some of us counted cars going in one direction, like to Mount Horeb, and the rest counted cars going the other direction.

SN: Why did some people get numbers that were so much bigger than others?

SG: Well the first time we counted, some kids might have counted by 2s or 5s instead of 1s. And then they might have gotten mixed up or something.

November 7

Our number line plot (shown in Figure 3.5) showed how the traffic patterns had changed over the past 4 weeks, but a bar or line graph would show the same information in a different, and perhaps more visual or obvious, manner. By offering multiple analogies of data modeling, I was hoping that children would come to a better understanding of the relationships that we had found in the traffic flow and rely less on the isolated attributes (Brown, 1989). We could graph the traffic as we counted it, either going to Mount Horeb or Madison, or we could combine traffic from both directions. Because there were many children in our classroom who were content to count by ones and use Unifix cubes, I decided to combine traffic counts and push the issues of place value and the use of manipulatives that were most effective.

I was curious to know if the students would look for a number in the middle to represent traffic each way. I expected that they would want to add all the numbers together, even though four or five groups counted the same traffic. As we worked with our data, the following discussion took place:

T: Wow, we certainly have a lot of information here about how the bypass changed the traffic in Verona. Do you think . . . the [local paper] would be interested in our findings? What could we tell them about the patterns we found? Did we ever find out how much traffic goes through Verona? . . .

    . . . Show me where our information tells how much traffic goes through town. Does that [points to number line plot in Figure 3.6, representing the traffic to Madison] tell us how much traffic went through Verona? . . . What can we do with this information to make it less confusing to other people? If we're counting traffic, does direction make a difference or not? To someone who's reading an article in the newspaper about

Figure 3.5. Traffic counts on November 3, plotted on number lines (work by two classes).

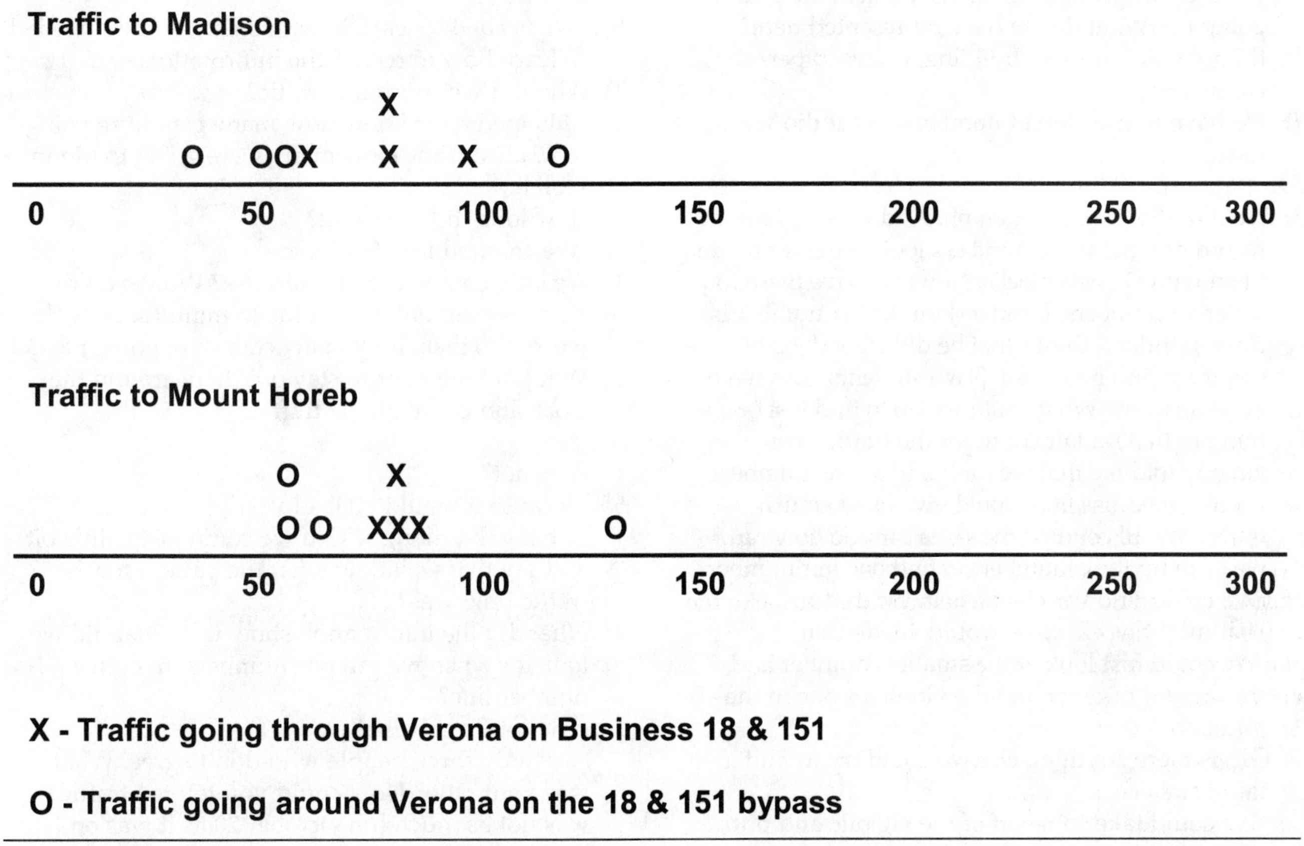

Traffic to Madison

```
                        X
        O    OOX    X      X        O
   |_____|
   0         50         100       150       200       250       300
```

Traffic to Mount Horeb

```
              O      X
              OO   XXX              O
   |_____|
   0         50         100       150       200       250       300
```

X - Traffic going through Verona on Business 18 & 151

O - Traffic going around Verona on the 18 & 151 bypass

how much traffic goes through Verona, does it matter which direction the traffic is going? [Eleven children vote that direction does not matter. One of those opposed says, "Then it would be harder."] . . .

. . . What should we do with this big number, 320, way out here?

S1: X it out.

T: Why do you think we could X it out?

S1: Somebody might have just counted the cars probably twice as much as the other ones did.

T: What's a fair number of cars? How could we put the numbers together? We've got the information, how are we going to put it together?

S2: We could pick any two lines and add those together.

S3: We could add all the traffic together.

T: Would that work?

S3: Use a calculator to add it all up.

T: If we added it all up, would that tell us anything?

S3: How much traffic was all together.

T: OK. Here, we've got one group of people counting the traffic that went to Madison. And this X shows another group of people who were counting cars going to Madison. Were these two groups counting the same cars, or were they counting different cars?

All: Oh, oh!

T: We have four groups who counted different numbers for the traffic going to Madison. Which one is the right number? How could we find one number that we all agree on, or that seems fair? How can we even them up, so we'll have one fair number? Let's build the numbers and see if we can find some way to make them seem fair or even.

Figure 3.6. Traffic counts on October 13, plotted on number line (class work).

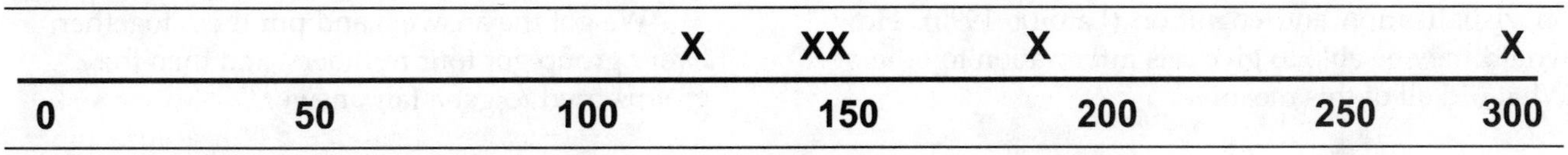

```
                        X     XX         X                      X
   |_____|
   0         50         100       150       200       250       300
```

T: What did we represent here? Look at the numbers. Look at our grid going across. Look at the grid going up. What do we have represented here? [Many wild ideas—a building, a skyscraper, an *f*, a gun, etc.]

T: We have four different numbers. What did we make?

S4: A graph.

T: We did. We have a bar graph. And we also have a record of what those numbers look like if we made them with Diene's blocks. Now, we have these four different numbers. [Student] thinks her number is right. [Student] thinks that he did a good job of counting, and he's right. [Two students] also have good answers. What could we do to find just one number that's a fair count for the traffic? You already told me that we can't add all the numbers together because that would give us too much traffic. We all counted the same cars. So how can we even up these numbers to find one fair number?

S5: We could find which one is in the middle.

T: That might work. How would we do that?

S5: We could just look at the smallest number and the biggest number and then look for one in the middle.

T: OK, is there anything else we could try to find a fair number?

S6: We could take some off of the big pile and put them on the little ones?

T: Could you show me what you mean by that? [Student removes a 10–rod from the largest pile and places it with the smallest pile.]

T: Do you mean that we could make all the piles the same?

S6: Yeah.

T: What would happen if we evened up the piles and there were two 10s too many? What could we do with those 10s?

S7: We could get 20 little cubes for them. Then put maybe two more on each pile.

T: Go ahead. Show us how you could trade them for ones and even them up.

November 28

Someone from the local paper was to interview our class on the following day, so I was interested in knowing exactly what the students could tell her about our survey, the information we had gathered, the reasons for doing it, and what the data represented. I was looking for what Latour called "holding the focus steady" on visualization and cognition (Latour, 1990). How would they be able to give this information to others? What did all of this mean?

T: How did you survey the traffic? What did you do and why?

S1: We needed to learn how to count, and we needed to learn how to record the information.

T: Why did we count the traffic?

S2: It helped us to know how many cars were going to Madison, and how many were going to Mount Horeb.

T: How long did we count?

S3: We counted for 15 minutes.

T: We only counted for 15 minutes? Wow, you're right, we did only count for 15 minutes. How do we know, then, how many cars were going past? Wouldn't we have to stay out there around the clock and count all the traffic?

S4: No.

T: Why not?

S5: Because it would take all year.

T: Is that valid though? Can we count just a little bit and say that we know what the pattern for the traffic flow was? . . .

T: What did the information show us? What did we look for when we put our numbers up on the number line?

S6: The traffic got smaller.

T: I see only three people who don't agree. What was your clue? How could you tell the traffic was not as much [on October 20 as it was on October 13]?

S7: Because the Xs tell how much there is. The other two weeks have like 200 cars, and these two weeks only have 100.

T: Why do we have blue Xs on November 3?

S8: They were counting on the bypass.

T: I'm going to ask you to work together in small groups. Each group needs to write one question that you think [the reporter] should ask us tomorrow and be ready to give us a good answer to your question.

The students came up with the following questions and answers:

Group 1: How did you count the traffic?

"We put one slash for each car that goes by. One slash can equal 5 cars, too. We got a piece of paper and decided how we are going to count, 5s, 10s, 1s, or 2s."

Group 2: How did you get a fair number?

"We got the answers and put them together. Every group got four numbers, and then the groups tried to get a fair answer."

Group 3: What does your graph show?
   "Our graph shows the number of cars. It shows the dates. And it shows the traffic."

Group 4: How did you record the information?
   "We wrote down tallies on a piece of paper. One tally could stand for 5, 10, or 1."

20/20 HINDSIGHT

How do I change my own thinking and teaching practices in order to help students learn? The process of predicting, describing, and recalling described by Kelly and Lesh (2000) offers a very practical model for practice and reflection on the process of teaching and learning. The big open-ended questions are more difficult for me to find. Next, I am curious to know what my students will transfer from this project with data collecting to other projects. If we set up an experiment with force and motion by putting the class toy frog in a little

wagon and observing the reactions to a simple push, what will students learn? Will they predict what will happen? How will they record the information? What patterns and relationships will they look for in the data? What conclusions might they draw?

REFERENCES

Brown, A. L. (1989). Analogical learning and transfer: What develops? In S. Vosniadou & A. Ortony (Eds.), *Similarity and analogical reasoning* (pp. 498–531). New York: Cambridge University Press.

Kelly, A., & Lesh, R. (Eds.). (2000). *Research design in mathematics and science education.* Dordrecht, Netherlands: Kleuwer.

Latour, B. (1990). Drawing things together. In M. Lynch & S. Woolgar (Eds.), *Representation in scientific practice* (pp. 19–68). Cambridge, MA: Massachusetts Institute of Technology Press.

Chapter 4

What's Typical?: A Study of the Distributions of Items in Recycling Bins

CARMEN CURTIS

Country View Elementary School, Third Grade
Verona, Wisconsin

Our third-grade class counted the number and type of items in each family's recycling bin during the month of February. I had several goals in mind. First, I hoped that the class would construct data displays as responses to questions that they posed about the contents of the bins. Second, I intended to find out how students might think about structuring data and how these different ways of structuring data might influence their ideas about qualities of distribution, especially measures of center. This apparently simple investigation of recycling bins initiated many investigations and conversations that I didn't anticipate, but that in retrospect were important for grounding students' thinking about data.

THINKING ABOUT DATA IN THE CONTEXT OF RECYCLING

What Counts?

The opening question posed by the class was straightforward: "What can you expect to find in a Verona recycling bin?" Before the data collection could begin, the class had to come to a decision about what would and would not be included in their data. For instance, the class chose to include glass bottles, alumi-num cans, and plastics in their counts, but not newspaper or cardboard. An important part of the data collection planning process was to make explicit the categories and information that would be included in the students' counts. We found that there's more to recycling than meets the eye. For instance, recycling companies distinguish among several different grades of plastic and glass. So, even our initial question proved more complicated than we thought, but thinking about the nature of the data helped students think about recycling. I find that questions about the nature of data often provoke thinking about the phenomenon itself.

What's Worth Measuring and How Do We Go About Measuring?

Once a week during the month of February, each student recorded the number of items in his or her family's recycling bin. Several students wondered what might be the "typical" or "usual" count for the families in the class, perhaps because they noticed that the counts were often very different. After four weeks of data collection, the class had a data set composed of seventy-one values, each representing the count in one recycling bin for each week in February. Students explored ways of manipulating, organizing, and describ-

Investigating Real Data in the Classroom: Expanding Children's Understanding of Math and Science. Copyright © 2002 by Teachers College, Columbia University. All rights reserved. ISBN 0-8077-4141-8 (pbk.). Prior to photocopying items for classroom use, please contact the Copyright Clearance Center, Customer Service, 222 Rosewood Dr., Danvers, MA 01923, USA, tel. (508) 750-8400.

ing these data in order to let them better answer the question they started out with: What is the typical number of items in a recycling bin?

"I've Got the Information, but What Does It Mean?"

At the end of the month, I asked students to write their counts for each week on a sticky note. I put the resulting 71 sticky notes on the board in no apparent order. I wondered what kinds of structures students might consider, so I asked, " "Is the way they're displayed right now a very helpful way to show people what we found out when we collected data about our recycling bins?" Several students answered, "No!" Abby suggested ordering the data according to days on which it was collected (students collected data on Mondays or Thursdays—both are recycling pickup days in our community). "Mondays could be in a separate column from Thursdays." Another student suggested arranging the data by week, so that it would be clear which pieces of data were collected during which weeks. To both of these suggestions, I responded by asking them, "What that would let us see that we can't see now?" By probing in this way, I encouraged students to think about how different organizations of data might "spotlight" different aspects of what was interesting about the relationships within the data. Several students noticed missing data. (There should have been 84 bin totals, but there were only 71.) Katie made the insightful comment that if the data were displayed in terms of days and weeks, the class would be able to identify the days on which some students did not bring in their bin totals (perhaps because they were absent from school, they forgot, etc.). This exchange, and others like it, helped students come to see how different arrangements of data could "show" different things about the data set.

Structuring Data to Answer a Question: Initial Strategies

We returned to our original question of "typical or usual" number of recycled objects. I asked questions such as "So how can we use those pieces of data that we collected to try to give our best-guess answer to someone who says, 'So what'd you find out? What is pretty normal, or pretty usual, for a recycling bin in Verona?' You've learned a lot about what's normal for your family. Is what's usual for your family the same as what's usual for everyone else's family?" The students talked a little bit about what was normal or typical for their family and decided that it would not necessarily make sense to say that what was normal for Natalie's family would be normal for Paul's. The rela-

tionship between unique cases versus the distribution of the whole data set became important for the class to think about.

I asked students to imagine different ways of arranging the set of recycling bin totals in order to help them "pick a number that's a good fit" for the data set as a whole. In the class discussion about this, three main strategies were offered. Eric proposed *ordering the numbers from smallest to biggest*, so that they could see the *range of the numbers* in the data set. Natalie offered another suggestion—grouping together all the 21s and all the 34s, that is, *group together all the values that occurred more than once*. This strategy involved ideas of frequency and mode. Natalie commented that this strategy would allow them to see "which ones [numbers] are most common and which one's aren't." Another way to arrange data was suggested by Abby, who proposed *ordering the numbers in intervals of 10s*, because "if you do that, it would help understand if the 20s or the 30s or the 40s are more popular." Through the discussion of these strategies, students were beginning to touch on issues of frequency and distribution: Which numbers and ranges of numbers would be "most popular" and perhaps even "typical?"

To summarize, the strategies that emerged in the whole group discussion were

- Arrange the values in order from smallest to largest (in order to see the range of numbers).
- Arrange like values together (all of the "21s" together, etc.) in order to see which ones occur most often.
- Arrange values from smallest to largest, grouping intervals of ten (in order to see what range of numbers was "most popular").

Hence, children's initial ideas corresponded to reorganizing data as ordered lists, as line plots, and as histograms. I next moved to small-group work as a setting for choosing among these senses of structure.

Small-Group Explorations of Data Structure and Distribution

The three kinds of strategies developed in the whole-group discussion served as resources for students when they broke up into seven small groups. Each group decided on ways to structure the data for the purpose of coming to a decision about what might be typical for a Verona recycling bin. I gave each group 71 paper squares with a count written on each square and asked each group to decide on a way of structuring the data. Many of the groups seemed to build off the initial three strategies, modifying and extending them in a variety of ways. During my interactions with small groups, I asked students to talk about why they proposed a particular strategy or agreed with one offered by another student. I consistently asked students to defend their contributions and to be as explicit and clear as possible while explaining their reasoning to the group. This emphasis on explanation was an important part of the small-group discussions. It encouraged students to think about the various reasons one might have for modeling data in particular ways, and it also encouraged them to keep their main research question in mind as they explored ways of manipulating the data. The ultimate task of the small-group work was to find a *defendable* number to represent a typical recycling bin.

What Do We Do with the Data?

All the groups, with the exception of one, eventually structured their data on the floor as a line of cards with totals arranged from smallest to largest, left to right. Some groups immediately started arranging all the data from smallest to largest; for other groups arranging the data was a two-step process. For these groups, the first step was to arrange the data set into subsets, each one an interval of 10. (This, too, was a suggestion from the class discussion.) After arranging by intervals, the groups then combined all the intervals in order, from smallest to largest, so rows of ordered numbers were common to all groups. The students did not leave any spaces between cards to represent potential values, so I inferred that they had explicit awareness of the order, but perhaps not of the interval.

One question that was raised in ordering the numbers was what to do with the totals that occurred more than once (the "doubles" and "triples"). At first, these numbers were simply represented as part of the sequence. Yet this did not seem "right," so students placed the repeated numbers in a column, so that the row was changed to a two-dimensional structure with columns depicting values that were repeated. This arrangement combined ideas that were presented in the whole-group discussion, that is, the idea of arranging the data from smallest to largest, and the idea of arranging the data by like values.

There was one group, however, who displayed their data differently. This group (Abby's) began by arranging the data in clusters in intervals of 10s until they had 10 different clusters of numbers spread out on the floor. Next, they proceeded to order each cluster from smallest to largest, ending up with 10 stacks. Because they were having trouble deciding which number was most typical for a Verona recycling bin by looking at randomly placed stacks of ordered numbers, I suggested that perhaps they could come up with a display that would move the data closer together, taking up less space. The group decided that it would be too difficult to make sense of one tall stack of 71 numbers, so they decided to keep the 10 stacks separate, but to arrange them differently. As Figure 4.1 shows, they ended up with a display consisting of 10 stacks (or columns) next to one another, ordered from left to right (with the smallest interval of 10 as the first stack on the left). Furthermore, each individual stack was ordered with the smallest number on the bottom to the largest on the top. This second step in arranging their data in order (both the stack itself and the grouping of stacks) was also a variation of the ideas that were presented in the whole-group discussion, that is, the idea of arranging them sequentially so as to capture the range (of each interval, in this instance). Notice, however, that as with many groups, the separation in value between the highest value and the remainder of the data was not explicitly represented as another bin.

So What's Typical?

After arranging the data, the students moved on to pick one typical number out of all 71 bin totals. In the effort to complete the task to come up with just *one* number that would best represent all the data they had collected, the students had to grapple with the various meanings that *typical* could have.

Some strategies to pick a typical number were abandoned more quickly than others. One group (Eric's) immediately looked at the range and halved it, coming up with 59 (the range was 0–119). The closest number to that in their data set was 61. However, on looking at their data, they realized that there were too many numbers below 61 for that to be a representative number.

Figure 4.1. A stacked display of data invented by Abby's group.

			39						
			38						
			38	47					
		28	38	47					
	18	28	37	46					
	18	27	37	46					
	17	24	36	44					
	17	24	35	44					
	16	22	35	43					
	15	21	33	43					
	15	21	33	43					
	15	21	32	42		66			
	14	21	32	42	56	64			
8	12	20	31	41	52	62			
6	12	20	30	40	52	61			119
0	10	20	30	40	51	61	72	80	106

Another group (Leah's) initially used this same strategy because it seemed "number-wise," but eventually decided that it wasn't only the *value* of the number that was important. They also needed to consider other values in relation to their selection of a typical number. For example, one group noted that the highest number (119) was *much* higher than the rest and occurred only once, because someone was cleaning out their cabinets. They thought that values such as 0 and 119 were "not very likely." Therefore they decided that it would be more valuable to look at numbers that were grouped together: "It's not the number [that's important], it's what's around it."

Another strategy was to look at the number that occurred most often. In fact, every group at one point considered 21, the mode, to be the best representative of a typical number. However, each group then decided that there were too many numbers above 21. It was not close enough to the middle of all the numbers in the data set to serve as the typical number. So, I inferred that children's first preferences might be for most (mode), but after considering the entire distribution, they wanted to find something that would be closer to "middle."

There were a variety of strategies for finding the middle. One group tried to find half of the entire set of values, and so found the median by "counting in" from both ends. They met at the 36th case, which had a value of 34. The children in this group had a sense of middle as splitting the data into upper and lower halves. Other groups also focused on "half" as a ready means of thinking about the middle, but they proposed that only the distinct entries in each bin should be counted. They wanted to ignore "copies" (multiple instances of the same value) and so proposed finding the value of the bin associated with the middle of the 44 distinct counts. Finding this sense of middle often lead to choices of "between 35 and 36," or arbitrary selection of one of these values

Abby's group also chose 34 as the typical number. Because they had arranged their data in intervals of tens, they noticed that the interval containing bin counts ranging in the 30s was the most frequent or "most popular" group. Since there was an even count of numbers in this stack (16), they had difficulty deciding which number to pick (34 and 35 were the two center numbers). In the end, just like the other four groups, they picked 34 because this number split the data in half.

One interesting thread that occurred in the search for the typical number was the mixing up of the *value* of the actual numbers and the *total number* of bin totals. For instance, Eric's group had decided that 34 was the typical number, based upon the idea that it seemed to be in the middle of the 71 counts. However, they decided to double 34 (perhaps to check their answer) and

came up with 68. This bothered them because they knew that there were 71 separate bin totals. So they chose the typical number to be either 35 or 36 because, when doubled, this total came closest to 71. (They noted that there was no actual value of 35.) Similarly, another group switched their typical number after seeing that the value of their number, when doubled, did not equal the total number of cases. Hence, the sense of half that some of the children entertained about the data seemed to oscillate between the order of the bin count in the group (the 36th case) and the idea that the resulting value (34) should be half as large as the total (71).

SUMMARY AND REFLECTIONS

Trying to answer the question "What can you expect to find in a Verona recycling bin?" provided my students with an interesting context for data construction and display. I wanted to shift the classroom emphasis from answering questions about a pre-made display of someone else's data to working with data generated in response to a question posed by students. Working with recycling data collected over an entire month gave my students the opportunity to manipulate a large amount of data. The sheer quantity of data created a need for summary and display. It also provided me with an opportunity to find out how the data arrangements or displays created by students might be similar to or different from the tables, charts, and graphs provided by textbooks and teachers. Although student displays converged toward those provided in textbooks or newspapers (like the student groups of 10 and histograms), students' efforts to make sense of these data helped them see the rationale for conventional displays such as frequency plots or histograms.

Even though the data displays created by the students were very similar (six of the seven groups had nearly identical arrangements at the end of the lesson), I knew that there was a great deal of thinking behind those displays. The class wrestled long and hard with the problem of how to arrange these data to answer our questions before small groups started to "play" with the data set. Students' initial ideas about how to structure the data were fairly unsophisticated, but questions that I asked and questions the children asked of one another focused everyone's thinking on the job that the final display needed to do. I found that asking "What do these data tell us?" quickly led to responses focusing on "has the most" or "has the least," but often did not go much further. Asking the whole class to consider the issue of "typical" seemed to stimulate consideration of the entire data set as a distribution (how the data were clustered), rather than as a mere collection. Over the course of discussion, students began to see that various arrangements of the bin totals (i.e., various ways to structure the data) could be a *tool* for helping them think about a fair number to represent all of their recycling data. Once each group of students had a chance to arrange and rearrange the data, they used their displays to convince the rest of the class that their choice of a typical number made sense.

If I were to try this task again, I might add some data from some hypothetical bins to distinguish more clearly between the range of the data and the number of cases (In this set, by happenstance, they were the same). This might help children keep better track of some important distinctions as they create representations of data. I would want to focus more on what to do about multiple instances of a value when considering typical numbers (indicators of center). I might also think of ways to characterize the variation that children dealt with in their construction of "typical," perhaps by posing questions comparing one week's data to that of another. These and other distinctions might be profitably mined, so children could learn to reason about distribution in the primary grades.

Chapter 5

Shadows

SUSAN WAINWRIGHT

Country View Elementary School, Second Grade
Verona, Wisconsin

I had several coordinated objectives for the shadows project that I pursued with my second-grade class. First and foremost, I hoped to increase students' awareness of shadows and what causes them. I planned to pursue this objective by having students investigate relationships between geometric solids, the position of a light source, and the resulting shadows that were cast. We followed these investigations with research on how the length and position of our own shadows changed throughout the day. Both of these investigations provided motivation and opportunities for data collection and recording. Having students conduct an investigation by collecting, representing, and interpreting data was my second objective for the unit. My third objective, related to the first and second goals, was to introduce data modeling as a tool for learning. We completed this project over 2 weeks, working for about 90 minutes each day.

FIRST STEPS

Before beginning the investigation, I wanted to learn about my students' initial beliefs about shadows. I was pretty certain that they were well aware of shadows and suspected that they would have some interesting preconceptions about what causes them. I also guessed that they were aware that the sun changes position during the day, although I was not confident that all students knew that changes in shadows co-occur with shifts in the sun's position.

First Discussion

To get a sense of students' initial thinking, we read a children's book titled *Bear Shadow* (Asch, 1985) together as a class. This provided a ready context for asking my second-graders what they knew in general about shadows. As new ideas were raised during the group discussion, I listed their ideas on a large piece of paper. Here are some of the ideas that they generated:

- Almost everything has a shadow, and the shadow is part of the object.
- Shadows look like the object making the shadow.
- There is a connection between what causes shadows and reflections, for example, in a mirror. This is because both shadows and reflections "look like the object that is making them."
- Shadows aren't always in the same place.
- Shadows are caused by blocking light.

I noticed that some of these ideas (such as the last two on the list) would serve as very useful foundations for our inquiry. Others ("Shadows look like the object that casts them") are not always right, and could provoke some interesting challenges for children to struggle with as we proceeded with our investigations. It was very helpful for me to have this briefing on children's initial beliefs, because it helped me think ahead to the kinds of questions that students might be likely to raise when we began our shadow work.

Investigating Real Data in the Classroom: Expanding Children's Understanding of Math and Science. Copyright © 2002 by Teachers College, Columbia University. All rights reserved. ISBN 0-8077-4141-8 (pbk.). Prior to photocopying items for classroom use, please contact the Copyright Clearance Center, Customer Service, 222 Rosewood Dr., Danvers, MA 01923, USA, tel. (508) 750-8400.

Preevaluation

Next, I asked my students to write and draw pictures individually to answer a series of targeted questions about light and shadows. My purpose was to find out how widely the ideas expressed by the group were shared by individual children. I also suspected that drawings might be a better medium for explaining certain ideas (for example, how light travels) than group discussion.

The first question I asked was "How does light travel from a flashlight?" I provided a picture of a flashlight and asked students to draw a picture that would answer this question. Most of the second-graders drew the light traveling out from the flashlight in straight lines. The lines proceeded out at various angles, as shown in Figure 5.1a. However, to my surprise, a couple of the students drew the light going *toward* the flashlight (Figure 5.1b).

Figure 5.1. Student depictions of light from a flashlight.

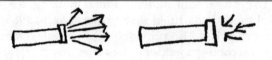

The second question I asked was "What causes shadows?" Once again, students' replies showed varying levels of understanding and detail. Some students mentioned only the role of the object or agent that casts the shadow. In these replies, the object and its shadow were not clearly differentiated. For example, one simply claimed, "People make shadows." Another said, "You can make animals with your hands. Shadows are you. What you do, your shadow does."

Other students mentioned the role of light, without saying much about how light is implicated in shadows. Figure 5.2 is a good example of replies in this category. However, some students explicitly mentioned the *blocking* of light. As one explained, "If you shine a light on a person it will make a shade spot because it blocks the light. The light hits your body and makes a shade spot." Another said, "If you put your hand up by a wall and shine a light on the wall, the light will go past your hand and not through it."

Some of the replies to this question included references to reflection, suggesting that, as the whole class discussion had implied, some students might be unsure about similarities and differences between reflection and shadows. Perhaps children knew that both phenomena had something to do with light. Perhaps children had in mind their idea that both reflections and shadows are in some way "similar" to the object that

Figure 5.2. Student's response to the question, "What causes shadows?"

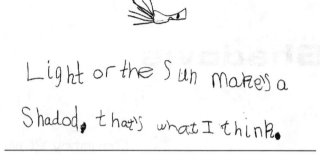

Light or the Sun makes a Shadod, that's what I think.

casts them. Alternatively, they might have heard that light is reflected off an object that casts a shadow, and they might therefore believe that reflection is involved somehow in shadows, without being sure how. For example, one child wrote, "Shadows are made of light. It reflects off your body. It can be any kind of light. It can be sunshine, regular light, or any kind of light there is." Another claimed, "A shadow is caused by a light. It reflects by the light and it needs light to proceed. A shadow can be made by dark sometimes. That's all I know about how a shadow is caused." As in this last remark, I noticed that some students apparently think that "dark" is a quality that is somehow different from the mere absence of light (just as many students believe that "cold" is a positive attribute that is the opposite of "hot").

DARKROOM ACTIVITIES

We began our work with shadows in a "darkroom," basically an empty classroom with as much light shut out as we could accomplish. First, we spent some time investigating light. We compared candles to flashlights as sources of light and discussed ways of talking about different kinds of light. We eventually agreed that we could describe the candles as "dim" and the flashlights as "bright." We also discussed how light travels away from its source. My ideas for these activities came from a chapter called "Me and My Shadow" in a tradebook by Roth, Cervoni, Wellnitz, and Arms (1998).

Our next step was to explore the properties of shadows and silhouettes. We had fun using the flashlights and finger play to make a variety of kinds of shadows. This common experience naturally led to a discussion about what causes shadows. We finally concurred on the following definition: "A shadow is when something blocks the light so it can't get through." We shone the flashlights on one another to project our silhouettes onto the wall and cut out dark "silhouette" shapes from cardboard. This activity helped us notice that the shape of our shadows differed when we faced the light sideways versus head on.

GEOMETRIC SHADOWS

The next set of investigations were adapted from TERC's *Investigations in Number, Data, and Space* (Battista & Clements 1995), particularly the Grade 4 unit titled "Seeing Solids and Silhouettes." I began by using a variety of three-dimensional geometric forms and the overhead projector to help my students understand that three-dimensional geometric solids project shadows that are two-dimensional shapes. Then, with the overhead projector light turned off, I placed a shape on the glass so that the face of the solid I had just shown the students was facing down. Students were asked to predict what they thought the shadow would look like by drawing that shape on their paper. Then I turned the projector on so that they could see the actual shadow cast by the form.

Right away, students caught on to the idea that the shape of the shadow depended on which side of the form was placed on the glass. One student volunteered to explain how the shadow got on the screen: "It's like a reflection. It bounces up there." After some discussion about our previous "light-blocking" investigations, the class decided that the *light* bounced up, not the shadow. When I put the cone on the glass with the point up, it cast a shadow shaped like a circle. I asked where the point was. One student said that it was in the shadow. Another proposed that the point could not be seen because "the circle part is bigger."

We had a "big time" discussion about whether a light could cause a shadow by itself. One boy was thoroughly convinced that it could. He pointed to the chalkboard, which wasn't being hit by light from the overhead, and said that the dark spot was a shadow. We discussed whether being in a room with no light was the same as being in a shadow. Students decided that this would be "darkness," not a shadow. Once again, students came to the conclusion that to have a shadow, we needed two things: light and something to block it.

OUR OWN SHADOWS

On the next day, students went outside at 9:15 with their fifth-grade "buddies" to measure their shadows. When they returned, I asked, "How does your shadow change during one day?" I explained that they would be repeating the shadow measurements four more times during the day. Although student replies varied, all seemed to feel that they expected some kind of change.

As Figure 5.3 illustrates, some expected changes in size, whereas others mentioned changes in position.

One student wrote, "I think my shadow will get biger at 9:15 and then get smaller at 11:00 becase sometimes the sun will shin darectle on me and make it big and when it's not shining darectly on me I think it will make my shadow small." Another stated, "What I think will happen is my shadow will get smaller, and towards the end of the day it will get bigger and bigger. I think that will happen because, when the sun is down in the sky, we block the sun. And when the sun is up high in the sky, it comes straight down so there is no shadow. But when the sun comes down, so we block the sun again." A third student demonstrated through his drawings how he expected his shadow would move during the day. The movements he expected, however, were very sporadic. His shadow started at his left, moved farther to the left at 11:00, then was in front of him at 12:15, was behind him and to the right at 1:20, and finally was directly behind him at 2:30.

Data Collection and Recording

My second-graders worked in pairs with fifth-graders to trace their shadows on paper at five different times during the day. The fifth-graders outlined the second-graders' feet with chalk and initialed the outline. Each time the shadow outlines were made, data was recorded on the time of day, position of the sun, and length and position of the shadow.

The fifth-graders were very conscientious about their task. A data sheet that included space for drawings and measurements was used by each pair, as illustrated in Figure 5.4. The fifth-graders started out as the primary recorders, but were encouraged to include the second-graders throughout the day.

After the second shadow drawing, the second-graders began to notice some unexpected changes. When I asked them to write comments about their measurements, they produced a mix of observations, predictions, and interesting attempts to consolidate what they were observing with things that they had obviously heard (but incompletely understood!) about the movement of the sun and the earth.

- "The shadow is pointing in different places. It's turning right because the sun is turning left."
- "The shadow got smaller while it moved because the sun got closer. The earth is moving around the sun and it's like the sun is moving but it's not. Because the next one will be only one hour in between it won't move as fast."
- "The shadow is smaller because the sun is moving upward. Because the light is more on you rather than around you the shadow's smaller."

Figure 5.3. Children's responses to the question, "How does your shadow change during one day?"

(a)

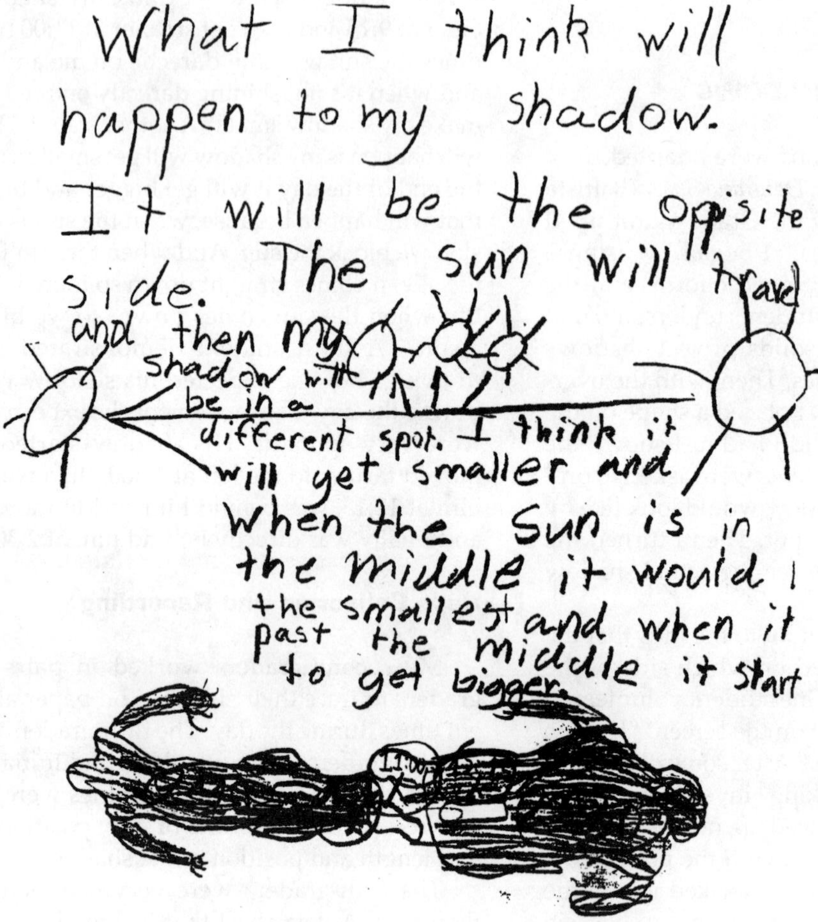

(b)

Figure 5.4. Data sheet used by students to collect data on shadows at different times of the day.

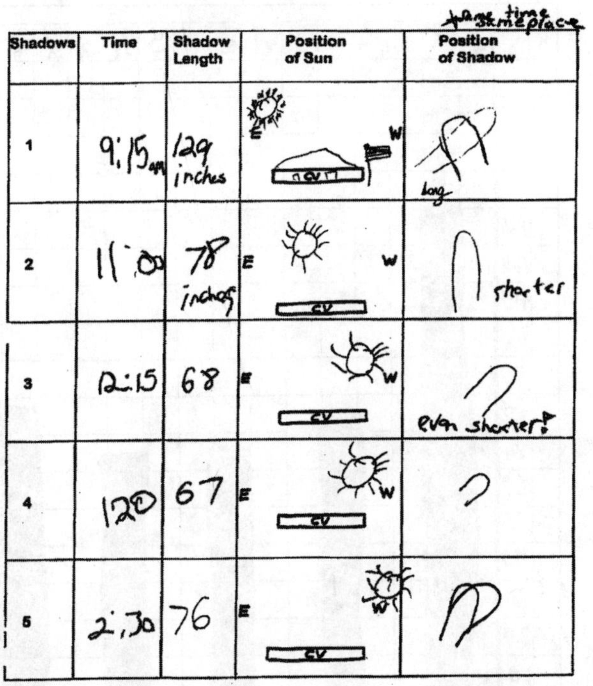

Table 5.1. Children's ideas about shadows before and after modeling.

Before Modeling	After Modeling
"I thought shadows disappeared at noon."	"It just shrinks. It's below your feet."
"I thought it would go fast around."	"It went slower."
"I thought my shadow would keep shrinking."	"The sun was opposite my shadow."
"I thought shadows stayed the same."	"It went smaller."

- "Since 9:15 it was out front. It will be to the right side when we go out at 2:30."
- "It was really long. Then it got shorter. Then I made another prediction to get even shorter. I'm not sure what will happen this afternoon.

The comments were particularly helpful in making it evident to children that their ideas were changing as they conducted their measurements and observations. Although it is common for second-graders to change their minds, they often forget that they have done so. Because I wanted them to be aware of the role of the data in their thinking, it was important to me that they consciously represent what they used to think and how their thinking was changing. Table 5.1 presents some examples.

Graphing Data

The fifth-graders joined us again the next day. Together, we reviewed our data and discussed how they had helped us to understand more about how shadows change. Then I asked students how they thought we could record and share the data we had gathered. We constructed a bar graph together step by step, discussing the need for each component of the graph as we went. Figure 5.5a shows our first graph. Then the fifth-graders helped the second-graders make a graph of

their own data (see Figure 5.5b). Most of this process seemed clear to students. One thing that came up was the need to line up information correctly, especially from the bottom up, so the information was in the correct column. There was good discussion about why a graph is a clear source of information and when we need to use a different tool. Our technology aide demonstrated how to use a computer program to make bar graphs of their data.

Modeling Activity

At the end of the week, after a brief review of the week's activities, students were given the task of building a model (with a fifth-grade partner) that showed how shadows change during the day. Then they were to ponder the big question—*why*?

Assorted supplies were made available—and without delay, they were off. Ideas were flowing almost immediately. The students were not at all intimidated by the task at hand. They seemed to feel they had plenty of knowledge and experience to carry it out. Many variations occurred. There was a very simplistic model using only a stick-and-block figure and a flashlight. Other students branched out to try to show a scale of measure for length and time. One boy explained carefully, using his model, why shadows don't really disappear at noon: ". . . usually . . . as the sun is still at some kind of angle." Another told me, "It is like your shadow is sitting up. [He demonstrated with a pencil.] That's why it gets shorter." Many of the children talked about short shadows being due to the fact that less of a given object blocked the sun. I asked the group what was unrealistic about the moving flashlights in their models. One boy explained that he knew the sun didn't really move, but that they needed to do it that way for

Figure 5.5. Class bar graphs based on shadow data: (a) fifth-grade graph; (b) second-grade graph.

(a)

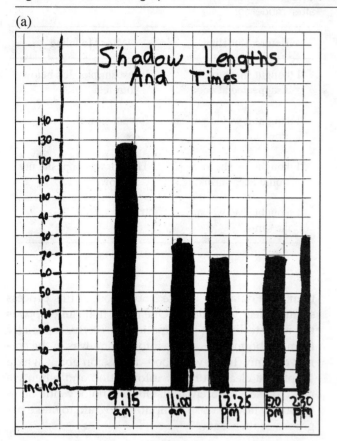

(b)

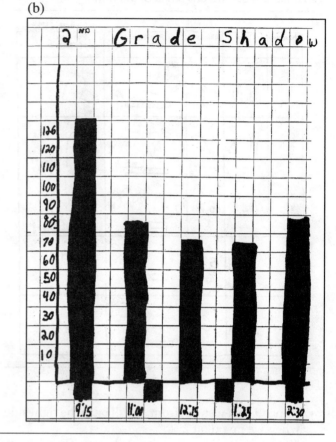

their models. I challenged them to think of a way to make their models more realistic.

Revisions and Sharing of Models

The fifth-graders returned to our classroom for a final episode of sharing models in groups and discussing revisions. The students took great pride in their models and the knowledge that they shared. It seemed very natural to them that no two models were alike, even though they had all been working on the identical task.

A lively discussion about the "fake sunlight" from the flashlights emerged. One second-grader explained that candlelight is more like the sun because it radiates out. A fifth-grader had ideas about taking off the head of the flashlight to see if that would result in a source that radiated a full 360 degrees. To avoid this perceived limitation, other students used a "pretend" light source such as a balloon or Styrofoam ball. They didn't feel it was a problem that they didn't use actual light in their model.

As one might expect, the fifth-graders had more ideas than the second-graders did about how shadows

appear on different parts of the earth. One boy, who had a very simplistic model, used it to explain that Wisconsin sun angles were different from those at the equator. In his model, a slanted stick-and-block toy cast the shadow. One girl felt strongly that the toy should be straightened up in order to get accurate results. Others felt that as long as it was always slanted in the same way, it would be OK. Someone mentioned that "things in nature like trees" are slanted.

Groups used measuring devices, drawings of shadows during the day, imprints of shadows in clay, and compass roses to make their models demonstrate their ideas.

LEARNING OVER TIME

I gave my students a written postevaluation that consisted of three questions. The first was identical to one of the questions asked before we began our investigations. The questions were "What causes a shadow? How did your shadow change in one day? Why do you think it changed?"

As you can expect, and as Figure 5.6 illustrates, the responses varied. About half of the class were able to explain that a shadow is caused by light being blocked by an object. Others just showed sources of light that caused shadows, and some drew pictures of a light source and an object blocking the source, causing the shadow.

Because the second two questions were listed together, many of the students went into the *why* part without telling me what changes they saw in the shadows. Therefore, the next day I again asked the first part of the question (How did your shadow change in one day?). This time, most of the students mentioned size, position, or both. Three mentioned the process of the

Figure 5.6. Children's post-unit responses on written evaluation.

shadow growing shorter and then longer again. They proposed many interesting explanations about *why* shadows change.

- "Because the earth moves around the sun, and every time you go out the sun is in a different place which makes the shadows go down and up."
- "I think the sun is moving and the shadow moved the opposite way." "Because the earth moves around the sun, the light goes to another place so the shadow moves because the tree block the sun from a different direction."
- "The sun moves."
- "Why I think my shadow changed is when the sun moved it made my shadow change. And I think my shadow changed because the earth really moves but it makes the sun look like it's moving."

I think many of these ideas were greatly influenced by the conversations between my second-graders and the fifth-graders. The fifth-graders had been studying shadows in their own classroom for some time before they came to work with the second-graders. It might be more beneficial next year for my students to do their own modeling and then share their ideas with the fifth-graders. They might then be more comfortable dealing with some of the basic changes rather than trying to grasp the *why*.

Reflection: This project took a great deal of planning time, but it was time well spent because it led to some exciting learning opportunities for my students and a

very rewarding teaching experience for me. The combination of the fifth-graders and the second-graders was perfect for activities such as these. My students didn't get bogged down by the measurement/recording tasks, and they had natural encouragers in their fifth-grade partners. The fifth-graders seemed impressed with the second-graders' knowledge and added to their discussions without overpowering them.

I do hope to revisit shadows in January and possibly April for a mini-session dealing with more outdoor measuring so that the children can get some thoughts going about the changes during different times of the year.

It was wonderful to see the enthusiasm the students had for each activity and also to really feel like a guide rather than an instructor—they were so self-directed and motivated. The discussions, model building, and revision ideas just "oozed" with learning. I feel that my objectives were met and that students' work extended beyond them.

REFERENCES

Asch, F. (1985). *Bear shadow*. Englewood Cliffs, NJ: Prentice-Hall.

Battista, M., & Clements, D. (1995). Exploring geometric shapes [curriculum unit]. In TERC [Developers], *Investigations in number, data, and space* (Grade 4). Palo Alto, CA: Dale Seymour.

Roth, C. E., Cervoni, C., Wellnitz, T., & Arms, E. (1988). Me and my shadow. In C. E. Roth, C. Cervonia, T. Wellnutz, & E. Arms, (Eds.), *Schoolground science activities* (p. 37). Lincoln, MA: Massachusetts Audubon Society.

Chapter 6

Graphing

JENNIE CLEMENT

Sugar Creek Elementary School, Second Grade
Verona, Wisconsin

Graphing is a way for children to explore ideas about organizing and representing information, to compare quantities, to map change over time, and to visualize relationships. In this chapter, I describe some of the big ideas in the development of children's knowledge about graphs, show how some of these big ideas can be realized in classroom activities, and document some of the highlights about children's ways of thinking about these big ideas. In particular, I explain how I help second-grade children develop knowledge about graphs. Although my experiences are with younger children, they apply to older children as well, especially if the older students have not had the chance to develop their own understanding of graphing.

BIG IDEAS ABOUT GRAPHS

The structure of any graph relies on a number of related, but important, ideas. These include the following:

- *Communication*. Children often do not understand that graphs are a means of communication and that graphs need to be designed to communicate effectively. This means that the selection of a *title*; the *labeling* of the axes of a graph (for graphs with axes); and the selection of *colors*, or different shading patterns, are all important to consider explicitly. I often talk with children about the meaning of graphs and set up situations where other children, teachers, and parents see and try to make sense of their graphs.

- *Function*. Different graphs have different functions. Children often think that bar graphs are the only kinds of graphs, and they further believe that bar graphs fulfill all functions. But I like children to be aware of, and to think explicitly about, what bar, circle, and line graphs are good for. (I also used to think that one type fit all.)

- *Number Sense*. Graphs often rely on children's ideas about number. For example, children's decisions about the number of partitions that a circle graph should include are based not only on their knowledge of circles, but also on their understanding of fractions. Graphs often represent quantities and differences among quantities, so they can be good tools for helping children reason about comparisons among quantities (e.g., compare problems often seem to invite bar graphs). Graphs can also help children develop language, including concepts such as *more*, *less*, *above*, *fewest*, and *most*. The placement of numbers on a graph is often problematic for children. They have absorbed conventional ideas that graphs include numbers, but they are usually uncertain about just what functions numbers serve.

- *Data Visualization*. Graphs are the predominant form of representing and visualizing data, so they play a key role in any activity involving the posing of questions and the collection of data (see chapter 1 about data). Graphs are representational forms, but children's initial thinking about them is more often rooted in visually realistic drawings. So graphing is a representational "step away" from the "reality" of drawings.

Investigating Real Data in the Classroom: Expanding Children's Understanding of Math and Science. Copyright © 2002 by Teachers College, Columbia University. All rights reserved. ISBN 0-8077-4141-8 (pbk.). Prior to photocopying items for classroom use, please contact the Copyright Clearance Center, Customer Service, 222 Rosewood Dr., Danvers, MA 01923, USA, tel. (508) 750-8400.

- *Construction.* Construction of a graph relies on many assumptions. Some of these include
  - (a) Big ideas in measurement (e.g., identical units). For example, children sometimes draw units of different dimensions, such as different-size rectangles, to represent quantities. So, the quantity 10 might be represented by a "stack" of 10 differently sized rectangles. Children's problems with identical units also extend to the size of the intervals they use on line graphs: Some children think that intervals of different size are appropriate, just as long as the final number is where they want it to be. The function of equal intervals is not obvious.
  - (b) Scale. Children often are uncertain of the relationship between the quantity in the world and the quantity on the graph. For example, sometimes they believe that if something in the world measures 10 inches, then a graph showing, for instance, the length of plants, must also be scaled in inches. The idea that 1 inch might be represented by ¼ inch on a graph paper square is sometimes hard for children to see.
  - (c) Origin. When we construct a two-dimensional line graph, we have in mind that the origin is the zero point of the scale or scales that we are using (often this number actually is zero). Children usually aren't sure about what number should go there.

GRAPHING IN THE PRIMARY GRADES

In the primary grades, elementary school children are exposed to graphs as a way of sharing information about a variety of topics, from types of pets children have to where the first bites were taken from a gingerbread cookie. Picture graphs are very common in kindergarten. For example, children may be asked to illustrate the family pet—let's say a dog—on a precut square and glue the card in the row with the other dog pictures. The "graph" is pre-made: The format is set, the columns labeled horizontally and vertically, the title(s) given, and the measurement issues unproblematic. (Sometimes the graph format consists of columns for placement of objects by the children with no labels on the x and y axes and a sentence on the top of the graph describing the activity.) Once the picture graph is complete, children are very good at interpreting the information to answer comparison questions such as "Are there more families with dogs or fish?" "How many families have cats for pets?" "What type of pet do most families have?" and "What type of pet is found least often in families?" Listening to the children's answers

to these questions and their explanations for how they arrived at those answers provides good insight into children's mathematical understanding as well as their understanding of concepts such as *more, less, same, tallest,* and *shortest,* to name just a few.

Consider the question "How many families have birds for pets?" Children's responses, including explanations for how they arrived at the answer may vary from "I got 5 by counting the cards like this: 1, 2, 3, 4, 5," to "I looked at the top of the bird row and looked over and saw the 5, so my answer is 5." For the question "Are there more families with dogs or fish?" children's responses may vary from "Dogs have more because it's the tallest one" to "Dogs have more because that row has 7 and the bird row only has 3." Because the bars are built by stacking squares or rectangles one on top of the other, there are clear "division" lines that children can use to count in order to answer harder questions.

As children's mathematical understandings mature, they can begin to answer higher-level-thinking questions such as "We know there are more families with dogs than fish. How many more?" Moreover, graphs are visual and allow children who struggle with abstract mathematical concepts, such as the Join (Change Unknown) problems of Cognitively Guided Instruction, an opportunity to feel successful by offering them a very concrete model to interpret (especially Compare [Difference Unknown] problems). A Join (Change Unknown) word problem is of the form: $7 + \square = 27$. A Compare (Difference Unknown) word problem has the following form: Joe has 15 marbles. Melissa had 47. How many more marbles does Melissa have than Joe?

Picture graphs are used in first grade as well, but bar graphs, in which illustrations of the family pet are replaced by colored squares, become more common. Again, a pre-made graph is designed, and the kids glue squares in the appropriate columns. The children are still good at answering questions about the information on the graph, and more kids are able to answer higher-level-thinking questions like, "How many more kids ride the bus to school than walk?" and "How many fewer kids ride their bikes to school than get rides?" Children's responses to "How did you figure out that five more kids ride the bus than walk?" become more sophisticated as well and provide the teacher with a good assessment of where the kids are in their mathematical thinking. Children's responses can also be used to assess growth. The replacement of the concrete "pictures" with the more abstract "squares" does not seem to affect the children's abilities to interpret information about the completed graphs. Again, this is in part due to the division lines that are created by the way the bars are built.

EXPANDING CHILDREN'S IDEAS
ABOUT GRAPHS

As a second-grade teacher, I was curious about how kids would interpret other types of graphs, such as line and circle graphs. Picture and bar graphs are by far the most prevalent structure used by classroom teachers, and as I have suggested, these picture and bar graphs are often "predigested" for children. I wanted to know what kinds of knowledge kids would need if they were involved in the construction of graphs and if they were involved in both interpreting and constructing bar, line, and pie graphs. I also wanted to see if expanding the questioning part of my graphing activities to include questions about the "parts" of a graph, giving my second-graders opportunities to create graphs of their own, and using the unforeseen issues that I was pretty sure would arise naturally from these projects would expand the children's understanding of graphs and graphing. So I began to think about activities that would allow me to gain a better understanding of students and their knowledge about graphs while giving children an opportunity to construct some knowledge of their own about graphs and graphing.

I started by formulating the following teaching goals:

- Use line, circle and bar graphs with students.
- Design more varied and open-ended graphing activities to help kids construct knowledge about graphs and number.
- Formulate questions that would encourage kids to think about the conventions in bar, line, and circle graphs.
- Give students opportunities to collect data, to decide which graph is most appropriate to share the data, and to construct that graph.
- Based on the activities, kids' responses, and projects they complete, assess kids to see how their knowledge about graphs and graphing changes over time.
- Identify any developmental stages that emerge from the assessments.

What follows is a partial list of questions that I found myself asking kids about our graphing activities:

- What makes a graph a graph?
- Are there different types of graphs?
- What kind of graph is this, and how can you tell?
- Is this a graph?
- What would we need to do to make it a graph?
- Why are there numbers on a graph?
- Where should those numbers go?
- Should those numbers be labeled so that we know what the numbers stand for?

- Are there times when a bar graph is more useful than a line graph or a circle graph?
- How can we decide which graph is best?
- Do graphs, like books and maps, need titles to tell us what they're about?
- If graphs need titles, where should the title go and why?

Most of these questions were generated in response to the answers children gave to my initial questions. Yet other questions became part of our discussions as I attempted to build a vocabulary that would help us communicate ideas about the graphs. I also wanted to keep the kids thinking about the conventions of line, circle, and bar graphs so that the concepts they were constructing along the way could be confirmed, changed, or challenged.

I was a little concerned that some of my questions would be too leading and elicit responses that were prompted by the nature of the question, as opposed to eliciting responses based on the knowledge children had about a particular concept. I found that most of the time, my questions had the children grappling with an idea, and I found them using great communication skills to justify an answer. Yet there were times that I challenged ideas the kids offered by posting another solution so I could be sure that they could justify those ideas as well.

Reflections: Listening to the children's responses to my questions taught me about misconceptions children had about graphs, and I realized there was a need to develop a common language we could use about graphs and sometimes to develop a common understanding of that language. We learned in the study of number that questioning plays a very important role in children's mathematical growth and in a teacher's ability to make better instructional decisions. The same is true for graphing.

It became clear to me that even though my second-graders had been graphing for 2 years and had lots of background knowledge to draw on, I would need to emphasize certain critical parts of instruction if the children were to go beyond interpreting graphs for their "basic" information. These included examining the features of a graph, constructing graphs, being exposed to line and circle graphs, comparing and contrasting the three basic types of graphs, and deciding when one type of graph is more useful than another (based on the information the graph was showing).

GRAPHING ACTIVITIES

In the following sections I describe some of the graphing activities I have completed with my classes over the past 3 years, including examples of some of the dialogue that took place during the activities. Note that the dialogue is critical to understanding students' ideas about graphs, the ways these ideas change over time, and, as it turns out, understanding their ideas about number, as well. The excerpts of dialogue I have provided are typical of the responses children have given me and are not intended to be inclusive.

Bar Graphs

How Do I Feel? On the first day of school, I invited the children to explore the room. I asked them, as they did so, to take cards from the table, write their names on the cards, and, using pushpins, place the cards on the bulletin board next to the word cards that best described how they were feeling. Figure 6.1. shows what our "graph" looked like on Day 1.

On the 2nd day, I asked the students to gather in front of the board where the cards had been placed the day before. Then I reviewed with the kids what they had done. I began asking some of the questions I listed at the beginning of this chapter to see what knowledge the kids had about the conventions of graphs, and then I asked questions particular to bar graphs.

I first asked students if what they were looking at was a graph. Their answers varied from "Yes" to "No" to "Sort of." I called on a student to talk about his answer ("sort of") to see if I could draw out what he meant. He said something about numbers ("So we can tell how many there are in the rows"). This idea about needing to add numbers caught on, and we began to talk about where the numbers should go.

The cards labeling the "feeling words" were on the *x*-axis and the "bars" (composed of the cards unevenly placed by the children) were on the *y*-axis (see Figure 6.1).

Figure 6.1. Card "graph" of feelings.

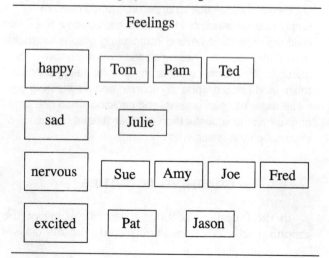

Feelings

Like the responses to the initial question, the kids' responses to where the numbers should be placed varied. Some suggestions about the placement of the numbers included nondescript answers of "over there" and "pretty much anywhere" to more specific answers of "on the side" and "on the bottom." Most kids seemed to like the idea of putting the numbers on the bottom, so I suggested that we try adding them to the bottom to see how it looked. I then showed the kids the cards I had and asked them if they could help me decide what numbers I should write and guide me in the placement of the cards. They did this by directing me to place the number 1 card under the first name card in the "happy" row at the bottom of the "graph," the number 2 under the second name card at the bottom of the "graph," and so on until the longest row had been numbered.

The kids seem pleased with the results, so I asked them if it would work to have the cards on the side, and one person answered by saying, "No, because then you wouldn't be able to tell how many there were." Someone else countered by saying that we could still find out how many by counting. So I began asking the kids questions about the graph, such as "How many kids said they felt silly yesterday?" and "Did more kids feel nervous or mellow?" They were very adept at answering the questions and explaining their answers. When I asked the kids to explain how they got their answers, most kids said they counted the cards. When I asked if there was another way to find the answer, one person suggested finding the end of the row and looking down to see what number was there. This explanation was accepted by the children and seemed to make sense, yet counting the cards seemed to be the preferred strategy. Going back to the placement of the numbers, I asked the kids if they would be able to answer questions about the graph if the numbers were on the side where they couldn't count, and they said no.

I then asked if there was anything else we needed to add, and the kids seemed to struggle with being able to give me any more specific answers so I began to suggest a few. I asked if they could see that the cards with kids' names were sometimes close and sometimes had spaces left in between. They concurred, so I asked them if that mattered, meaning did it make the rows easier or harder to read? Again, answers varied, so I took a card from a short row and moved it to line up with the number 7 and asked if that was OK. Many hands went up and one person said, "You can't do that because there aren't really more in the 'silly' row." The kids then suggested that the cards should either be placed right next to each other with just a little space between or side by side with no space. We went with no space.

I had to continue to prompt the kids in this manner to add the other conventions like labeling the numbers, labeling the bars, and adding a title to the graph. These ideas were easily accepted by the children, and they made logical suggestions for placement of and wording for the rest of these graph "parts" as well as reasons for these parts. The last question I asked the kids was "What kind of a graph is this?" They definitely recognized the format, but were unable to come up with a name. I told the kids it was a bar graph. Later I transferred the graph to a piece of tagboard and hung it on the wall so we could refer to it later.

Reflections: I think it is important to note here that, with the exception of the numbers, the other missing graph conventions, which were not as easily identifiable for the children, were the same graph parts that are usually preset by the teacher and were the parts the kids were least involved with when adding their square to the class graph or when answering questions about the graph.

After reading the book *Tall City, Wide Country* (Chwast, 1983), I asked the kids to *think* about where each of them would prefer to live, in the "tall city" or in the "wide country." Several kids shared their thoughts and the reasons for them. On the board I had two small pieces of tagboard, one labeled "Tall City" and the other labeled "Wide Country." Using links, I asked each child to place a link on the card showing where they would prefer to live.

When we finished I asked the kids to tell me what the links showed. It was quite obvious to the kids that most preferred the country over the city, that chain being quite a bit longer than the city one. I asked the kids to tell me how many kids preferred the country and they began counting the links. We found that there were 17 links. We repeated the process for the city card and counted 4 links. I asked the kids to tell me how many more kids felt at home in the country than in the city. Counting up and using facts, the kids determined that the answer was 13.

I asked the students if what they were looking at was a graph. I was surprised to hear many kids say, "Yes" and "Kind of," and "No." While asking the kids to explain their thinking, I ended up writing the things on the chalkboard around the links (see Figure 6.2).

I gave each child a piece of graph paper and asked them if they could take the information on the board and make a graph. I thought this would be relatively easy, but I found interesting variations in children's ideas about constructing this graph. Some children just copied the drawing of the links shown above. Others substituted bars for links, but did not pay any attention to the size of the units constituting the bars. Some children did pay attention to the size of each of the units making up the bar but thought that the orientation needed to be the same as the drawing. Other children worried less about the original orientation of the links and de-

cided that either horizontal or vertical depictions would work better (see Figure 6.3).

I developed a scoring rubric to capture my sense of similarities and differences in the children's work. The rubric assigns a point scale from 0 to 5 and shows a progression from literal copy to a graph as a representation:

0. Made no attempt.
1. Drew a picture of the picture.
2. Drew a picture of the picture but used squares on the graph paper to represent a link.
3. Attempted use of a bar to represent the number of children who preferred the city to the country. The bar shows a more continuous view of the quantities.
4. Changed the orientation from vertical to horizontal (showing that they recognized that the orientation of the paper clips did not have to be preserved in the graph).
5. Conventional bar graph with labels.

Reflections: Children's ideas about visual representation seem to begin with literal depictions, as in their artwork. Over time, they seem to be able to create greater "distance" between the items being depicted and the graph. Eventually, children learn to reason about which parts of graphs serve which functions, and they learn the value of certain conventions, such as equal-sized intervals and orientations where greater height means greater quantity, and so on.

Circle Graphs

Holding a piece of tagboard on which I had drawn a circle divided evenly into 20 pieces, I asked the students to tell me what they saw. Students' responses varied from "a circle" to "lines" to "pizza slices" to "a rectangle." They pointed to the spot on the graph they were looking at or explained verbally.

I then asked the kids how many "pizza slices" there were. They counted quickly and told me 19 and 20. We counted as a group and agreed on 20. I asked them if they thought there was a reason for that number, and someone suggested that it was how many people there were in our room, kids and adults together.

I asked if they thought we could use the circle *to tell a story* about how many boys and how many girls there were in our room on this day. They were sure we could and began to offer ideas of how we could. One idea was to write names inside the slices; another was to put marks inside the slices (Xs for girls and Os for boys); someone else suggested we color the slices one shade for girls and another shade for the boys.

To extend this idea, I asked if that meant we would have the girls use a color such as green and the boys use

Figure 6.2. Graph: of children's preferences of places to live.

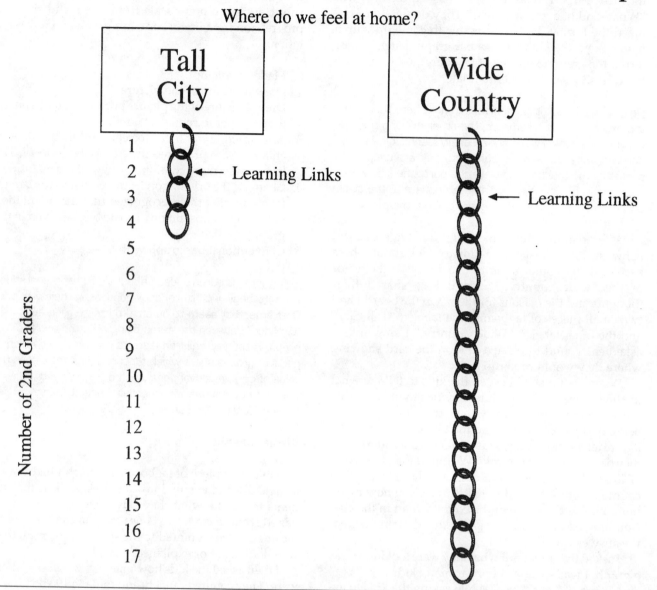

Tall City, Wide Country-Turning "it" into a Graph

Where do we feel at home?

a color such as red. They said yes, so I asked what I should do. They said I should color a slice green because I was a girl. I asked if I could color two sections, and they said no, that each person could only color one or we would run out. So I pointed to a specific slice and colored it. Another student came up next and asked whether she should color one a bit away from the one I colored, or whether she should color one next to mine. There was some discussion of which of these ideas was best, and they agreed that if they were going to be able to use the final product to see if we had more boys or

girls in our room, then the student and I (two females) should color slices next to each other. Some still thought we would be able to count the slices even if the differently colored slices were all over the circle, but many agreed the first plan would be easier, so that was the one we stuck with.

When the kids and adults had each colored a slice and we were all sitting on the floor, many noticed that "it was even." I had someone explain what was meant by even. One child showed how there was a line down the middle of the circle that broke it in half and half were

Figure 6.3. Horizontal and vertical variation in children's graphs.

(a)

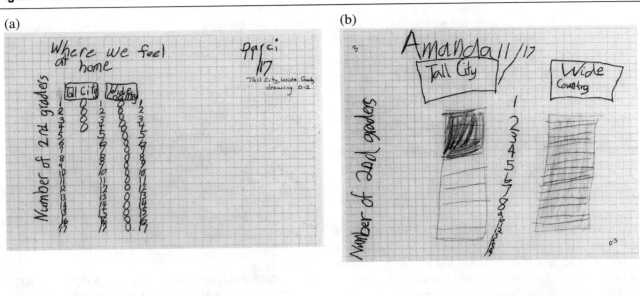

(b)

(c)

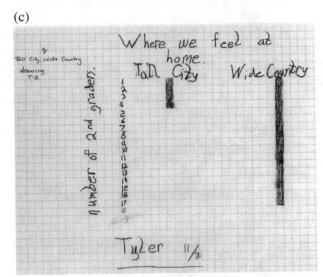

(d)

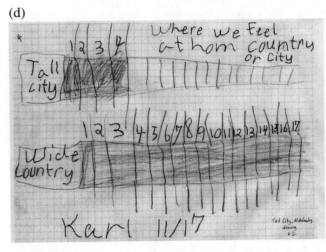

(e)

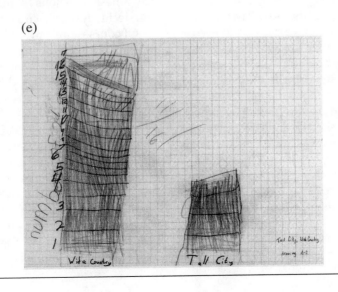

red and half were green. We counted the number of green slices and found there were 10, and they knew that meant there would be 10 red slices, too.

I asked if we needed to put something on the paper to show what we did and what the colors stood for. I asked the kids who said yes if they could offer any ideas to the group. Many suggestions were offered, ranging from writing sentences to writing words on the pizza slices. Pulling down a state map, I pointed to the key and asked students what it was. The majority of the kids correctly identified it as a key. I asked what the purpose of the key was. When someone mentioned symbols, I elaborated on the idea, and we practiced by finding a few symbols on the map and reading the key to find out what each symbol stood for.

I asked if adding a *key* would help us label our colors and what they stood for. Wanting to give it a try, the children had me write the word *key* on the paper and draw a red square under it, write the word *girl* next to it, and repeat the process with the green square for the boys. They were pleased with the way this turned out but thought some of the other ideas would have worked as well.

At this point, I began referring to our bar graph, titled, "How We Feel," and asked the kids to think about the things we added to the graph and the reasons we added those things. I then asked if there was anything that we added to that graph that we needed to add to this one. Someone suggested adding numbers so once again, we could tell how many. I asked where the numbers should go. One person suggested the side, so we discussed how that might work.

As a child was explaining how to look over from a section to a number, it became clear to that this wouldn't work, and they explained, showing that if we tried to find a section and look straight over, we wouldn't get the number that showed how many red sections there really were. Someone else then suggested we write numbers around the circle. Again, they saw flaws in this idea as we discussed it further, so we decided to leave numbers off. The other convention we added was a title at the top. Again, they were able to make reasonable suggestions for the wording. Referring to the bar graph once again, I asked if they remembered what we called this kind of graph. Some read the title, and then someone said "bar graph." I then asked the kids if they could guess what kind of graph this was, and after various ideas someone said "circle graph." Because the overall shape of this graph is a circle, this name made perfect sense to the kids, unlike a "bar" graph, where the bar shape was not as obvious to them.

Reflections: The circle graph was a little more difficult to use in terms of conventions because it didn't seem

obvious even to me that there are as many consistent conventions in circle graphs as there are in bar graphs. However, the ideas of what we should and shouldn't add, where we should add a particular convention, and how it should be added were just as varied as those that emerged during the construction of the bar graph. Even though we ended up using only one idea, I'm reasonably sure the students would have been happy to use any one of the others. This would be one place for me to watch for changes in understanding. If you read Erin DiPerna's chapter (chapter 8) on the use of pie graphs to show how categories of eye types (circle, oval, other) of children's drawings of themselves changed with grade, you will see that there are other important questions to consider, such as, How can a circle be partitioned into n pieces? Should each partition be the same size?

COMPARING AND CONTRASTING BAR AND CIRCLE GRAPHS

Shortly after Halloween, I invited the kids to help me construct a graph of my leftover Halloween candy from home. I told them that when kids came to my door in their costumes, they chose their favorites from all the types of candy that I offered. I asked my students to look at the numbers of different kinds of "leftovers" and then make some inferences about the kinds of candy that were most frequently chosen (that is, the favorites). My purpose was to provide a new reason for organizing data in a graph, namely, for drawing new conclusions that are not given in the original information. The way I posed the task to children was that they should identify the numbers of each kind of candy that was left and think about whether they could answer such questions as these: "How much of the leftover candy is jawbreakers?" "How much is gum?" Some children tried to address these questions by making a bar graph, but several decided to try a circle graph.

Of course, circle graphs are a good choice, because they go beyond showing frequencies of items to showing proportions of a total. Apparently, then, even young children have good intuitions that circle graphs can show relations between an overall amount of something and the categories that make it up. However, children also had clear limitations in understanding *how* circle graphs work. In particular, they did not necessarily understand the need to partition their circle graphs into equal portions (the idea of equal units, once again). And those who knew they should partition their circle equally, did not know how to. Most children simply drew a circle and began to partition it ad hoc. Some of the children were obviously concerned with making equal-sized partitions, but had no way to make their number of partitions come out to the desired total.

Other children successfully generated an appropriate number of partitions, but only by ignoring the need for equal size. Erin DiPerna's chapter on data classification with body portraits contains detailed accounts of these very same issues in her fourth-grade class. Her chapter also contains some excellent suggestions for how to address these issues in instruction, so I will not repeat them here (see chapter 8).

LINE GRAPHS

Graphing Excitement

Line graphs are good for showing relationships. With line graphs, I emphasize that they are good for showing something that changes over time. Because we read a lot and like to talk about what we find interesting in a story, I decided to use graphs to help children develop reading ability. So, while we were reading stories such as *Rainbow Crow* (VanAllen, 1989) and *Stellaluna* (Cannon, 1993), I asked children to identify key story events, for example, the beginning event, the problem in the story, the events leading up to the solution of the problem, and the ending event. I then ask children to rate how exciting they found each event. There are many ways of obtaining these ratings, and each provides opportunities for children to think about measurement and mathematics. For example, sometimes we use a number such as 10 to represent the very most exciting event, and then we rate all the other events in relation to the 10. So, for example, a moderately exciting event might get a rating of 5 or 6. You can see how such conversations as these can include ideas about fractions and even ratio (e.g., is a moderately exciting event half as exciting as the most exciting? Three fourths as exciting?). Conversations about what numerical system to use also raise consideration of the fact that in this case, "10" stands for a level of excitement, not 10 of anything (a quantity). This idea is challenging, especially for young children.

How to represent the story events and the relationship between excitement and these events poses problems in representation, communication, and visualization. Where should we put the story elements? What should be their order? (Or should there be any order?) What's the other axis (the vertical axis) good for? Should we use intervals on the vertical axis? Should we use numbers to label these intervals?

In their first attempts to make these graphs, children tended to use pictures and words to order the story events, but their graphs did not communicate the scale that they used to represent changes in their excitement. After trying to interpret these graphs, they discovered that they needed some revisions. On their revised graphs, they again used pictures and words to communicate the story events, but they also made more explicit their scale and intervals for representing changes in excitement.

Weather

During my unit on weather, my class made line graphs. One, shown in Figure 6.4, displays the relationship between temperature and day (the same time each day—the noon recess). As part of our work with line graphs, I also asked children to write interpretations of the graphs (see Table 6.1).

Ways of Thinking About Line Graphs

Children's thinking about line graphs develops during the course of activities such as these. The following are important transitions to look for:

Measure. Children's ideas about measuring excitement usually begin with words such as *a lot* or *a little* or *boring*. The very idea that excitement can be represented with a number is usually a new one. Then children need to decide how to map their feelings onto number quantities in a meaningful way, so depending upon how you talk about this, they can consider such ideas as using a 5-point scale, using a 10-point scale, or even using no scale. And, as I mentioned before, is a feeling such as "fine" half (e.g., a 5) as exciting as "awesome" (e.g., a 10)?

Purpose. What's the purpose of the graph? Children's ideas about showing the relationship between a story event and how excited they are by that event rarely (never?) includes the idea of a line graph. When I've posed this problem to children, their suggestions are usually unidimensional—they have ideas about measuring excitement or about identifying and ordering story events, but usually I have to suggest that they try to use a line graph to show how these things go together. This gives us an opportunity to see the line graph as having a purpose, and we try out different ways of clearly communicating how our excitement changes as we read the story.

Using Coordinates. The use of line graphs requires thinking about coordinates and describing position with coordinates (X,Y), typically a new idea for children. I usually begin with a colored sticker and ask children where I should put it. Sometimes I link this challenge to locating places in a game or to my use of geoboards labeled with letters and numbers.

Figure 6.4. Class line graph: A visual display of temperature.

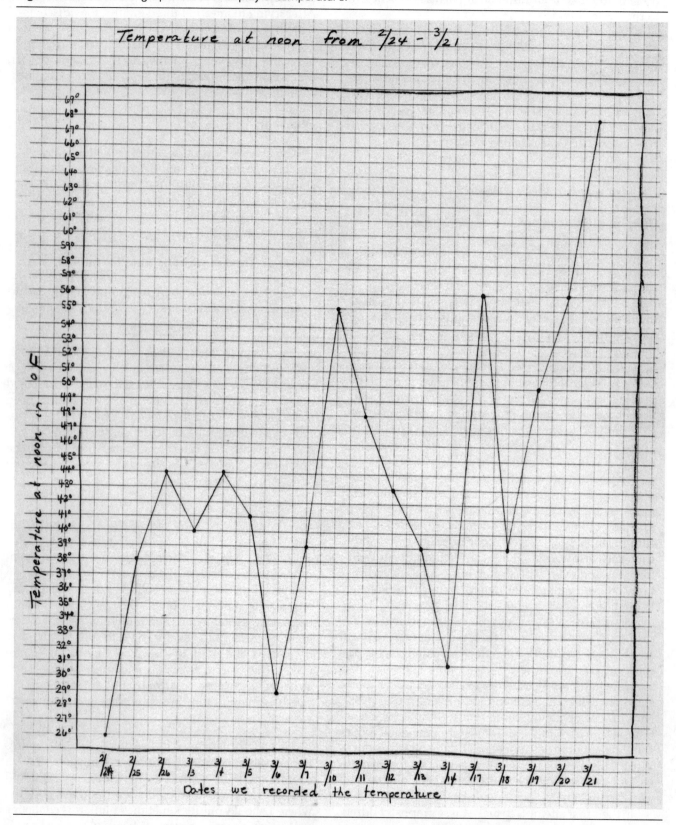

Table 6.1. Sample of students' interpretations of weather graphs.

Line Graph Temperature	Bar Graph—Weather
1. The loest temperature was 26°F.	1. There where more cloudy days then snowy days.
2. The highest temperature was 68°F.	2. Windy and sunny days had 6.
3. There were les in the 60 then in the 40.	3. There where no rainy days.
4. There where 2 days that where 44°F.	4. There where 4 more cloudy days than partly sunny days.
5. There where 3 days that where 39°F.	5. There was 1 more snowy day then rainy days.
6. There were 6 days that were in the 40.	6. There where 6 more sunny days then rainy days.
7. There were 2 days that were 57°F.	7. There were 2 snowy days.
	8. Partly sunny neaded 1 more to have 5.
	9. We had les windy days then cloudy.

Reflections: Initially, I think that children just "don't get" line graphs, but after doing these activities, they have a lot better understanding of why we might use these graphs. They might, however, also develop a bar graph of excitement (because the story events are discrete, not continuous). However, I think this is one of those times that a line graph is fine, even if line-graph apologists might disagree, because it helps children get the basic idea of line graphs and their uses. Something that I've thought about, but haven't tried, is to try out some of the things that Deb Lucas has done using data modeling with literature (See chapter 7). I might have children read and, after every minute, have them rate their excitement, mark where they are in the text, and continue reading until the next rating. Then I would have them graph their excitement versus time of reading. The interesting question for literacy would be to have them reflect on the events in the text that corresponded with different levels of excitement. And, if we did this for several stories, we could investigate questions such as whether stories "typically" follow the same pattern of rising and falling excitement. For older grades, you might even try different kinds of stories, some of which build excitement gradually, and others that build excitement more quickly.

CONCLUSIONS

Graphing is a form of spatial visualization that facilitates different forms of quantitative reasoning. I have found that it is important for children to work in ways that help them understand graphs—how they are constructed and what they are good for. In the primary grades, children's first ideas about graphs seem tied closely to their ideas about drawings, and it is through progressive experience that they come to understand the use and value of graphical conventions, such as titles, labels for axes, and the use of units to represent quantity. If children are provided with experience in representing different situations, they can come to understand the functions of three primary types of graphs (bar, circle, and line) during the primary grades. These understandings provide a firm foundation for later mathematical development.

REFERENCES

Cannon, J. (1993). *Stellaluna*. San Diego: Harcourt Brace Jovanovich.

Chwast, S. (1983). *Tall city, wide country*. New York: Viking.

VanAllen, N. (1989). *Rainbow crow*. New York: Knopf.

Chapter 7

Graphing Artistry: Data Displays as Tools for Understanding Literary Devices

DEBORAH LUCAS

Jefferson Middle School, Sixth Grade
Madison, Wisconsin

Designing and interpreting data displays are important forms of mathematical literacy. One of my goals is to help middle school students develop fluency and flexibility, so that choices and criteria for data display become visible parts of students' mathematical learning. Because I am also a teacher of language arts, I try to foster synergies between mathematical and linguistic literacies. Consequently, when learning mathematics, students keep journals, write "math biographies," and engage in related forms of writing to learn. As counterpoint, I also look for opportunities for students to engage mathematics as a tool for developing literacy about language and performing arts. In this chapter, I describe how construction and interpretation of data displays were used as tools for developing student understanding of genres, such as cinema and poetry. Students used data representations to better understand how writers and movie directors use plot devices to increase and maintain audience involvement.

DATA MODELS OF PLOT DEVICES IN CINEMA

The idea for this project began after I watched the movie *Contact*. I was excited to share this movie with my classes because, as mentioned, I emphasize mathematical literacy with my students—writing their mathematical autobiography; writing their questions, interpretations, understandings, and explanations of the math we do; writing summaries of their learning; and developing "thinking trails" that demonstrate how they arrived at a particular mathematical conclusion. *Contact* is a popular movie with a strong female hero who engages in high-level mathematics and espouses the premise that mathematics is a language, literally the one universal language. Indeed, in *Contact*, communication across the universe is through mathematics. Further, the pervasiveness of mathematical application is peppered throughout the film.

I divided the movie into 15-minute segments. Longer than that would stretch my challenged students beyond their capability to recall information, and shorter than that would break up the movie too much. At the end of each segment, I stopped the movie and gave students time to write a very brief summary and to list associations with their own experience and new ideas stimulated by the film. For example, there is a scene in *Contact* where the main character tells the other characters that part of the aliens' "message" is a series of primes. The character proceeds to describe and list primes. This scene was met with high excitement by my

Investigating Real Data in the Classroom: Expanding Children's Understanding of Math and Science. Copyright © 2002 by Teachers College, Columbia University. All rights reserved. ISBN 0-8077-4141-8 (pbk.). Prior to photocopying items for classroom use, please contact the Copyright Clearance Center, Customer Service, 222 Rosewood Dr., Danvers, MA 01923, USA, tel. (508) 750-8400.

classes, who were in the middle of a *Connected Mathematics* unit (titled *Prime Time*) on factors, multiples, and prime and composite numbers. They were able to see an aspect of their mathematical learning in the action of the main character.

For each 15-minute segment, students drew upon their knowledge of other forms of literacy to speculate about devices used by the author/director to get and keep interest. These devices included foreshadowing; repetition; point of view; mood through music, camera angle, color or brightness; tone; humor; anomaly; surprise; character; event—special effects, violence; idea—complexity, new, confirming, oppositional information; and setting. Last, I asked students to rate how interesting each section was, on a six-point scale (1 = dull; 2 = little; 3 = some; 4 = very; 5 = exciting; and 6 = wow!). I hoped that the display of interest ratings would provoke exploration of the text devices and cinematic techniques responsible for patterns that we might see in displays of our ratings. I also asked students to rate each segment for the relative number of "connections" with their experiences, to set the stage for exploration of covariation between associative memories and interest in the events of the film.

Students worked individually and then in small groups. The work in small groups provided opportunities for students to extend, clarify, and "fill in the gaps." Individually, students proceeded to answer questions and follow instructions such as

1. What does your data tell you?
2. How can you make the data meaningful?
3. What kinds of statements can you make based on your data?
4. How could this data help you if you were a movie producer/director?
5. You are a movie critic. Give the movie a single interest rating. Use the data to justify your rating. Explain your reasoning.

The first question was intended to provoke students to make observations about the raw data that could be justified. This is an important step in helping students distinguish between what they believe and what can be justified by appeal to data. Question 2 was intended to provoke structuring of data, such as lists, tables, and charts. Question 3 required students to have effectively observed and organized the data to note trends, and like the first question, to justify conjectures. The fourth question invited students to consider purposes of data collection, and the fifth item provoked consideration of center of the responses (e.g., "typical" level of interest). I asked students to create visual displays of their data

that would support their responses to questions and instructions such as these.

During their small-group interactions, students compared their conjectures and displays, trying to reach agreement about "effective" displays. Several students wanted to see the entire class's data because "we need everybody's numbers to really see if the small-groups' representations were right," said Mona. We decided to create a collective display of our data, represented by Figure 7.1.

The move to a group display evoked further consideration of the nature of the data. For example, when I asked students, "What do the data tell you?" many suggested that they had rated many of the intervals the "same." This was followed by discussion of *same* as identical (modal), or as values within a range. The idea of values within a range suggested that for some purposes it might be appropriate to create intervals or "bins" for further analysis. As we discussed these senses of *same*, some students reflected that "there are only a few outliers," an observation that allowed us to think about criteria for "out."

Other students were more focused on trends in the data, rather than variation. Many noticed that if we summarized individual ratings with measures of center, such as the mean, "the ratings get higher as the movie plays." Their explanations of this apparent trend focused attention on some of the plot devices that I had hoped would be stimulated:

- The opening was boring because of little action. (Plot)
- We didn't know the characters yet. (Character)
- We didn't understand in the beginning and then "got into it." (Plot)
- It got really exciting when Ellie received the first signal. (Plot)
- That stuff about primes was cool. (Plot, connection to experience)
- That guy out in space had been watching and helping her forever. Who was that guy? (Character; anomaly; setting)
- I thought it was rotten when Ellie wasn't picked to go. (Surprise; anomaly)
- Yeah, that other guy just took over, like he did before. (Character)
- Did she go or didn't she? (Anomaly)

During this conversation, I repeatedly asked students to draw data-based conclusions (i.e., "What kinds of statements can you make based on your data?"). Many students were particularly drawn to visible peaks of interest, debating about their sources and the aspects of data that were most compelling. A slice of this dialogue follows:

Figure 7.1. Class display of ratings of interest by episode.

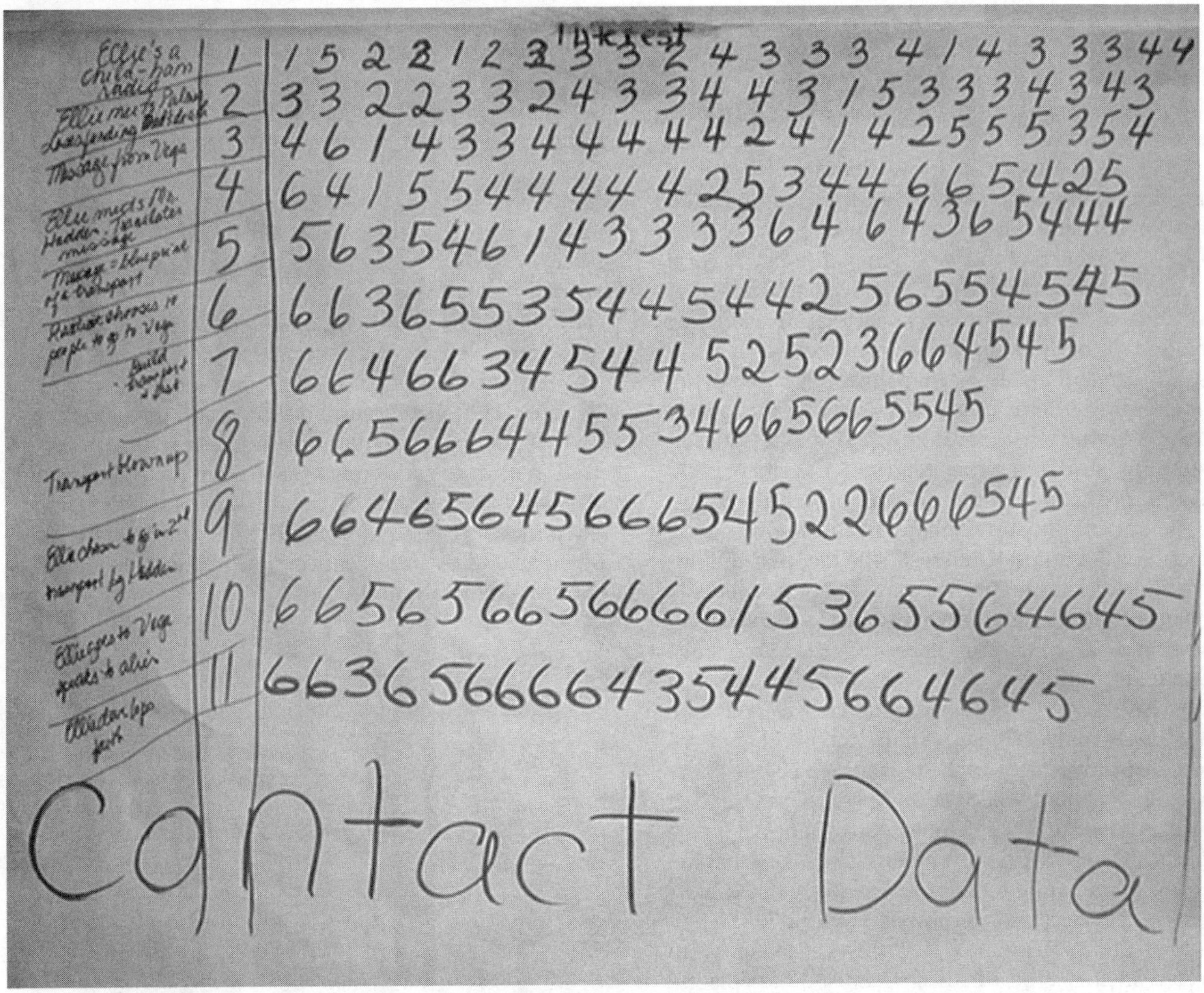

Mona: We know that the movie started getting exciting when Ellie hears the aliens because most of the numbers go up there and the mean is higher, 4.2.

Brett: Yeah, but some people gave that section a 3. One's even a 2.

Matt: But the mode is higher than that. It's 5. That means exciting and it's only one away from the top.

Teacher: We've studied about rising and falling action in stories and mapped those. In most stories, the tension rises continuously until the climax, then falls with the resolution. What happens in Contact?

Students: The end is high too. It was still exciting.

But movies are different from stories.

I mean, they're stories, but you tell them differently.

Yeah, people expect a lot of action and stuff.

The director probably didn't want people to walk out.

People are used to a lot of action and they'd get mad if there wasn't any.

Teacher: So there isn't any falling action or resolution in Contact.

Students: Yes, there is. Right at the end.

It's real short.

The part in the courtroom and how she's (Ellie) sorry that she didn't believe him before and now she does.

Teacher: Do your ratings show that?

Students: No.

Because it's too short.

Movies have to keep things exciting right to the end.

Here was an opportunity to use data to address artistry. What makes the numbers rise? When pressed, students cited interesting characters, even ones they didn't like, and getting to know characters better as reasons for higher ratings later. Action, as represented by rapid event sequences, violence, and special effects, accounted for much of the variation in interest. Several also mentioned surprise when Ellie was not chosen to go to Vega or when another character, Mr. Hadden, interceded on her behalf. Students suggested that settings on Vega and inside the machine were noteworthy as maintaining interest. Anomaly (did she make contact or not?) was hotly debated. Clearly, with guided questioning, students were "reading" the story, picking up literary and cinematic devices used to get and keep their attention, and mathematically analyzing the devices' impact on their interest. The fact that the impact was remarkably similar across students struck them as both surprising and expected. Surprising, because it hadn't occurred to them that they could use mathematics in this way. Expected, because "it was a really good movie" and "we liked it."

Student displays of interest varied, both in the type of graph employed and in the measure of center. Most argued that the mean would be the "best" representation of the group because "everyone gets a chance. It's *per*" (referring to the ratio). Other students suggested that the mode would be far better because it represented majority preference. Figure 7.2 represents the kind of display most small groups generated. Two senses of change were indicated in this type of display. Episode-to-episode change was marked by changes in height, and change within each episode was compared visually to a benchmark of the mean rating across all episodes. Covariation between ratings of connections to other ideas and interest was displayed by juxtaposing the bars representing each mean rating. Some students were surprised that connections ratings didn't "track" interest ratings, but most thought that the plot devices were better explanations of interest. (This beginning look at covariation could have been profitably explored in greater depth. The balancing act of teaching took us in other directions.)

One small group brought an alternative form of display to the attention of their classmates (see Figure 7.3). They proposed that line segments would make changing interest "easier to see." This display provoked discussion of what we might be assuming about the intervals of time (assumptions implicit in the use of the bar charts, but not talked about explicitly). I drew students' attention to the scale used (especially because the rating scale had a maxi-

mum of 6), and we talked about potential effects of changes in scale on how we might see transitions in interest (alterations of slope with choices of scale).

The students often referred to their notes summarizing the action at various points to determine why they liked, were interested in, or felt the excitement of a particular section. Students asked that brief plot summaries be added to the class rating chart so that they could more easily relate their ratings of interest to what was happening in the movie. They then used the summaries to justify the ratings and the ratings as reflective of the effectiveness or interestingness of the plot devices. For example, "People like action and special effects, and that part has action."

Students also repeatedly mentioned that they "learned a lot." They learned a lot about different types of mathematics, that mathematics is so important and used in so many different ways. They were really impressed with the idea that mathematics is a language and could be used to communicate. This type of literacy was a new idea, and they spent a considerable amount of time talking about it.

Figure 7.2. A display representing mean ratings of interest and connections across the eleven episodes of *Contact*.

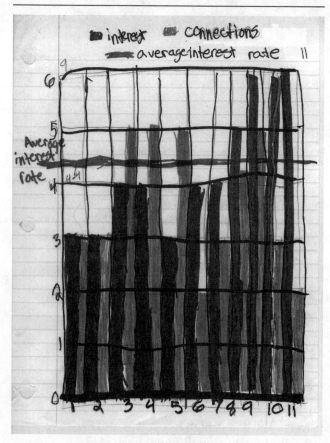

Figure 7.3. A line graph of transitions in interest across episodes of *Contact*.

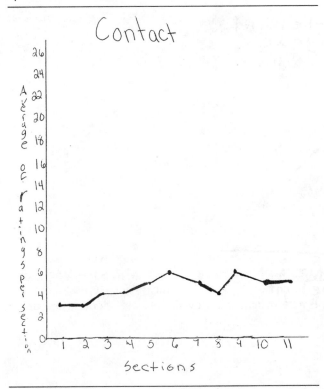

We revisited the ideas developed for *Contact* in ratings of other movies. We were able to see whether rising and falling trends of interest, and the ways in which directors and screenwriters used literary devices, were unique to *Contact*. Not surprisingly, students' efficiency and effectiveness in using the rating scales and representing outcomes improved dramatically. Student discussions then moved quickly to gathering individual scores; "eyeballing" trends; computing mean, median, and mode; determining the best graphic display; and arguing for interpretations.

DATA MODELS OF LITERARY DEVICES IN TEXT

We followed similar procedures to track trends in our interest in literature. We used the Tennyson poem *Charge of the Light Brigade*, a work in a very different format from that of film. Finding a poem of sufficient length that sixth-graders could understand and find interesting was a challenge. The *Light Brigade*, though not a great poem, has many of the same action sequences that students identified as appealing, and it isn't terribly obscure. Some

background teaching of the history behind the poem preceded the reading, as well as some vocabulary instruction to aid understanding. Students had copies of the poem before them as I read it aloud twice.

The literary devices that students identified in the poem were plot, repetition of words, figurative language, rhyme, imagery, and meter. The fact that the charge actually happened and was the result of an error (*blunder*—stanza 2) really affected them (anomaly). They were appalled that so many died because of a mistake (surprise). Students also had difficulty understanding why men would ride into that valley against cannons when they had only sabers and single-shot guns (stanza 3). It was the language that affected students the most. They cited *the flashing sabers, blundered, volleyed*, and *thundered* as adding tension to the poem (stanzas 4 and 5). Many students stated that the poem was "intense." They also felt that they could really see and feel the action because of the words chosen. They liked the repetition of words and phrases, especially *six hundred*. All these preferences were reflected in their ratings.

Students showed greater sophistication about data display here. They went directly from their individual ratings on literary devices and interest to noticing peaks, flat stretches, lows, and trends in small-group data. They compared their scores to those of others and, noticing identical scores for some stanzas, suggested that the entire class's scores would reflect the same. Some groups graphed immediately so they could compare their displays with those of other groups. Most used a line graph instead of a bar graph. Again, the class requested compilation of class data so they could see overall ratings. Also, they immediately noted patterns of ratings and began to compute measures of center. Figure 7.4, for example, represents modes of interest and devices perceived across the stanzas of the poem.

Using measures of center from their interest ratings and arguing about the relative merits of these measures, students identified stanza 3 as having the most literary devices. Certainly the tension in the poem noticeably increases here. But they were most interested in stanzas 4 and 5 because they were drawn to the action, the language, the mental pictures, and the knowledge of casualties (also literary devices). The totality of the poem's story hit them at this point and their interest ratings jumped to reflect that as well. "Not the six hundred" and "Left of six hundred" were listed by them as devices of both repetition and change that were effective (stanzas 4 and 5). In typical sixth-grader fashion, the majority of students declared that they didn't *really* like the poem, although they noted that it was "intense" and "cool" and that "the words made me see it." They supposed that Tennyson had done the best he could,

Figure 7.4. Modal ratings of interest and literary devices

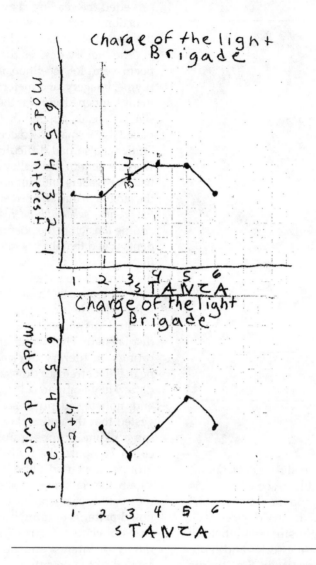

considering it was written so long ago. "It is a poem, after all," said one.

These sixth-grade students successfully used data displays to capture such qualities as interest. Their explorations of "best ways" to show trends and to represent the group deepened their mathematical literacy, even as it served as a tool to orient them toward the devices and techniques, such as plot, character, setting, tone, and mood, that authors and directors use in their work to get and keep interest. They saw the advantages of data displays demonstrated in their activity. Together, they used their knowledge of literary devices to judge the representativeness of their data displays and their data displays to confirm their assessment of interest. Multiple, mutually reinforcing literacies—graphing artistry.

Chapter 8

Data Models of Ourselves: Body Self-Portrait Project

ERIN DIPERNA

Country View Elementary School, Third Grade
Verona, Wisconsin

As part of the Human Body unit that I regularly teach with my third-grade class, I had planned for my students to take part in a 2-day data collection project designed to answer some of their questions about how children's body self-portraits progress though the elementary school grades. Little did I realize the potential this project had! I started out by sending a letter to all the classroom teachers in our school, pre-K through fifth grade. In the letter, I asked if their students could draw a "full-body self-portrait." I also requested that the students note their grade level on their portraits. As my third-graders reviewed the resulting portraits, we commented on the dramatic differences between the portraits drawn by prekindergarteners and those made by fifth-graders. I challenged my students to identify a set of characteristics that could capture the differences between the self-portraits made by young children and those made by children in older grades. Moreover, I asked, could we identify and describe these characteristics in sufficient detail so that we would be able to accurately predict the exact grade of the artists of a new set of self-portraits?

As we became more involved in the project, big mathematical concepts began to surface. While collecting data, the students gained experience with data abstraction in order to make the data collection more meaningful and manageable. They made predictions regarding the progression of self-portraits and then developed models to prove or disprove their predictions. Once they tested their model, they were faced with the challenge of revising their models to see if their models could be improved. Through this 6-month project, I learned a great deal about my students' mathematical thinking.

Before I begin to describe what we did in greater detail, I will first outline the top-level goals that I hoped to achieve with my students in this work. Above all, I wanted the project to involve students in an inquiry in which *data modeling* would be central. This objective entailed three major subgoals. First, students needed to decide which critical *attributes* of the portraits to focus on. As I will explain, we eventually settled on eye shape, head shape, hair, and hands, but this was far from a foregone conclusion. Having decided that these attributes might help us diagnose the age of the artists, we then, second, had to decide *how to measure the attributes*. For example, how many categories of eye shapes did we observe, and what level of description was most useful for predicting the grade of the artist? The third subgoal was deciding how to display our data so that they would clearly communicate what we observed at each grade level and make it easy to compare one grade level with the others. Finally, I wanted my students to use these data models to make predictions about new portraits, to check the accuracy of their predictions, and then to go through the process of testing and refining their models.

Investigating Real Data in the Classroom: Expanding Children's Understanding of Math and Science. Copyright © 2002 by Teachers College, Columbia University. All rights reserved. ISBN 0-8077-4141-8 (pbk.). Prior to photocopying items for classroom use, please contact the Copyright Clearance Center, Customer Service, 222 Rosewood Dr., Danvers, MA 01923, USA, tel. (508) 750-8400.

At different times throughout the study, the students were faced with concepts they had no prior knowledge of. Whenever this occurred, I simply taught a minilesson on the concept and then integrated what they learned into our study. For example, when I realized that the students had to compare large-number fractions with uncommon denominators, we worked with small-number fractions with common denominators and then uncommon denominators. Once the students felt confident with fractions that had uncommon denominators, they applied their knowledge to the fractions that were a part of the data collected.

INITIAL BRAINSTORMING ABOUT MEASURABLE BODY PARTS

On the first day, I asked the students to come up with some questions regarding the development of self-portraits throughout the grade levels. Eventually, we turned our attention to one question in particular: "What are some body parts that will show progress from pre-K to fifth grade?" As you might expect, a variety of possibilities were volunteered. One student suggested that it might be useful to look at head shape. This student thought that the portraits of the younger children tended to feature circular heads, whereas those of older students tended to include heads that were more oval. Another student mentioned body shape. The body shape drawn by the younger artists was described as a kind of "stick figure," while those made by students in the older grades were "bubbled out." Someone noticed that hands were portrayed in less or more detailed fashion, an observation that led to questions about whether the portrait included five fingers on each hand, and whether fingernails were drawn. Others proposed that eye shape might be diagnostic, as might the inclusion (or lack!) of eyelashes and eyebrows.

To my surprise, one girl suggested that we could study voices. I asked the rest of the class how they thought we could do that, given that the self-portraits were the only information we had to work with. Many agreed that pictures would not permit us to study voices.

IDENTIFYING ATTRIBUTES

After this initial brainstorming session, I proposed that students start off by collecting data on "hands." I chose hands because they had come up during our brainstorming session, but also because I thought that hands would definitely show progression throughout the grade levels. I placed students in groups of three, and each group was responsible for a certain grade level's hands.

My second suggestion was a study of eyes. In retrospect, I probably should have had the students choose which body part they wanted to research. I was very hesitant to let the students choose at this point because I wanted to make sure that they were collecting data on a body part that would really show progression. I was concerned that if I had let the reins go too early in the study, they would have collected data that would not show them anything. Now I am inclined to think that it would have actually been helpful if some of the attributes had turned out to have predictive value, while others did not.

For the third study, the students voted on the body part they wanted to look at—hair won. In the back of my mind, I was not sure about hair being a very informative body part, but I figured that if it ended up not being informative, we would find that out later when we tested our data model.

Collecting Data from the Self-Portraits/ Dealing with Data Abstraction

Hands Study. The students recorded every possible type of hand found in their grade level's self-portraits. In fact, some groups ended up with 15 different types of hands. Once they were finished collecting their data, I asked them if they could tell me anything about the way their grade level illustrated hands. The students shared with me that "six students had four stick fingers," or "two students had fingernails." Although their observations were very finely detailed, they had difficulty generalizing. I finally suggested that they tell me how many portraits had five fingers on each hand and how many did not. As the students embarked on other body parts, I hoped that on their own they would be able to come up with the "broad categories." As we progressed through this study, I intended to ease off more and more in terms of suggestions for "broad categories."

Eyes Study. Once again, the students recorded every eye shape they could possibly find. Once the students had their data, but still could not make any generalizations, I focused our discussion on coming up with broader topics, as we did for the hands. Our discussion went through the spectrum of possible broad categories. I asked the students first what the most "basic" eye shape and then what the most "advanced" eye shape would be. One student suggested that we could break down the eyes into "eyeball shape" and "circle shape." The rest of the class was very impressed with this student's cut-and-dried suggestion.

Then we got into a lengthy discussion about what would be considered a "dot" eye. About three of my students took that as an invitation to come up with about 15 other possibilities. I made it a point to refocus the group by telling them that we needed broad categories that would clearly show progress in self-portraits over the elementary years. I asked the students if they felt it was necessary to get really technical about dots, eyelashes, and so on, or whether we could focus on the shapes of the eye. Unanimously, the students felt that we could stick to the outer shape of the eye, because, they argued, a "circle" eye is less advanced than a "football-shaped" eye. I asked them what we would do with an eye that did not fit into either of those two categories. There was no response to this question.

So then I asked the students if we could have more than two categories. Many of the students felt that we could. I asked them what this category could be called, so that every other eye besides the circle and football shape would fit into it. One student suggested that we call it the "neither" or "other" category. The rest of the class seemed to be at ease with this suggestion. So, after the extensive discussion, the class agreed on having "football-shaped eyes," "circle eyes" and "other eyes," which weren't "football-shaped" or "circle-shaped." We called the "other" category our "safety net." The students proceeded to categorize portraits into the three categories.

Another interesting point came out of this discussion when I asked, "Let's say that when we are doing the circle graph for eyes: 'football' = blue, 'circle' = red, and 'other' eyes = green. Will we have any white areas on our graph?" I asked the kids to shut their eyes and vote: thumbs up for yes, there would be white areas; and thumbs down for no, there would not be white areas on the circle graph. About 90% of the students voted no. I asked someone to explain. One student said that with our categories, there was not a single eye shape that would not fit into at least one of them. I asked who disagreed. One did, and I asked this student to draw a picture of an eye that would cause some white areas on our graph—a kind of an eye that would not fit in any of the three categories. He came up and drew a bizarre-looking eye shape. I asked the kids if this would fit into "football" (they all said no) and "circle" (they all said no). I then asked if the eye shape that this student had drawn would fit into the "other" category. The student who had drawn it bashfully answered that it would—that eye would be a green mark in the circle graph under the "other" category.

Hair Study. My students broke into their groups and started to record the type of hair each portrait had. They recorded "wavy," "curly," "straight," "short," and so on. I called all the groups together and asked them to restate our question about hair. I asked them if collecting data on "what kind of hair" someone had would show how self-portraits changed as students progressed

through the grades. Only one group chose to do "hair" or "no hair." I asked this group to share what they were doing with hair. They commented that they chose to use the categories "hair" or "no hair" because they guessed that the older the students were, the more likely they were to put hair in their self-portraits. I sent the rest of the groups back to look at "hair" or "no hair" in the portraits.

Reflections: It became quite evident to me that data abstraction is a very complex issue for students to deal with. As our study continued, I did see an improvement in some students' abilities to generalize categories and ideas. A helpful question that I observed students asking themselves when coming up with their broad topics was "What would I most likely find on a pre-K portrait and also a fifth-grade portrait?" I am pleased that my students were given opportunities to work with data abstraction, but I feel that this concept is not something that should be dealt with only one time in a school year. Exposing children to data abstraction in various situations during their elementary years is very beneficial in helping them build a solid foundation for making generalizations.

PREDICTING WITH CIRCLE GRAPHS

I was curious to see if my students understood what they were truly looking for in their eye study. In order to do this I asked them to predict what they thought a circle graph would look like once they collected their data on eyes. The students predicted (using circle graphs) what a pre-K eye circle graph would look like if red = football-shaped eye, green = circle-shaped eye, and blue = other eye shape. All the students predicted that hardly any pre-K students would have football-shaped eyes, and they showed that by including little to no red on their prediction graphs. My students predicted that the chance for more red (football shape) would increase as artists progressed to higher grades. They also predicted that there would be less green (circle shape) and blue (other shapes).

An interesting discussion arose from one student's prediction, illustrated in Figure 8.1. As we looked at this graph together, I asked students, "How much of the circle is red?" The students guessed from 1/4 to 1/16. One student said, "1/2 of a 1/2 of a 1/2." For the next 20 minutes, we talked about what that value was worth. We tried to figure it out using a rectangle on the chalkboard. (If I did this again, I would make sure every child had a clipboard with paper, so that all students could actively try to figure this out.)

One of my students used the following reasoning, illustrated in the left panel of Figure 8.2:

Figure 8.1. A student's prediction of eye shapes drawn by pre-kindergarten students. Red = football shapes; green = circular shapes.

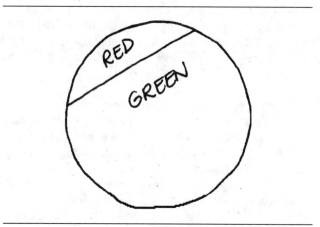

1. She cut the rectangle into 1/2.
2. She cut the 1/2 in1/2.
3. She cut the 1/4 in 1/2.
4. She then lost track of part-whole relationship.

This student claimed that there was no such thing as a 1/2 of a 1/2 of a 1/2, because all of the pieces were unequal. Another student partitioned her rectangle differently, as shown in the right panel of Figure 8.2. She concluded that 1/2 of a 1/2 of a 1/2 was equal to 1/8. She said, "One side is just like the other." When I asked the class how they felt about the two different rectangles, about two thirds agreed with the second student's reasoning. The other third didn't seem to have an opinion. My original intention had been to get the students to realize that shaded circles are very difficult to measure.

Reflections: I thought that it was very interesting for the students to make predictions on their data, especially by using circle graphs. Their predictions showed me that all the students were very aware of the trends that they

might find in the data. I also learned a lot about the students who graphed their circles as in Figure 8.1, where the student did not use the center of the circle as a point of reference. Those students had difficulties later on in the study when determining a quarter or a third of a circle.

Sharing Data

The students shared their data, and then I put it on the board. Table 8.1 is a facsimile of our table. The kids determined whether each of the fractions was less than 1/2, equal to 1/2, or more than 1/2. They jotted their answers down on a sheet of paper and then showed me their responses. I asked the students, with their eyes closed, to do "thumbs up" for >1/2, "thumbs down" for <1/2, and "hands level" for = 1/2. Through this, I got a chance to do a quick assessment of each student and his or her understanding of fractional value as I called out a particular fraction. Then I asked for volunteers to explain their answers. Usually, the explanation would be something like (for 9/15), "Well, I doubled the top number and got 18, and 18 is larger than 15, so 9/15 is greater than half." By the time we got to the hair study, there were very few errors with the fraction votes.

When we got to the hair study, we continued to vote with "less than," "equal to," and "more than" 1/2, but after the students voted, I asked them questions such as "Is this closer to 1/2 or 1/4?" For the most part, my students had difficulty deciding. It seemed that they didn't quite know how to figure the 1/4 out. Instead of telling them how to do it, I continued to raise the question about 1/4. We got to a more difficult fraction in the eye study. All the students knew that 11/45 was less than 1/2, but when I asked them if this fraction was close to 1/4, no one had a definite answer. I proceeded to ask them what they did to find out if something was "half." The students agreed that they doubled the top number. I then asked them what they thought they would do if they wanted to find out if a fraction was

Figure 8.2. Students' use of rectangles to figure out "1/2 of a 1/2 of a 1/2."

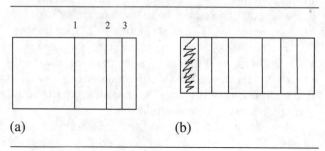

(a)   (b)

Table 8.1. Number of artists in each grade making each category of eye shape.

Eyes	Football	Circle	Other
Pre-K	*0*	*6*	*9*
Total N	15	15	15
Kindergarten	*2*	*33*	*1*
Total N	36	36	36

1/4. I prompted by asking, "How many pieces are in a circle that is divided into fourths?" Four was the unanimous answer. One student said, "You do the top number four times." So that's what they did: 11 four times was 44. We continued to work on fractional values.

Making Sense of the Data

As we looked at our "hand data," I asked the students to look at the Table 8.2 to determine which grade was most likely to include five fingers in their self-portraits. For the most part, the students thought that fourth grade had "better" results than fifth grade (that is, fourth-graders were more likely to include five fingers). I asked the students how they could prove that the fourth grade did better. One child said that fourth grade had only six kids who didn't include five fingers. I pointed out that the fifth grade had more self-portraits than fourth grade, and asked if there should be more fifth-grade self-portraits that did not include five fingers. This question seemed to be over their heads, so after a short discussion I decided to end the discussion. I wanted our next activity to focus on equivalent fractions and comparing fractions, and I decided to do that with much lower numbers.

Partitioning Fractions with Same Numerator. The following day, the students partitioned and shaded in fractions with the same numerators on circle graphs. I chose to use the same numerators because that seemed to be all that my students were looking at when comparing fractions. After partitioning and shading the circles, they then made comparisons of the fractions (see Figure 8.3).

The examples had the same numerators and had denominators that were either 2, 4, 6, 8, or 10. (These

Table 8.2. Proportion of students in each grade who drew five fingers on hands.

Grade of Artist	Proportion of Students
Pre-K	1 out of 15
Kindergarten	3 out of 38
First Grade	7 out of 45
Second Grade	24 out of 38
Fourth Grade	32 out of 38
Fifth Grade	52 out of 67

numbers as denominators were least frustrating for the students.) All of my students were able to figure out which fractions were "worth more" once they shaded in the circles. When they agreed that 3/4 was more than 3/8, I asked how that was possible, because both circles had the same number of pieces shaded. One student surprised me by her answer. She said that the circle with eight pieces had more pieces in the circle, so that made each of the pieces smaller than the pie that only had four pieces. So I asked the students if, when looking at fractions, they looked only at the top number. After many of our examples, I felt as though the kids understood that they needed to look at the top number and the bottom number.

Partitioning Fractions with Different Numerators and Denominators. I then gave the students fractions that had different numerators and denominators. For one example, I purposely chose 1/2 and 3/8, because I thought that my students would think that 3/8 was larger because the numerator 3 was larger than the numerator 1. After partitioning and shading, my students realized that 1/2 was larger than 3/8. However, one student, whose shading is represented in Figure 8.4, concluded the opposite. The other students gave suggestions about ways of changing her circle so that she could get the correct answer. They suggested that she partition more carefully so that the pieces would be all the same size. They also suggested that she shade pieces right next to one another.

At this point, we again discussed whether the "top" number alone determines if one fraction is larger than another. After a few more comparison questions, most of my students were able to explain that they needed to compare the "top" number along with the "bottom" number when comparing fractions. Then we looked again at our "hands" results. By this time, the students still felt that fourth grade had better results, but they were able to explain their reasoning more clearly and accurately. So that they could justify their thinking, I asked the students to construct circle graphs to display the results.

Reflections: I feel that this mini-lesson on fractions was incredibly important for the continuation of the study. At first, the students were convinced that the higher the numerator, the higher the fractional value. During these 2 days of working with fractions, my major focus was for the students to verbalize and understand that fractions are a comparison of the top and bottom number. After the two days, it seemed clear to me that almost three quarters of my class had a very firm understanding of comparing fractions. I made a point throughout the rest of the study to reacquaint the class with comparing fractions whenever the chance arose. As the study

Figure 8.3. Comparing fractions of circle graphs.

Kindergarten

Pre-Kindergarten

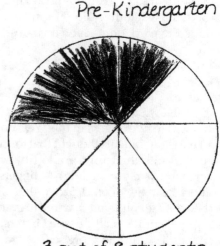

3 out of 4 students in
Kindergarten had 5 fingers
in their portraits.

3 out of 8 students
in Pre-K. had 5 fingers
in their portrait?

Did Kindergarten or Pre-Kindergarten
have BETTER results? ___Kindergarten___

Explain your answer:

___because they have half as many as___

___the   pre Kindergart-ns.___

progressed, the students came up with other strategies on their own when comparing fractions, which I will discuss further later in the chapter, especially when the students developed their own models.

Displaying Data

I decided against handing the students perfectly partitioned circles, because I felt that they needed to struggle with figuring out the process themselves. So, to start out, I gave the students a blank sheet of paper and told them to construct a circle divided into 15 equal parts. The students were very excited about this task. During this assignment, I learned a lot about their thinking. Most students just went about partitioning very blindly, but others put great thought into it. One stu-

dent came up to me with her circle cut in half. She told me that there was no way to divide the circle in half and still come up with 15 equal parts, because 7 pieces would be on one side and 8 pieces on the other. I asked her what she could first divide her circle into to get 15 pieces. After wrestling with this for a couple of minutes, she thought that drawing a Y in the circle would make 3 pieces in the circle. I asked her how many smaller pieces would go into each of the 3 pieces to make 15 total pieces. She drew four lines in each piece and then realized that 5 tiny pieces would be in each of the 3 pieces to get 15 total. Her circle looked more accurate than a lot of the other partitioned circles.

Once everyone had given the partitioning a try, we critiqued different students' circles. I held up one circle that clearly did not have equal pieces (see Figure 8.5). I

Figure 8.4. Partitioning and shading 3/8 of circle graph.

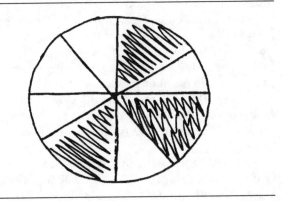

asked the students if it was important to have equal pieces. Some said yes, others said that it didn't matter. I asked them, if this were a pizza, and I ate A and B (two out of four pieces) and someone else ate C and D (two out of four pieces), would that be fair? The unanimous answer was that it would not be fair. So then I asked again, do the pieces of our circle need to be the same?

By this time, everyone agreed that in order for it to be fair, the pieces had to be equal in size. I explained to the students that it is nearly impossible for someone to divide a circle into 15 perfectly equal pieces. I continued by telling them that there is a computer program that constructs "perfectly" divided circles. Many of my students had worked on LogoWriter in their second-grade classrooms. I explained that in order to divide circles perfectly into equal pieces, we needed to know more about circles.

Then I asked the kids if they knew how many degrees are in a circle. One student answered that there are 360 degrees in a circle. I asked the students to stand up and turn around 360 degrees. All the students, except one, did the 360. I asked if someone could explain what 360 degrees meant. One student said, "If you have a circle and go the whole way around it, that will be 360

Figure 8.5. A circle graph with unequal pieces.

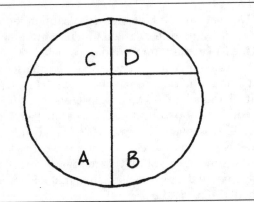

degrees." I then drew a circle on the board and asked, "Well, how many degrees would be in each piece if I had four equal pieces?" With that, I cut the circle into four equal pieces. Hands shot up, and many kids said 90 degrees. I asked them how they got that answer. One student commented that four 90s are in 360.

I asked how many degrees would be in each piece if I cut the circle in half. I erased one of the lines in my circle. Most of my students had their hands in the air, ready to give the answer 180 degrees. The explanation was that there are two 90s in a half of a circle and 90 two times is 180. I asked if there were another way to get 180 degrees in half a circle, hoping that they would say, "Oh, half of 360 is 180." No such luck, so we continued. I divided my circle on the board into eight equal parts. I asked the students if they could tell me how many degrees were in one of these eight pieces. One student answered that it would be 45 degrees because 45 is half of 90. I then questioned, "How can you check your answer, that in a circle that has eight equal pieces, that each piece has a degree of 45?" Another student said to add 45 eight times. So on the board, we added 45 eight times. The students seemed impressed when it added up to 360.

After determining how many degrees would be in each piece of a circle that had 8 equal pieces, I drew a rough sketch of a circle that had 15 pieces. I asked the kids to respond with thumbs down if they thought that the degrees of each piece would be fewer than 45, or thumbs up if they thought that the degrees of each piece would be greater than 45. (Hands flat if they really didn't have an opinion yet.) About 50% of the class thought that the degrees would be fewer than 45 degrees, 25% thought that the degrees would be greater than 45 degrees, and 25% of the class didn't have an opinion yet. I asked for a thumbs-up person to explain his or her answer. One student said that the degrees would definitely be fewer than 45 degrees, because there were more pieces in the pie and all the pieces had to add up to 360. I asked the kids if they could make a guess about how many degrees would be in each piece. Some guesses were 20, 30, and 26. I asked how we could find out the correct answer. One student suggested that we do 20 × 15. So on the board, we calculated 20 × 15 (300). I asked if our degrees would have to be higher or lower than 20. Unanimously, the kids felt that we needed our degree number to be higher in order to reach 360.

One student suggested that we try 22. We calculated that and got 330. The kids became excited because our guess was even closer. After this, a student with some difficulty in math suggested 19. Instead of questioning, I decided that we would figure out 19 × 15. When the student saw that this equaled 285 degrees, she seemed embarrassed and said, "Oh, I meant 29." After trying

29, we gradually made it to 24 × 15. This, as a surprise to the students, worked out perfectly.

To determine the degrees in each piece of a pie that was divided into 38 equal pieces, we started out by reviewing how many degrees were in a circle with 8 pieces and 15 pieces. I asked the kids, "Knowing the degrees in circles with 15 pieces and 8 pieces, will our degrees for a circle with 38 pieces be higher or lower than the 15 and 8?" Everyone agreed that the more pieces you get in a circle, the lower the number of degrees would be. I then opened the floor to suggestions for 38 pieces. We started off with a suggestion of 10. None of my kids could see automatically that 10 would be too high. So we started out doing 10 thirty-eight times. A student pointed out that we could also do 10 × 38. We quickly figured out, with column addition, that 10 × 8 = 80 and 10 × 30 = 300, which gave us the answer of 380.

Next, a student suggested trying 9. I asked students, if 10 × 38 equaled 380, what we could do easily to get 9 × 38. A suggestion was made that we simply take 38 away from 380. So I asked the kids what 380 take away 30 is (350). We then took away another 8 (342). The students realized that nine 38s was too low. So then I asked, "If 10 is too high and 9 is too low, then what could the answer be?" Many students came up with 9 1/2. This became tricky, because I wasn't sure if the kids would know to take half of 38 to find half a degree. So I asked them, "What have we been adding together to count as one degree?" They answered, 38. "So how much would a half of a degree be?" About one third of the class raised their hands. One student said, "What is half of 38?" Many did the calculation in their heads. Another student said, "Well, half of 30 is 15 and half of 8 is 4, so the answer is 19." So then I asked, "What do we do with the 19?" One student said to add it to the 342 (361). The kids were disappointed that they didn't get 360, but I explained that 361 was as close as we had to get to 360. So then I questioned, "How many degrees are in a piece of a pie that has 38 equal pieces?" The unanimous answer was 9 and a half degrees. I asked them, "How do I write that in numbers?" One student responded with 9 and then 1 over 2. I asked them how else I could write it. No one seemed to have any suggestions. I finally wrote on the board that it could be written as 9.5, and that the .5 stood for half of a whole.

To find the degrees in a piece of a pie that had 67 equal pieces, the process was basically the same as for one with 38 pieces. I was initially interested in asking if the number of degrees would be larger or smaller than for the circle with 38 equal pieces. One of my quietest students said that the pieces in the 67-piece circle were smaller than the pieces in the circle with 38 pieces because there were more pieces in the 67-piece circle. Everyone agreed with her. I asked if some-one had a suggestion for a number of degrees that we could start with. One student said 7. I asked him what we were supposed to do with the 7. He answered that we had to add 67 seven times, which we did together (469). The kids shuddered at how "off" that guess was. I asked them, "How far off are we?" One student, who had very good number sense, said that we were a little more than 100 off. I asked them, "How many 67s can we get out of 100?" Another student said that we could get one 67 out of the 100, so that would take us down to six 67s.

I wanted to see if any of them would say, "Just take 67 off 469," but no one did, so we added six 67s (402). Many students immediately said, "Six is too high, so let's try 5." We tried 5 and got 335. A roar of "5 and a half" came from the class. I asked them how we were supposed to find what the half degree was worth. A student said to take half of 67. All of a sudden, the room was quiet, and then someone finally said, "You can't take half of 67, because it is an odd number." I asked them what half of 66 or 68 was. They immediately said 33 and 34. I questioned, "What number comes in between 33 and 34?" Someone said 33 and a half. I told them that 33 and a half is half of 67. Then a student said to take 335 and add 33 and a half on to it. They came up with the answer 368 and a half.

Truthfully, I was about to call it quits, but the kids wanted to get closer to the 368. I asked them, "What do we know about the degree?" One student said that "5 was too low and 5 and a half was too big." Then he said in the same breath, "I bet it's 5 and a quarter." Then the question was, how do we find a quarter of the degree? The same student said that half of the degree was 33 and a half, then asked "So what is half of that?" Another student said that half of 30 was 15, and that half of 3 is one and a half, so half of 33 was 16 and a half. (I didn't point out that he still needed to take half of the other half, thinking that it might be too overwhelming.) So then I posed the question, What do we do with the 16 and a half? The first student, still on a roll, said that we had to add it to the 335, which was the 5 degrees. Together we found that 335 plus the 16 and a half was 351 and a half.

Once again, the kids seemed disappointed that we didn't get right to 360. I asked the students if they could tell me where this number of degrees fell. A student said that it was somewhere between 5 and a quarter degrees and 5 and a half degrees. I then asked, "How do you write 5 and a half?" The answer given was 5.5. I then asked, "How do you write 5 and a quarter?" The answer 5.3 was given, along with 5.2. I finally told the kids that it is what a quarter (the coin) is worth. The figure 5.25 was then given. I told them that the exact number of degrees of the piece was 5.35, so that it is somewhere in between 5.5 and 5.25.

<u>Reflections:</u> This was probably one of my favorite parts of the study. Together as a class, we established how many degrees were in each piece of a pie within a circle graph. At first I didn't see a need for the students to be a part of this process, but now looking back, I feel that this benefited the students in a number of ways. First, it gave us an opportunity to work with addition and multiplication and the way these two operations interconnected. This process also allowed me to learn a lot about my students' number sense. Finally, it gave me an opportunity to reacquaint my students with the notion of fractional pieces in a circle.

Interpreting Data

Hands Study. I started off by asking students how pre-K and kindergarten compared on their results for hands. The students looked at their shaded-in circles. All but one claimed that kindergarten had more of their circles filled in green. The shading of this student's circle, shown in Figure 8.6, made it difficult for her to prove her answer when I asked her about it. I asked her if she thought having her shaded areas all over the circle made it difficult for her to make sense of her graph. She said that she thought her circle was shaded in just fine. I then showed her another student's graph, which had three pieces shaded in right next to one another. I then asked her to compare the pre-K and kindergarten graphs again. Her answer this time was that kindergarten had more of the circle filled in. She proved that by placing the pre-K graph over the K graph and explaining that you can see extra green from the K graph where the pre-K graph is white.

As a class we came up with conclusions for the Hands graphs. This process of coming up with conclusions was very difficult at first. The students kept wanting to offer me numbers, not generalizations. I had to introduce words such as *likely*, *not likely*, and so on. These are the conclusions that the students came up with:

Figure 8.6. Partitioning and shading in fractions of circle graphs.

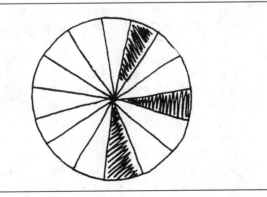

1. It was *not likely* that pre-K students would include five fingers. One student added, though, that there was a small chance that they would.
2. It was *not likely* that K students would include five fingers, but more likely that they would than pre-K. I asked one student, "If you had a portrait that had 5 fingers on it, could it possibly be a kindergartner?" She said that it could, "because in our graph for K, there were a few that did have five fingers."
3. It was *not likely* that first-graders included five fingers, but they were more likely to do so than kindergarten and prekindergarten.
4. A little more than *half* of the second-graders included five fingers.
5. It was *very likely* that fourth- and fifth-graders would have five fingers in their portraits.

The big debate, though, was "Did fourth grade have better results than fifth grade?" The students concluded by looking at their graphs that fourth grade did indeed have better results than fifth grade. I asked the kids what some reasons were that fourth grade did better than fifth grade. Here are some of their ideas:

a. Some portraits had hands in pockets.
b. They rushed through it and didn't take their time.
c. They didn't want to do the assignment.
d. They didn't have enough time to complete the assignment (i.e., "It was time for recess").

Eyes Study and Hair Study. Using their circle graphs, the students were going to interpret their results. The interpretation of data took on a new twist because the kids had made "predictions" before they collected data. So, my goals for this interpretation of data were three-fold. First, I wanted students to take their prediction sheets and compare their prediction circle graphs to the actual, data-collected circle graphs. Second, I wanted them to come up with conclusions about "Self-Portraits and Eyes" through the grade levels using their data. But with these generalizations, I wanted them to be a little more specific than "more likely/less likely." I wanted them to focus in on what part of the circles were a particular eye shape (i.e., in second grade, football shapes were most popular: 1/2 of the second grade had football-shaped eyes, 1/4 had circle shaped, and 1/4 had "other" eyes.) Third, after the interpretations with more specific information were made, I planned on asking them "comprehension questions" regarding their graphs.

Comparing Predictions with Data

My students and I had an enjoyable time making comparisons between their prediction sheets and the actual data displayed on circle graphs. I emphasized,

"What did you predict correctly?" First, we started with the pre-K graph, and I had the kids tell a partner what they did well. After they had time to share with a partner, I asked for volunteers. Many volunteers came forward and shared what they predicted accurately and even not so accurately. Two very interesting comments came out of this activity. One arose when a student said that, with first grade, he had predicted "circle eyes" correctly and "football eyes" correctly, but he was incorrect about "other eyes." Another student told him that that was impossible. I asked him why he thought that. The student said that on the circle graph with three colors, he could either predict one eye shape correctly, no eye shapes correctly, or all eye shapes correctly. He then added that if two colors were predicted correctly, then the third color had to be correct as well.

The second interesting comment was made by a student with difficulties in math. After all this comparing with the prediction circle graphs and data-collected circle graphs, the student said, "No one's prediction is truly correct because the circles are two different sizes. The circles and the pieces have to be the same size to be equal." I then looked at the prediction sheet. She was right. The circles that I had made were much smaller on the prediction sheets than the circles on the data-collected circle graphs.

Making Conclusions about Eyes

Because I wanted the conclusions to be more specific than those made in the hands study, the students were a little shaky at first. It took some examples as a whole class for them to get the gist of what I meant by "more specific." Here are some ideas that my students had in terms of making conclusions about their portraits.

Pre-K: "A little more than half of pre-K had 'other' eye sockets and there are no 'football' eye sockets. > 1/4 or <1/2 of the pre-K students had 'circle' eye sockets."

Kindergarten: "In kindergarten, there is, 1/6 of football eye sockets." [The 1/6 was challenging in that the kids went right for < 1/4. I asked if they could get more specific than that. I asked them, "How many of the red sections could you fit in the circle?" Some students got down to 1/6, whereas others were comfortable with staying with 1/4.] "There are even less 'other' and 'football' shaped eyes. For 'circle' sockets, we got more than 3/4 of the circle." [With the "circle sockets," many of the students said "more than 1/2" immediately. I asked if they could get more specific. I questioned, "Is it closer to 1/2 or the entire circle?" They agreed that it was somewhere in between those. I then drew a circle on the board with four pieces, and I asked for a volunteer to shade in the circle so that it looked like the red section of the kindergarten circle. The volunteer shaded in a little more than 3/4 of the circle. I asked, "How many

parts of this circle are filled in?" "Three out of four pieces." "What would the fraction look like for this circle?" One student gave the reply 3/4.]

First Grade: "The first grade has 1/4 of 'football' shaped eyes and the 'circle' eyes are very close to 1/2 of the circle. Blue is very close to a 1/4, but a little less."

Second Grade: "More than half of the second grade circle has 'circle' eyes and the 'football' eyes are in between 1/4 and 1/2 of the circle. There were hardly any 'other' eyes on the circle."

Third Grade: "Almost exactly 3/4 of the eyes were 'football' and 1/4 of the eyes were 'circle.' Hardly any 'other' eyes were in third grade, but more 'other' eyes were in third grade than second grade!"

Fourth Grade: "Fourth grade had less 'football' eyes than third grade. They only had a little more than 1/2 that were 'football.' They also had a little more than 1/4 of 'circle' eyes. They had less 'other' eyes than third grade, though."

Fifth Grade: "Fifth grade had more than 3/4 of their circle 'football' shaped eyes. They had the best results for 'football' eyes in all of the grades. They had almost the same amount of 'circle' and 'other' eyes, but a little more 'circle' eyes."

Comprehension Questions Using Circle Graphs

My students did an outstanding job on this section of interpretation of data. Here are the questions that I asked and the answers that I received:

1. *Which grade level is most likely to have portraits with "football" eyes?*
   "Fifth grade is, because they had more than 3/4 of their circle with 'football' eyes. No other grades had more then 3/4 of their circle with 'football.' "
2. *Which grade level is most likely to have a portrait with "circle" eyes?*
   "Kindergarten is, because they had the largest section of green on their circle graph."
3. *Who is more likely to have "circle" eyes on their portraits, first or third?*
   "First grade is more likely, because they had more than 1/2 for 'circle' eyes, and third grade had about 1/4 for 'circle' eyes."
4. *Who is less likely to have "other" eyes, fourth or fifth?*
   "Fourth grade is less likely, because they had only two students with 'other' and fifth grade had four students with 'other' eyes." I asked this child if it was the actual number of kids that mattered. She seemed to catch what she had said and changed her answer to "Fourth grade is less likely, because their section of blue was smaller than the section of blue on the fifth-grade circle."

5. *At which grade level did almost exactly 1/4 of the students have "football" eyes?*

   "First grade." When I asked how the student knew that, the reply was that "the section of red could be placed four times around the circle with the size that it is."

6. *Did more or fewer than 1/2 of the fourth-graders have "circle" eyes, and how could you prove that?*

   "More than 1/2 had 'circle' eyes. I know this because if I would cut the circle graph in half, the red would take up more than half of the circle. Also, 22 out of 38 students had 'circle' eyes, and if I would double the 22, I would get 44, which is more than 38. That makes it more than half of my graph."

7. *Did you have any white sections on your graph? Why did or didn't you?*

   "No, I did not have any white areas, because the 'other' category would take care of any eyes that didn't fall into the 'football' or 'circle' categories."

Reflections: The students demonstrated deep understanding of fractional values 1/4, 1/2, and 3/4. I felt comfortable that all the students had moved beyond simply looking at the graph and instead used the numbers to prove their answers. Some students did continue to "eyeball" the graph initially, but then they all gradually made a natural move toward using the numbers.

PROCEDURE FOR CONSTRUCTING AND TESTING A MODEL

In order for the students to make sense of their data, our next step was for them to organize their data and construct a data model. To test the accuracy of their model, I gave them "mystery portraits" never seen by any of them, such as the examples in Figure 8.7. The steps taken to construct the model are explained next.

Establishing the Parameters for the Model

I asked the students to make up a set of rules or guidelines that would tell us how much of a shaded area on the graphs we could use to represent "likely," "unlikely," and "sometimes." One student began the discussion by saying, "If the top number is lower than 5, then it will be unlikely. If it is 5 or 6, it is sometimes. If it is 7 or above, then it will be likely." Playing devil's advocate, I asked this student and the class, "If my fraction was 4/6, then would that be unlikely, likely, or sometimes, according to your theory?" The class agreed that it would be likely because the fraction took up more than half of the circle. The student went back to the drawing board with his idea. I asked the class if the top number is the only number that really counts with fractions. Another student said that fractions were really a comparison of two numbers—the top and the bottom.

The first student rethought his theory and said, "I am going to lower the top number to 3. If the top number is less than 3, then it is unlikely. If it is 3 or 4, then it is sometimes. If the top number is greater than 4, then it is likely." Once again, I asked the class, "What if we had the fraction 2/3, would that be likely, unlikely, or sometimes?" The student had a tough time admitting that it would be likely, but he finally did, with the help of the entire class.

Another student suggested that if 1/4 of the circle or less was filled in, that would be unlikely. If the shaded area was more than 1/4 but less than 1/2, that would be sometimes. If the shaded area was more than

Figure 8.7. Examples of self-portraits classified by students into grade levels.

1/2, it would be likely. Many of the students thought that this student's idea was great.

At this point, the first student came up to the board and said that he thought that we should have four symbols. He drew on the board what he was thinking. He said, "With four symbols, we can be even more specific as to how big the area on the circle graph is." Another student immediately disagreed. He thought that the three symbols were causing too great a headache, and that we should go down to two symbols—likely or unlikely. I asked the class how they felt about two symbols. There weren't many responses to this idea. I showed them our symbol sheet for hair and no hair. Using two symbols, every single grade level was a – (unlikely) for no hair and + (likely) for hair. I asked the students, "Using the symbol sheet for hair, tell me which grade level a portrait would most likely be from if it had hair." One student said, "It could be from any of the seven grade levels, since they all have a 'likely' for hair." I then asked, "Do you think that we will be better off just having two symbols?" Another student said that with only two symbols, the grade levels would look too much alike, and that we needed to be more specific.

At this point, other students were coming up to the board to share their ideas. Most were very similar to the initial idea of looking at how much was shaded in. I asked the kids if they were ready to vote on the way we were going to decide on unlikely, sometimes, and likely. Three fourths of the class voted for the shaded-in idea. (The student who suggested two symbols voted for two symbols; the student who wanted four symbols voted for four symbols.) I told the kids that we would try looking at the shaded areas first; if this didn't work, we would have to come up with another idea. We also decided on the symbols in Table 8.3 to stand for the three categories of "unlikely," "sometimes," and "likely."

Constructing the Model: Determining Symbols

We started to go through the eyeball section together to decide which symbols went in each grade level. When we reached kindergarten, there was a controversy over "other" eyes and "football" eyes. We noticed that 1/36 children drew "other" eyes; 2/36 drew "football" eyes, and 33/36 drew "circle" eyes. Circle eyes were a given because they took up more than half of the circle. Some students gave football eyes a "sometimes" and other eyes an "unlikely." One student explained, "All three eye shapes should have a different symbol. If we find that "other" and "football" are both unlikely, then we aren't being as specific as we need to be." His point was well taken. I said, though, that if that's what we were going to do, then we wouldn't be following the shaded-in strategy. Some other students felt as though we needed to stick strictly to this strategy. We voted, and the majority ruled that we would go with the shaded-in plan. So, "other eyes" and "football eyes" got a – for unlikely; and "circle eyes" got a + for likely.

Later on, as we continued to review our results for eyes, the students discussed the fraction 11/45 for first-grade "football" eyes. Many of the students tried to "eyeball" the graph and ended up guessing whether 11 was 1/4 of 45. I found it interesting the way one student determined if 11 was 1/4 of 45. He explained, "I just doubled 11 and got 22 and 22 is less than half of 45, so 11 is less than 1/4 of 45." For the rest of any "close" 1/4, that was a common strategy.

We also came across the fraction 17/77. I think that the student got intimidated by the odd numbers in 17 and 77, so he tried a different strategy to determine if 17 was 1/4 of 77. He suggested that we add up four 17s, and if it equaled 77, then it would be exactly 1/4 of 77. Our total came out to 68. The class agreed that 17 was less than 1/4 of 77, so that particular body part got a – (unlikely).

Testing and Evaluating Model with Mystery Portraits

The next step was to test our model by finding out if it could accurately predict the age of the artists of a new set of "mystery portraits." As the students got started working with the mystery portraits, it was obvious to me that they were having a difficult time putting aside their own opinions to use just the model to guess the grade level of the portraits. So what I had them do was write down their gut-instinct guess and then, separately, their guess from the model.

For example, here is how we used the model to analyze mystery portrait #8. We saw that the portrait had circle eyes, hair, and five fingers. As they checked their model, students noticed that circle eyes were "likely" in kindergarten and first and second grades. They also saw that hair was likely for all grades. They decided, however, that the presence of hair should focus their guess on second, third, fourth, and fifth grades, because in prekindergarten, kindergarten, and first grade, "no

Table 8.3. Class criteria and symbols for likelihood of a feature at a particular grade.

	Unlikely	Sometimes	Likely
Symbol	–	O	+
Amount of Circle Shaded	Less than ¼	Between ¼ and ½	More than ½

hair" sometimes occurred. In the higher grades, "no hair" was unlikely. Students found that five fingers were likely in second, fourth, and fifth grades. However, they decided to restrict their attention to fourth and fifth grades, because fewer than five fingers occurred sometimes in second grade. We compiled our results on the chalkboard in a list like the one in Table 8.4.

The students concluded that this portrait was in the "second, fourth, or fifth [grade level] since they all are in two categories." (That is, at each of these grade levels, mystery portrait #8 had two features that were "likely" at that grade level.) When I informed them that it was a fourth-grade portrait, they seemed excited that their gut-instinct guess was more accurate than the guess based on the model.

Mystery portrait #10 had circle eyes, no hair, and fewer than five fingers. Our chalkboard table looked like the one in Table 8.5.

The students thought that this portrait was "kindergarten and first, since they are in all three categories." I informed them that it was, in fact, a kindergarten drawing. Then I asked, "Do you see any problem with our model?" One student said, "On our model, K and first grade are totally the same. We can't tell them apart." When I asked, "What might we do to help us in this situation?" he replied, "Collect data on other body parts." Mystery portrait #5 had "football" eyes, hair, and five fingers. As Table 8.6 suggests, these were features more likely to be observed in the portraits of upper-grade students.

Once again, my students decided to just put fourth and fifth grade for fingers because five fingers were "likely" in second grade, but fewer than five fingers also occurred "sometimes." Their guess was very accurate. The students thought that for this portrait, "fourth and fifth would be the best since they were in all three categories." I told them that the portrait was a fourth-grader's, but then asked them again what was problematic about our model. They thought that "fourth and fifth grade are totally the same. They aren't different in any way." When I asked again what we could do to improve our model, they said we should "study another body part."

Table 8.4. Grades at which Mystery Portrait 8's features were considered "likely."

Eyes	Hair	Fingers
K	2nd	4th
1st	3rd	5th
2nd	4th	
	5th	

Table 8.5. Grades at which Mystery Portrait 10's features were considered "likely."

Eyes	Hair	Fingers
K	Pre-K	Pre-K
1st	K	K
	1st	1st

Finally, mystery portrait #6 had "football" eyes, no hair, and five fingers. Table 8.7, which resulted from our analysis of this portrait, was particularly mystifying.

Students thought that this portrait really belonged to "no grade. since hair grades are so different from eyes and fingers," or that "fourth or fifth grades would be the best choices." I informed them that this portrait was from a fifth-grader—they were shocked that a fifth-grader would fail to include hair in his or her portrait. I asked the students if they felt that the hair category had really been helpful at all, because all the grades had "likely" and only prekindergarten, kindergarten, and first had a few "sometimes." Someone answered, "I do not think that hair was a good choice for a body part because first, someone may not have hair, and also it didn't tell us much about the different grade levels." (Remember, this was the body part that the students as a class chose to investigate.)

Reflections: I enjoyed this part of the study because the students finally had a chance to test their models and evaluate them. While determining the grade level that fit the various portraits, they used strategies that helped them be more accurate. The students also noticed fairly quickly that there were some problems with their model, and they were able to come up with solutions. Looking back at this section, I commented about asking the kids if hair was a good category for their study. I do feel that it was best for me to choose the first two categories for them at the beginning of the study, to ensure that they

Table 8.6. Grades at which Mystery Portrait 5's features were considered "likely."

Eyes	Hair	Fingers
3rd	2nd	4th
4th	3rd	5th
5th	4th	
	5th	

Table 8.7. Grades at which Mystery Portrait 6's features were considered "likely."

Eyes	Hair	Fingers
3rd	Pre-K	4th
4th	K	5th
5th	1st	

would be looking at body parts that would clearly show progression throughout the elementary years.

REVISING AND TESTING MODEL

Choosing New Body Parts

I felt it very necessary at this point for the students themselves to select the body parts, and we had a very lengthy discussion about the body parts we could do. Students came up with scenery in a picture, noses, lips, and eyes. We discussed each one to try to come up with those that would be most informative. I asked the students which grade level they thought would have more scenery than others. Everyone had an opinion. Some thought that kindergartners would draw the most scenery, whereas others thought that fifth-graders would. We looked through some portraits from various grade levels, and then I asked the kids if they noticed a trend. The students concluded that scenery would not tell us enough about portraits and the perspective grade levels.

Then we discussed noses. The kids had a field day coming up with different types of noses. One student finally suggested that we come up with only two or three, so that we could graph the results more easily and also decide which category they would fit into without a big mess. Overall, only a few big categories were discussed:

- "circle/dot"
- "side view"
- "other" [got this one from "eyes"]
- "nostrils/no nostrils"
- "front view"

Then someone said, "We should combine all of these with 'nostrils/no nostrils': 'circle/dot' with 'nostrils' and 'no nostrils,' 'side view' with 'nostrils' and 'no nostrils,' 'other' with 'nostrils' and 'no nostrils.'" Some kids began to groan that all those categories would make their job much more difficult, and that three basic categories would be good enough. The girls in the group

decided to go along with using these three categories: "other," "side view," and "circle/dot."

The student who had suggested using only two or three categories continued to say that he wanted to do "no eyes" and "eyes." The rest of the group refused even to discuss eyes anymore because "we have already collected data on eyes." To satisfy this student, we decided to look through some portraits just as we had with "scenery" to see if there was any real difference in different grade levels with respect to "eyes" and "no eyes." Quickly, we realized that almost *all* the portraits had eyes. There were just a few in prekindergarten that didn't, so students decided that "eyes and no eyes would not be a very informative body part."

Reflections: The students very naturally came up with two or three categories for body parts instead of jotting down every type of nose found or every type of ears found. This proved to me that data abstraction was beginning to solidify in the students' decision making.

Collecting Data

One group decided to use these categories for the nose: "side view," "other," and "dot/circle." Another group chose "ears" and "no ears." The "ears" group felt that the younger grades would most likely include ears, because older students pay closer attention to other things besides ears. I thought that their reasoning was interesting, so I let them go ahead with their plan.

The "nose" group made three piles for their three categories. The "side view" and "dot/circle" portraits were rather easy. When they got to a very advanced portrait that had a nose with a "frontal" view, they would put it in "other," along with portraits that may not have even had a nose. I asked one student if there was a type of nose that she was constantly putting in "other." She said, "The ones with the front view." I asked her which other noses were put in "other." She said, "No noses." I asked her if she saw those two "different" types of noses ("front" and "no nose") as being equivalent. She said that to her they were the same because they didn't fit in either of the other categories.

Reflection: I really struggled not to say anything more to the student about her three categories and the types of noses going into her "other" category. I wanted to see if she would change her mind on her own, or if testing the model would make it clear to her.

Constructing Model/Determining Symbols

Using the data collected, the students got started shading in their circles. Once they were done, I asked them to decide if the characteristics were "likely," "unlikely," or "sometimes." All but one of the boys in the "ears" group seemed to know what they were doing. To help the one student get back on track, I asked him what each section in the graph was. He said that each section meant a portrait. I asked him what he shaded in for the prekindergarten graph. He said nothing because there were no prekindergarten portraits with ears. I then asked him, if I were to give him a portrait with no ears, would it be likely that the portrait would be from prekindergarten? He said that it would very likely be from prekindergarten. They all remembered what the stipulations were for each of the categories.

Interestingly, one student used the numbers given instead of "eyeballing" the graphs for more than 1/4, less that 1/4, and more than 1/2. When he got the answer mathematically, I asked him to prove it by using the graph. This student was very successful in using the graph also, but I think that he was more comfortable deciding on the "likely," "unlikely," and "sometimes" using the numbers. For example, when the findings were 13 "ears" and 66 "no ears," he decided that "ears" was "unlikely" by adding four 13s and getting 52. He said that because 52 is less than 66, 13 is less than 1/4 of 66.

Reflection: The other boys in the group used the graphs more than this student, which was strange because in the previous model construction, almost none of the students "eyeballed" the graph, but used the numbers instead. I think that the other boys felt that just using the graph was more efficient as well as being accurate. Both ways ultimately seemed very effective for all of the kids.

As the girls determined the symbols for their model, some interesting discussions arose about sections of the circle graph that were very close to either 1/4 or 1/2. For example, for first grade, there were 10 portraits (of 44) with "circle" noses. I asked the students how much 1/4 of 44 was. One student responded that because 11 is 1/4 of 44, 10 out of 44 is less than 1/4.

In the second-grade results, discussions arose when we were trying to see if 8 portraits with "sideways" noses were less than 1/4 or more than 1/4 of 29. One student solved the problem by drawing four circles and placing a slash in each circle until she got a total of 29 slashes. She counted up 7 slashes in two circles and 8 slashes in two circles. She then commented that 7.5 would be 1/4 of 29, so 8 would be more than 1/4 of 29. For the fourth-grade portraits, we wanted to see if 19 was more than or less than half of 35. One student figured that 16 added to 19 was 35, so 19 had to be more than half because 16 is smaller than 19. Another student came up with her answer by dividing 35 in half and getting 17 and a half. She knew then that 19 was more than half of 35.

Testing the Models

The students used their initial model along with their newly constructed one (see Figure 8.8) to determine the grade level of the artist for a series of mystery portraits. We started with mystery portrait #18, which had "circle" eyes, fewer than five fingers, hair, an "other" nose, and ears. Table 8.8 summarizes the grades that were "likely" to use these features.

The students decided that first grade (the correct grade level) would be the best choice because first grade appeared in four of the five categories. The boys who did the "ears" study were very excited because they realized that they had finally found a way to find a difference between kindergarten and first grade.

Mystery portrait #12 had "circle" eyes, hair, fewer than five fingers, a "circle" nose, and ears. Table 8.9 shows the summary of our findings for this portrait.

The students decided that kindergarten or first grade would be the best guesses for the portrait because each of those grades appeared in three categories. The portrait ended up being a kindergarten portrait. Once again though, we discussed how our model could be improved so that we would not have two possibilities. The students felt that they could continue to study more body parts to try to come up with additional ways to tell the difference between kindergarten and first grade.

Mystery portrait #13 had "football" eyes, hair, five fingers, a "side view" nose, and ears. On the basis of Table 8.10, the students decided that the fourth or fifth grades would be the best guesses. The portrait was from the fourth grade.

Reflections: At the conclusion of our study, I asked the students if they found any use in revising our model. The boys were still very proud that their "ears" study found a big difference between the kindergarten and first-grade models. They also stated that it made our results and guesses more accurate, even though those guesses weren't perfect. They all still felt that thinking of more body parts and collecting data on those would make their models even better.

FURTHER DIRECTIONS

If I were to try this project again, there are a number of revisions or alterations that I might try. First, before the students ever see a portrait, I might have them discuss how they would go about making a rule to determine the grade level of an artist drawing a self-portrait. After they discuss it, then I'd have them actually do it. In this way, they would be able to compare their rule to the data that they collect later in the study.

Figure 8.8. Examples of constructed data model.

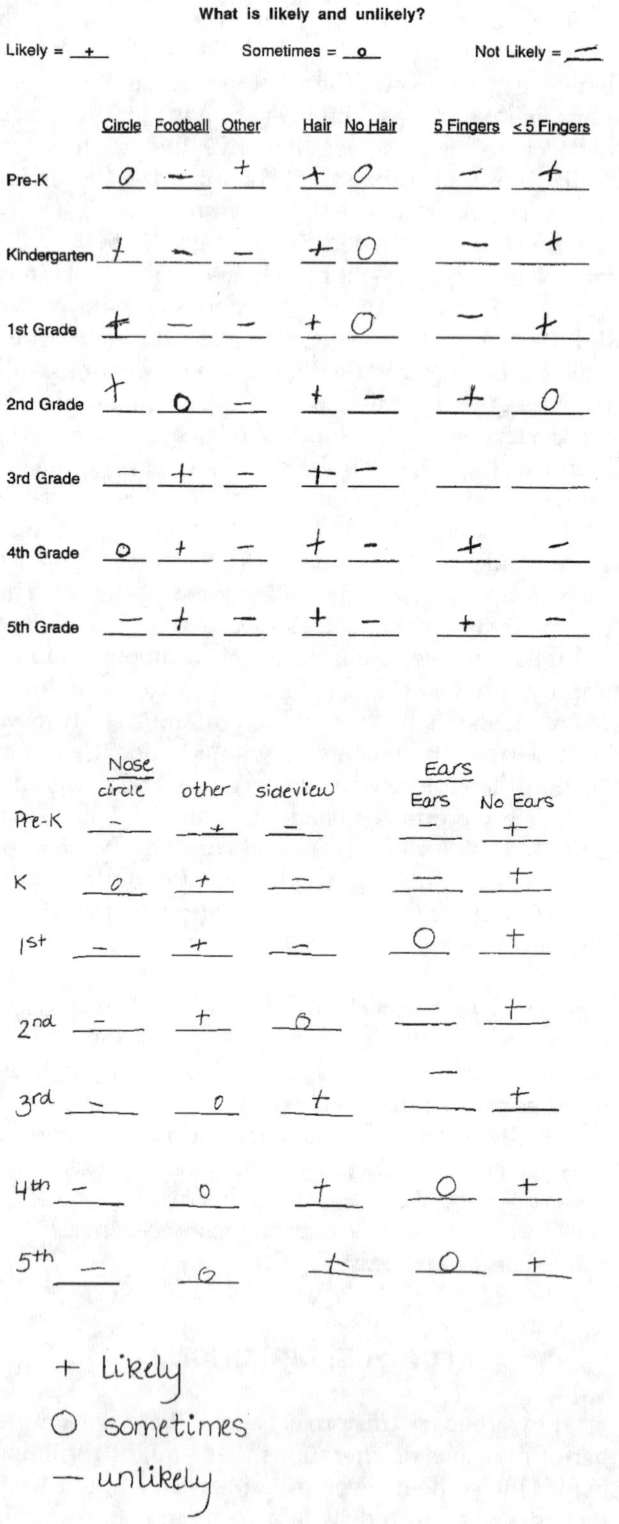

What is likely and unlikely?

Likely = _+_   Sometimes = _o_   Not Likely = _⌐_

	Circle	Football	Other	Hair	No Hair	5 Fingers	< 5 Fingers
Pre-K	O	—	+	+	O	—	+
Kindergarten	+	—	—	+	O	—	+
1st Grade	+	—	—	+	O	—	+
2nd Grade	+	O	—	+	—	+	O
3rd Grade	—	+	—	+	—		
4th Grade	O	+	—	+	—	+	—
5th Grade	—	+	—	+	—	+	—

	Nose			Ears	
	circle	other	sideview	Ears	No Ears
Pre-K	—	+	—	—	+
K	O	+	—	—	+
1st	—	+	—	O	+
2nd	—	+	O	—	+
3rd	—	O	+	—	+
4th	—	O	+	O	+
5th	—	O	+	O	+

+ likely
O sometimes
— unlikely

Table 8.8. Grades at which Mystery Portrait 18's features were considered "likely"

Eyes	Hair	Fingers	Nose	Ears
K	2nd	Pre-K	Pre-K	1st
1st	3rd	K	K	4th
	4th	1st	1st	5th
	5th			2nd

Table 8.9. Grades at which Mystery Portrait 12's features were considered "likely"

Eyes	Hair	Fingers	Nose	Ears
K	2nd	Pre-K	K	1st
1st	3rd	K	1st	4th
	4th	1st		5th

Table 8.10. Grades at which Mystery Portrait 13's features were considered "likely"

Eyes	Hair	Fingers	Nose	Ears
3rd	2nd	4th	3rd	1st
4th	3rd	5th	4th	4th
5th	4th		5th	5th
	5th			

Second, I would start the data collection with only 12 portraits at each grade level. This may ease the students into data abstraction, data collection, and so on much more gradually. Also, with smaller numbers to work with, the fraction issue could be dealt with within the study, instead of having to do a separate mini-lesson with made-up numbers. Next time, I might break the students into small groups, and have them each focus on the part they had selected. I did not do this at first, because I thought that it was important for us to have whole-group discussions, especially when we were dealing with data abstraction. I do think that after going through the entire data collection process once, students would be able to break into groups and conduct their own studies.

It would be worth allowing the students to revise their parameters for deciding if a trait is likely, unlikely, or sometimes. Maybe I'd allow students to come up with four categories. Then they can decide whether changing the parameters of likeliness will make their model become more accurate.

Finally, another extension would be to allow the students to conduct a cross-classification, to see if there were any connections or trends between two or three body parts and categories. For example, students might construct a cross-classification listing eye shapes across the top ("football," "circle," "other") and nose types down the side ("other," "side view," "circle"). By filling in the cells with their data, they will be able to see if, for example, circle-shaped eyes and circle-shaped noses tend to be drawn by the same individuals.

Chapter 9

Classification Models Across the Grades

SALLY HANNER, ERIC JAMES, AND MARK ROHLFING

Country View Elementary School, First/Second,
Fourth, and Fifth Grades
Verona, Wisconsin

The purpose of this chapter is to describe the learning experiences that occurred in three elementary school classrooms as students designed data classification models. The classrooms included a primary multiage room with first- and second-graders (ages 6–8), a fourth-grade class (ages 9–10) and a fifth-grade class (ages 10–11). Classrooms had approximately 20 students each, and instruction occurred over one week in the multiage classroom and over approximately a month in the two older grades.

The challenge for the students was to take a collection of drawings made by students from the school, kindergartners through fifth-graders, and to sort the drawings into groups corresponding to the students' best conclusions about the grade level of the artists. Basically, this task was a condensed adaptation of the one developed by Erin DiPerna and described in chapter 8. Here, we describe how this task, boiled down to its essence, provided an opportunity to compare students' thinking about data modeling at three different grade levels. Such comparisons can provide an important supplement to fine-grained accounts of change within-grade (like the one in chapter 8). Together, within-grade and cross-grade accounts can provide a compelling picture of the development of student thinking.

In the version of the portrait modeling task that we used, there were 12 drawings in a set, and the grade level of each drawing was not labeled. However, each drawing was labeled with a fictitious name so students could easily refer to specific drawings in their discussions. As we will explain later, the students were then asked to identify some common traits that drawings within their grade-level groupings shared, so that they could develop clear descriptive language to talk about those important traits, and more significantly, could come up with a model that would be useful for concluding that a specific drawing was done by a student at a certain grade level.

The drawings had lots of the natural charm typical of the work of young artists. There were two types of drawings. We call one of the sets the "near/far" drawings. To obtain these, the following instructions were given to students ranging from kindergarten to fifth grade: "Draw two houses in your picture, showing in some way that one house is near and the other house is far." We call the other set the "self-portraits." To obtain these, children were asked to "draw a full-body picture of yourself." The pictures were coded so that teachers would know the grade level of the artist, but the students working with the pictures would not know. The drawings were photocopied as black line drawings on

Investigating Real Data in the Classroom: Expanding Children's Understanding of Math and Science. Copyright © 2002 by Teachers College, Columbia University. All rights reserved. ISBN 0-8077-4141-8 (pbk.). Prior to photocopying items for classroom use, please contact the Copyright Clearance Center, Customer Service, 222 Rosewood Dr., Danvers, MA 01923, USA, tel. (508) 750-8400.

8½" by 11" white paper. Not all the pictures were used in every class, and they were not used in the same order in every class.

In all versions of the task, lessons progressed from being introduced initially as a classification task (e.g., "Sort these drawings according to the grade level of the artist who you think did the drawing") to a model-eliciting task (e.g., "Given the groups that you have formed, come up with a model that captures some shared characteristics of the group"). The models were assessed by giving the students additional drawings that had not been part of the original collection. Students were then asked to "use the model to determine which group this new picture belongs to, because it was drawn by an artist of the same grade level." Several test-and-revision cycles of models were undertaken as students tried to fine-tune their models to account for the available data. In the older grades, students often traded one anothers' models and attempted to apply the models generated by other students to classify new sets of pictures. This process allowed them to evaluate and provide feedback to one another about the utility and accuracy of the models and also served as a format for publicly considering the attributes of various kinds of models.

MATHEMATICS OF THE TASK

Students often had clear intuitions about the categories that drawings should fall into. For example, kindergarten drawings "look different" from third-grade drawings. But in this task, children were asked to generate a model that specified and explained their intuitions. In other words, they had to be clear about precisely how one category of drawings differed from another. Sometimes it was helpful to invoke an external audience, such as a "robot" or another person who was not familiar with the drawings, so that the model came to be regarded as a way of communicating with someone. The model had to be expressed precisely, so that distinctions such as "more detail" were acknowledged as too vague. This need for clarity pushed students to articulate precisely how they were thinking, including how they made decisions about which attributes were important to consider and how they could describe each attribute.

Often in the elementary grades, students are asked to classify objects that have defining features, such as square, red blocks versus round, blue blocks. So given any red, square block, it is easy to decide that it belongs with other red, square blocks. However, in the classification problem that we used for this investigation, a drawing could have attributes in common with more than one classification group. For example, both third-

grade and first-grade portraits could have "round" eyes. This meant that students not only had to identify attributes and decide how to describe them, but also had to decide how to combine and perhaps even weigh these attributes in order to make a correct classification.

Other mathematical ideas afforded by this model-eliciting task include the following:

• The notion of data structure (e.g., models with levels of the same attribute represented in every category or grade level have a table structure).
• The notion of fit of model to data (i.e., how accurate is the classification made by the model?).
• Generalization of the model to a new set of data (i.e., is the model too tuned to the specifics of the data set used in its creation?).

BENCHMARKS OF STUDENT THINKING

Here are some of the benchmarks we observed in our work that describe the major transitions in student thinking:

1. *Students need to recognize that creating a model is not the same thing as making categories "with your eyes."* Students often assumed that whatever they did to make categories would be evident to everyone.

For example, the first/second-graders were very confident that their classifications were correct—to the point where they often refused to use their models at all. In fact, when Eric asked one group to justify their classifications, they did not use their copy of the "group model." Eventually, he discovered that one child was standing on it. Similar issues were observed in the fourth- and fifth-grade classrooms. (These students, however, did not stand on the models.) In these classrooms, it was helpful to bring in an outside observer to make the need for clarity more evident. A "robot" who evaluated drawings or a visiting teacher who discussed the models with the children played important roles in helping students understand the need to ensure that classification was guided by the model, not by intuition.

2. *Students have to decide what is worthy of attention.* Deciding on attributes to attend to was very difficult for students, not only because they had to pick out some things and ignore others (an important step in abstraction), but also because they had to be able to describe the attribute that they had selected. We noticed many problems with describing attributes. Some of these included the following:

• Imprecise descriptors (e.g., "big hands," "simple," or " amount of detail"), which relied on a context for interpretation and were very difficult to make sense of for any particular drawing considered in isolation.

- Too many categories, so that there were almost as many categories for an attribute as there were drawings (e.g., football-shaped eyes with one eyelash, football-shaped eyes with two eyelashes, etc.).
- Descriptors that could not possibly be evaluated by looking at the pictures (e.g., "First-graders take less time than older kids" and "Plain, scribbled shirts, but that depends on the artist").
- Unrelated descriptors for each age group, so that the descriptors formulated for the first grade were not carried over to third, fifth, and so on. The first/second-grade models in particular showed this characteristic.

3. *Students evolve a language of description, which becomes more precise over model revisions.* For some children, this language came to be multirepresentational (i.e., some groups used drawings as well as words to exemplify an attribute). Most students came to realize (although not all agreed) that models with more words were not necessarily better.

4. *Students develop ideas about good ways to structure the data.* Initial models were often lists or paragraphs. These models were cumbersome to use, even when the descriptors were precise and unambiguous. Later models often included the important idea that the same attribute could be represented at more than one grade level, resulting in a table structure that enabled rapid classification.

5. *Students often ignore the need to combine information.* Failing to combine information left students with drawings that could fit into more than one category (grade level). To address this problem, the older students began to develop rules about classifying a drawing (e.g., classifying by the highest number of matches, meaning that the grade level that matched the greatest number of attributes was the correct one). Some students, however, were observed attending to certain of the dimensions on a model while ignoring others.

6. *Students learn to weigh attributes.* At the most sophisticated level, some children began to realize that some attributes were more important for model-fitting than others. In some cases, students tried to weigh these more important attributes more heavily in their "matching rules." Some children, however, explicitly said that this couldn't be done or was an unfair move.

7. *Students' ideas about model-fitting change.* At first, students thought that the model would fit the data perfectly. This was rarely the case. Occasionally they made

the model so particular that it fit the initial set of drawings without error. When they did this, however, they soon realized that they had "overfit" the model. When they were given new drawings at the same grade levels, these could not be classified with the overspecified models. For example, one fifth-grade student's model included the attributes: "Two have patterns on their shirts" and "One has a dress." Some symptoms of overfitting included students replicating the drawings in their "model" or making values of attributes that included "or."

Having described the major challenges and transitions in students' thinking across all three classrooms, we now turn to finer-grained descriptions of how these played out within each grade. Where it seems important, we emphasize comparisons across the age groups.

MULTIAGE FIRST/SECOND GRADE

Eric James, the teacher, began this one-week unit by reminding his students that 2 weeks before, they had drawn self-portraits without identifying themselves as the artists by name or by indicating their grade level. He explained that students at all grade levels in Country View Elementary School had also made similar portraits, so that there was now a large collection of self-portraits from children at all grades in the school. Then students were told that they would be given a small group of those portraits to decide which pictures were made by students at various grades. Figure 9.1, which includes a sample portrait made by a kindergartner and a fifth-grader, provides a sense of the range of the draw-

Figure 9.1. Examples of student self-portraits used in classification project.

ings. Eric explained that that the drawings made by students in Grades 2 and 4 had been left out of the set. Students then figured out that this meant there would be portraits made by kindergartners, first-graders, third-graders, and fifth-graders.

Classifying and Describing Portraits

Children were assigned to small groups to sort the pictures. The choice of small-group format was to provide a reason for children to articulate their thinking by communicating aloud to other members of the group. Each group of first/second-graders was accompanied by a fifth-grader who recorded their work and repeatedly asked the younger children for justifications of their placements (e.g., "What makes you think these are third-grade drawings?") However, the fifth-graders and adult observers noted that for every descriptor of an attribute that the children produced, they also produced an equal number of comments such as "It just looks like it was made by a third-grader."

Observers also noted that if a child commented on hair for one drawing, he or she did not necessarily look at hair on the next drawing. Instead, children jumped around from one attribute to another as they shifted their attention from picture to picture. This approach to the task suggested that they were regarding the portraits primarily as instances rather than as collections of attributes. Consistent with this idea, children picked up each portrait to inspect it individually and did not necessarily seem to be comparing new portraits to ones they had already classified. Previously placed pictures did not seem to help them figure out how to place new ones.

In general, children could easily come up with groupings that they confidently claimed were the kindergarten pictures, the first-grade pictures, and so forth. Moreover, they could fairly easily come up with observations about the portraits. However, their initial observations were limited to very general descriptors not useful for discriminating one picture from another (e.g., "good shirts," "weird hair," "funny bodies").

One group's initial list of descriptors (prepared with assistance from their fifth-grade recorder), shown in Table 9.1a, was merely a list of attributes, with minimal organization of any kind. The order of items suggests that they were simply mentioning observations about pictures as they appeared in the shuffled order provided by the teachers. Consequently, their list is an unordered set of descriptors with no regard for clustering them by the presumed grade level of the artists. A second group produced a somewhat more sophisticated level of organization, but note that their list, shown in Table 9.1b, failed to preserve order of grade or to carry attributes across the grade levels.

Table 9.1. Two samples of initial descriptor lists.

List A

IT DOESN'T HAVE WHAT A REAL PERSON WOULD HAVE

THEIR VERY CREATIVE PICTURES.

STICK PERSON.

NO BODY.

A POTATO BODY.

FOUR FEET.

REAL MODAL.

IT HAS A REAL BODY.

THREE FINGERS

LOOKS LIKE A CARROT

List B

KG	HEAD AND LEGS, NO FEET, WEIRD HAIR, LEGS TO HEAD, WEIRD
1	CLOTHS, NO HANDS
5	DRAWING SKILLS, CLOTHS, HANDS, PANTS, FEET
2	CLOTHS, LOOKS BETTER, BETTER CLOTHS, HANDS, EVERY THING A BODY SHOULD HAVE

Note. List A shows no apparent organization, and List B, although more "organized," does not show investigation of attributes across grade levels.

Evaluation of Feature Lists

After these first lists were completed, Eric explained that the next step would be to "give and get some feedback about which of the ideas seem really clear." To that end, he orchestrated a whole-class discussion in which the class concentrated on each of the descriptor lists in turn. This discussion seemed critical for turning the children's attention, at least momentarily, from whether they were "right" about grade authorship of the pictures to whether their features were clear and explicit. For example, two children included "potato body" as a descriptor for the kindergarten pictures. Eric asked them what "potato body" meant, and one of the children elaborated, "It means there's no feet and no body, and his arms are in his head." Eric repeatedly emphasized the need to be sure that terms such as "potato body" were being interpreted similarly by everyone.

Now the students questioned for the first time whether a proposed feature actually described the pictures assigned to it. For example, some students demanded to know whether they could really say that the kindergarten pictures had "no feet." The children noted that, to decide, they would have to determine explicitly what counted as feet. One child proposed that the authors of the list might have really meant "no shoes." To this suggestion, Eric responded, "Would that make their thinking clearer?" Another example of a clarifying question asked at this point is "Do we all know what 'no neck' means?"

This discussion also inspired some children to mention multiple features of particular portraits. For example, one child remarked about the picture labeled "Sam": "It has no fingers. It has no feet. You can barely see the mouth. And his hair looks like a hat." Another child's comments suggest that some students were beginning to compare portraits within a grade level on a common feature: "On all three of the kindergartners it goes, body, body, body. No body, then that tiny girl. So they go, like, kind of in a row." Yet even with these signs of progress, holistic judgments seemed more compelling to many of the children, who found descriptors less convincing than claims such as "I think this one looks like a kindergartner or a first-grader," or "I know what grades they were in, all."

On the basis of this discussion, Eric suggested that the children might want to revise their groupings, with an eye to more attributes and greater clarity. But after children had placed all the drawings into groups, it was difficult to move on to a next step because the students were reluctant to consider revising their categories.

Moreover, the descriptor lists they had generated were not regarded as a method for checking their thinking or as a guide for regrouping. As they looked at their categories, they did start to notice that there were portraits within each group that matched some of the descriptors for that group, but not all. For example, they might look at the kindergarten drawings and notice that although "no feet" fit three of the drawings, one drawing did have feet but was still considered a kindergarten drawing. The teacher pointed out, "We have to be careful if we're saying something for the whole bunch." Together, the group struggled with questions such as "Do we make only those statements that are true for every member of the group?" "Is it possible that portraits do not need to match all the descriptors to be included in a category?" "For example, could we decide that a picture fits as a member of the kindergarten group because it matches four of the six descriptors?"

To encourage consideration of these ideas, Eric offered the analogy of a good lunch. He explained, "I think a good lunch is one where, out of the four things you get, three of those four are choices you like." To push this idea further, he introduced the term *most*, rephrasing some of the children's descriptors into statements such as "Most of third-grade drawings have teeth." He also encouraged grouping the descriptors into vertical columns and looking for an arrangement that would permit tracing an attribute horizontally across the columns, and thus comparing portraits on that attribute across grades. As Figure 9.2 shows, this suggestion was only moderately successful, because the

Figure 9.2. Typical descriptor list used in classifying self-portraits.

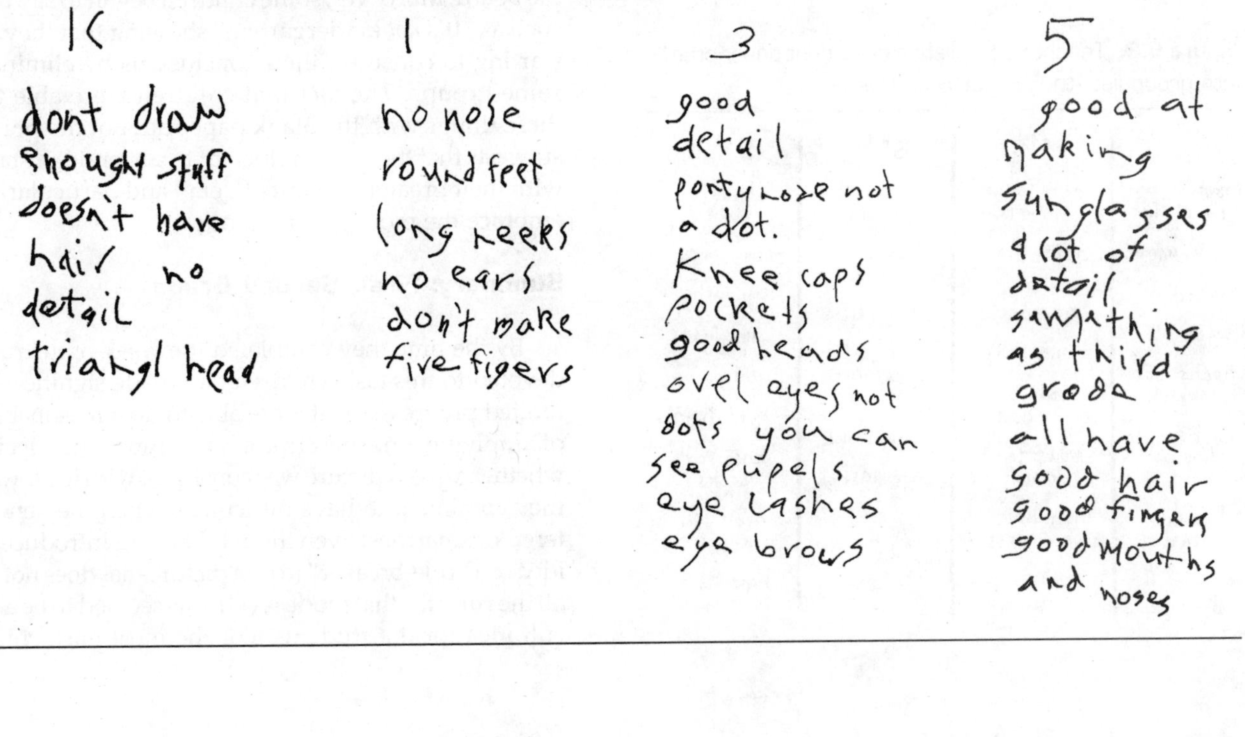

K	1	3	5
dont draw enough stuff doesn't have hair no detail triangl head	no nose round feet long necks no ears don't make five figers	good detail pontynose not a dot. Knee caps pockets good heads ovel eyes not dots you can see pupels eye lashes eya brows	good at making sunglasses a lot of detail samething as third grade all have good hair good fingers good mouths and noses

children's descriptor lists contained gaps, where they failed to comment on a variable at all grade levels, and redundancies, where the observation was the same across all grade levels and, hence, uninformative.

In fact, the idea that a picture might not fit all the descriptors in its category is a difficult one. As adults, we would be quite content with a model that does not get all the cases right. To us, it's less important that every picture be correctly identified and more important that our model does a good job of capturing what first-grade pictures are like *in general*. The children did not appear to assimilate this idea; instead, they were trying to identify a model that would assign every first-grade portrait to the first-grade column. Adults would be satisfied with a model if a portrait by a first-grader who drew with the sophistication of a third-grader ended up in the third-grade group. The children were more literal. For this reason, it may not have been a good idea to put so much emphasis on assigning the pictures and checking to see whether or not the placements were right.

Development of a Group List

On the 3rd day of instruction, Eric compiled children's lists into a "Super Smart" list, represented in Figure 9.3. When the group list was compiled, Eric suggested that children "might want to change your piles a little bit now that the whole class is thinking together." One child was heard remarking that one of the pictures designated as kindergarten in her group might actually be a third-grade picture. However, when asked to justify the proposed change, she retreated to, "Because it looks like third." An adult tried to turn her attention to the descriptors written on the board, but she appeared

satisfied with her "looks like" criterion. As this incident exemplifies, students continued to compare portraits to other individual cases, not to the Super Smart list.

Eric asked the children to review the Super Smart list to evaluate whether it was valid and useful. He also asked if any of the attributes might be especially powerful. He gave the children highlighter pens with individual copies of the list and asked them to use the list to check their proposed groups of portraits. Every time they used an attribute to assign a portrait to a category, students were to highlight that attribute with the pen. Children were asked whether there might be any variable powerful enough so that it might be sufficient alone to serve as a valid basis for a grouping.

Trying to Effect a Shift from List to Model

To help children overcome their dependence on the "way things look," Eric announced on the 4th day that he had some brand-new drawings. When he showed them to the class, they turned out to be blank, colored pieces of paper. He held up one (colored pink) and said, "See this picture of Rosie? I'm going to tell you some things about Rosie. See if you can figure out which group she's in. Let's pretend I said to you, 'Rosie has pants with pockets.' Raise your hand and tell me where Rosie would go." As he continued along this track (with "Peachie" and then "Greenie"), Eric also encouraged students to "keep their eyes open" and report "can't tell" if he used a clue that was not sufficient for deciding which grade "Rosie" belonged in. Eventually, the class began to call out, "Tell me more! Tell me more!" when Eric mentioned a descriptor that appeared under more than one of the grades in the Super Smart list on the board. Moreover, some children began to say things such as "It's *not* kindergarten," showing that they were starting to constrain their conclusions by eliminating some groups. The fact that children were able to do these things with the blank paper but not the portraits suggests that they were reluctant to surrender instances, with their greater amount of detail and particularity, to embrace the more general model.

Summary: First/Second Grade

By the time they completed the week of instruction devoted to this task, children had made significant but limited progress. Most were able to do a reasonable job of applying one descriptor at a time and deciding whether a given picture was consistent with it. However, they continued to have difficulties when they encountered mismatches. Even though Eric had introduced the idea of a "rule-breaker" (e.g., a picture that does not obey all the rules for that grade level), this seemed to be a difficult idea for the students. For the most part, children

Figure 9.3. Teacher compilation of student descriptor lists into group list—the "Super Smart list."

K	1st.	3rd.	5th.
mostly no clothes	details on shirts	pants with pockets	skinny bodies
stick arms	most have hair	fingers on hands	cool shoes
naked	no ears	oval eyes	eye lashes
eyes	long hair		sunglasses
looks like skeleton	good-shaped heads	decorated details	detail
no hair or dinosaur hair	bows or decorations	eye brows	good hair
triangle head	most have shoe laces	eye lashes	lines on socks
			heels on shoes
			hands with 5 fingers

appeared to be using the attributes as post hoc descriptions, and not really as rules. Rather than using attributes to categorize the pictures, children seemed to be using them to describe pictures in categories they had already assigned. Although a few children made progress in understanding the category system, these advances seemed very fragile and did not appear to "take hold" for the long term. For most of these young students, progress over the course of instruction consisted of changes in the quality of the descriptors themselves—from global, evaluative comments to feature-based descriptors that became more clearly stated, more differentiated, and more accurate as the activity progressed.

Comment: Laying the Groundwork

At the close of this chapter, we suggest possible modifications to this task, some proposed to make the task more challenging for older students and some proposed to make the task easier for young children to enter. However, many of the first/second-grade students found this task very challenging, and as argued above, most did not seem to be regarding their models as models. Hence, we conclude this first section of the chapter with some brief conjectures about fruitful ways of laying the groundwork in early grades for this kind of data-classification task later in elementary school:

1. *Avoid rushing too quickly past description to modeling.* It may be that we emphasized too early the idea of determining the grade level of the artists of the portraits. Instead, we might have been better served by encouraging piggybacking of comments about the pictures in order to elicit comments about what children notice about them. For example, if one child starts talking about shoelaces, another often will piggyback onto that idea and make a comment about some other aspect of shoes. We may have shortchanged that aspect of the activity by beginning the grouping too early. If children had had a more sustained discussion about what they saw in these pictures, possible groupings might have emerged (e.g., "I see a group who don't have feet," or "All of these are missing a head").

We might also present all the pictures in the group, ask children to sort them by one attribute (e.g., no fingers, some fingers, five fingers), then scramble the pictures, and ask children to re-sort by another attribute (e.g., no clothes, some clothes, detailed clothes). This kind of classifying and reclassifying activity builds nicely on familiar sorting activities frequently used in primary grades. It would probably serve to help turn children's attention toward the attributes and levels and away from correctness of grade-level placement.

Another way to do this might be to give the children a set of pictures already divided into grade groupings.

The class together could then be challenged to generate lots of observations about pictures in each group "to show that you really know what they're like." At that point, a new set of pictures could be introduced. Each new portrait could be reviewed, and children could decide whether to add each case to one of the existing sets by "tying it in" with already observed characteristics. To bring home this idea, children might be awarded one piece of tape for each attribute mentioned (e.g., "I think it belongs in the kindergarten group because it has no neck, no feet, and no clothes" would win three pieces of tape). As children use the tape to affix the new drawing, the teacher could then comment, "Great! This one ties in really well to the kindergarten category."

2. *Give children lots of experiences in noticing and using patterns, rules, and systems created by others,* especially in contexts that are familiar and show a need for a system of organization. A library, for example, is a familiar organizational system, and children can consider why it might be useful to have fiction separated from nonfiction, and books organized alphabetically, numerically, or both, within major sections. Asking questions such as "What does such an organization accomplish for a visitor?" or "Do we have intuitions about the 'right' number of categories within a familiar library, like the Country View Library?" can generate interesting discussion in the classroom. Some children might believe that there ought to be almost as many categories as books. A similar example might be to encourage children to think about the structure underlying the spatial layout of foods in the cafeteria: "Why are mustard and ketchup near the end of the line?" "Why are all the fruits presented together?"

Consideration of systems developed by others can also serve as the foundation for creating students' own systems and patterns. For example, children can write "rules" to describe the interactions of "Connecting People" and then set up physical models that embody those rules (e.g., "All the little people want to play outside and all the females want to play together"). Although these rules are descriptions and not models per se, practice with using and creating systems of rules that represent situations in the world can be useful experiences to then bring to challenging data-structure tasks like the one we tried in this study.

Note, however, that familiarity can be an obstacle as well as an advantage in these tasks. For example, one limitation of the task described in this study might have been that these young children could hardly help being influenced in their sorting by their personal knowledge of how their own portrait was drawn. In this case, children's perceptions that they already knew a lot about these drawings might have kept them from questioning their own assumptions. A possible route around children's overconfidence about their classifications might be to hand out drawings one at a time, deliberately sequencing them to provide "surprises." For example, a teacher might present a series of several drawings that look as if they were done by young students, and then, once children are sure these are all kindergarten drawings, present a drawing that looks *really* young. The purpose would be to shake up children's expectations and encourage them to question their intuitions about the age of the artists.

3. *Provide some experience with data models that feature nonoverlapping sets.* As noted later in this chapter, even the older students found it challenging that not all attributes fit every picture and that not every category was defined by a unique set of attributes. It could be valuable first to give young students opportunities that explicitly highlight the idea of nonoverlapping sets. For example, Angie Putz's first-grade class developed a graph to show "kinds of mittens." Children first classified their mittens by color and eventually were able to sort out the fact that a category system including "striped," "dotted," "green," and "other" was inappropriate, because the categories were not mutually exclusive. Similarly, Eric observed that children, while sorting his bottle-cap collection, often started with just a few very general categories (sometimes by brand name), which quickly differentiated into more fine-grained categories (e.g., diet and nondiet drinks). Deciding what works as a good category system depends on the use for it. For example, to decide what three or four kinds of soda would be best to order for a school party, students might first collect all the bottle caps from the school soda machine, then come up with a classification system that informed their choices. Given this situation, too many categories would be counterproductive. A different kind of use (and hence, category system) is suggested if students want to decide how many of the sodas should be diet soda and how many should be regular soda.

4. *Consider different forms of notational assistance,* especially for children who do not yet smoothly read. The rules games described earlier for the "Connecting People" can be supported with pictures of a house, a yard, and so on, into which the "people" are physically placed. Venn diagrams have an "overhead cost" (e.g., it is not trivial for children to understand their implications), but they can sometimes be used to clarify relationships among sets.

5. *Avoid overproceduralization.* Even though we are suggesting that it might be a good idea to begin data modeling in a simpler fashion, we wish to emphasize that we are not recommending a recipe approach. Very

often, teachers solve all the interesting issues for kids and present them already resolved to children, without giving children the opportunity to grapple with such questions as "What attributes should we include?" "How many attributes should we consider?" and "How should they be represented?" When teachers take over these decisions, all that's left is a cut-and-dried graphing or sorting activity, in which teachers have done all the intriguing and motivating thinking ahead of time. Our challenge as teachers is to avoid overpreparing tasks as much as it is to avoid overcomplicating them.

FOURTH GRADE

In Sally Hanner's fourth-grade room, we used only the near/far houses task because the previous year, some of her students had done the portraits task with Erin DiPerna. Figure 9.4 provides a sense of the wide range of differences among the drawings done at different grade levels.

Sally introduced the near/far houses project as a cooperative learning activity, with students working together in groups of four. Members of the group were assigned roles: material gatherer, reader, recorder, and reporter. On the first day, Sally presented four tasks that the group needed to complete:

1. Without discussion, predict the grade level of individual drawings.
2. Look closely at the drawings, and talk about why they might be in the same grade level.
3. Place the drawings into four piles by grade level.
4. Write descriptors for each grade level.

First Models

Sally then passed out packets that summarized the instructions. Packets included a data sheet on which students were asked to record their descriptors. The attributes identified on students' first trials are those written above the line in each box; the attributes below the line are revisions that the students added on a second occasion (see Figure 9.5 for typical descriptor sheet). It may be that the format of the sheet emphasized students' natural tendency to fail to carry attributes across the grade levels. Notice, for example, that although ways of representing "near and far" are discussed for each grade, "detail" is mentioned at some grades, but not at others. Notice also that the revisions all concern the way that size is (or is not) used to show which house is near and which is far.

During this phase, it was evident that children considered their first classifications entirely satisfactory. As might be expected, students tended not to be very criti-

Figure 9.4. Drawings done by students at different grade levels to contrast near/far houses.

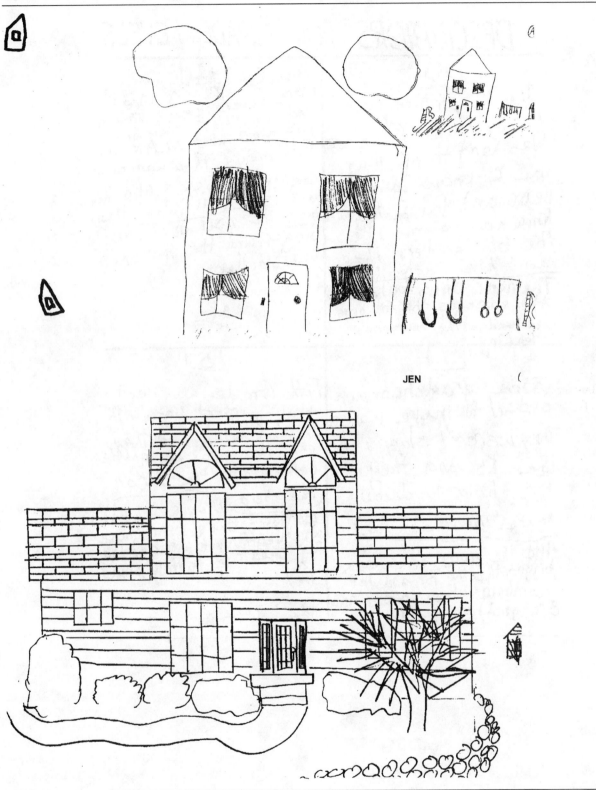

JEN

Figure 9.5. Typical descriptor sheet for the near/far houses task.

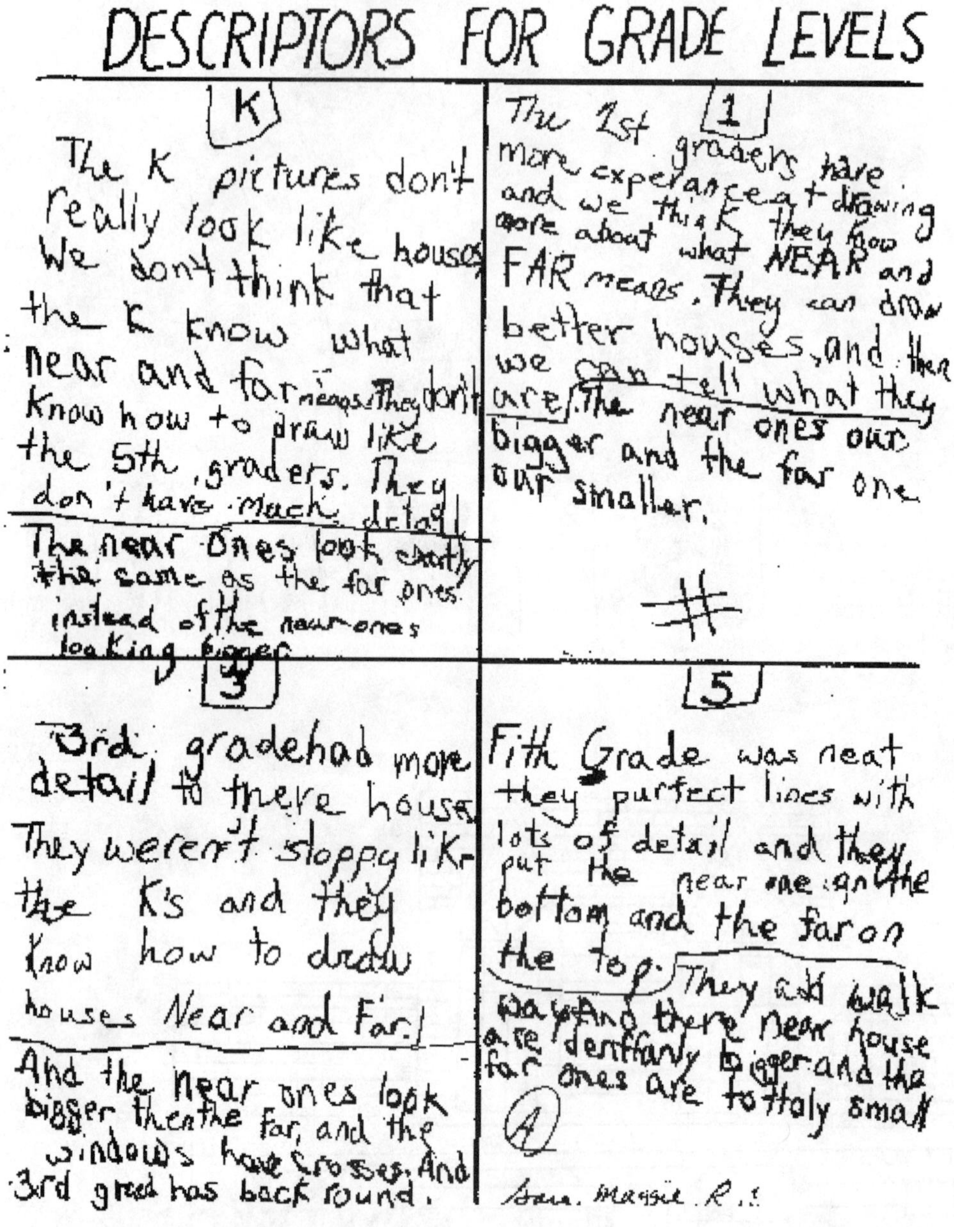

DESCRIPTORS FOR GRADE LEVELS

K

The K pictures don't really look like houses We dont think that the K know what near and far means. They don't know how to draw like the 5th graders. They don't have much detail. The near ones look exactly the same as the far ones instead of the near ones looking bigger.

1

The 1st graders have more experance at drawing and we think they know more about what NEAR and FAR means. They can draw better houses, and then we can tell what they are. The near ones our bigger and the far one our smaller.

\#

3

3rd grade had more detail to there houses. They weren't sloppy like the K's and they know how to draw houses Near and Far! And the near ones look bigger then the far, and the windows have crosses. And 3rd gred has back round.

5

Fith Grade was neat they purfect lines with lots of detail and they put the near one on the bottom and the far on the top. They add walk way and there near house are dentfany bigger and the far ones are tottaly small

Ⓐ

Sam. Massie R.S

cal of their own models. To assist children in the evaluation process, a researcher who had been observing the class served as a "robot" that read each of the model criteria and tried to apply each criterion to individual pictures. Of course, on many occasions, he could not do so (e.g., he had trouble deciding whether or not a particular picture had "detail," and he had no way of deciding whether a picture took a "long time" to draw). This was a big breakthrough for many of the children, who began to understand for the first time that the point was not just to describe a category already created, but to make a rule for placing pictures into categories. The "robot" exercise formed the foundation for revision, which the students otherwise would have resisted.

Instructional challenges during this portion of instruction included dislodging children from their initial gut-level categorization, that is, breaking them loose from what they had already done. They did not necessarily accept the notion of revising. Moreover, coordinating the work of the small groups took considerable planning. At the beginning, students were not listening to one another; instead, they tended to begin their work simply as individuals, each doing his or her own thing. In some of the groups, children argued about who was in control. Sally spent a great deal of time and energy encouraging their taking turns, listening respectfully, sharing the recording work, modeling thinking together, and so on. At one point, Sally called a class meeting and explicitly discussed the need for respect and for learning to accept criticism as an intellectual, not a personal, act. As the small-group work continued, especially after this meeting, children's behavior in these regards improved noticeably. It is important to understand that elementary school children do not necessarily take for granted such ideas as criticism, revision, evaluation, and working together without support, modeling, and practice.

In addition to struggling with changes in the classroom norms, there were conceptual challenges as well. Many of the children had real difficulties with the idea of combining attributes. For example, if they identified an attribute for pictures at one grade level, they would frequently be discouraged if they found that that the same attribute applied to pictures at another grade level. Similarly, they were discouraged if they found a picture that they had classified within a particular grade, that did not share all the attributes of that grade. These discoveries led several of the children to start over again many times, making no apparent progress. Moreover, several days into the work, all the children had what we called "box models," that is, models in which there was a separate list of attributes for each grade level—typically uncoordinated across grade levels.

The breakthrough came with a model generated by a student group one researcher was working with.

Somehow he got them to consider dimensions. Sally overheard him encouraging children to consider a continuum from "no detail," to "a little detail," to "some detail, " and, finally, to "a lot of detail." When their model was shown to the group, it was structured like a table, with dimensions across the top and grade levels listed down the side. The students did not spontaneously prefer this model to the others, which were posted around the room. In fact, some of the students wondered what the advantage was of the "columns and rows" in this model. One student explicitly objected that she believed the more "detail" a model had, the better. (This child apparently meant "words" because her group's model was easily the wordiest.) We conjectured that students might have been working on the basis of their writing instruction, in which they are continually advised to "add more information," "develop their ideas," and "write more."

Model Evaluation

At this point, children were so familiar with their models that they were again having difficulties stepping back from them to criticize and evaluate realistically. To address this problem, Sally invited Mark, the fifth-grade teacher, into the classroom to review all of the models, which were posted on butcher paper around the room. It was Mark's analysis that first helped the children think about the advantages of the "table" model.

After considering all the models, Mark suggested, "Speed is important. If you wanted to pay the sorter 25 cents per minute, we want them to be able to sort fast . . . if you start getting all those sentences in there, it becomes more confusing. . . ." At the end of this discussion, students agreed that the table model would be the easiest to apply quickly. Sally built on this idea by adding, "Is there a detail on your model that isn't helpful? Maybe it's true, but it's not that useful? Which are the really helpful details?"

Model Revision

The next round of revision was strongly influenced by these ideas. After this discussion, every group produced a dimensional model. One group, however, produced what was in essence two models, one dimensional and one a refinement of their original box model. Children who originally produced the wordiest model continued in their revision to retain a lot of extraneous detail, in spite of the fact that the data were now organized into a dimensional structure (see Figure 9.6).

During this final revision, students were especially concerned with good ways of combining attributes. Some of the groups began to consider how to represent

Figure 9.6. Students' revised model for near/far houses task. Note that much detail was retained in spite of the dimensional structure.

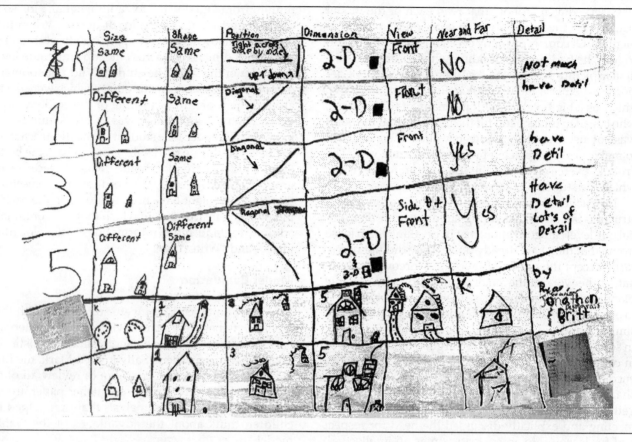

attributes that were seen in only certain pictures in an age group. For example, one group began to use phrases such as "1 out of 3" to describe the fact that only one of the three third-grade pictures contained three-dimensional qualities (see Figure 9.7). Similar conversations were heard in other groups.

Model Testing

A final phase of the task involved bringing in a third set of houses pictures (Set C) for testing the final models. The final models did a pretty good job of classifying the pictures, and for the most part, children were satisfied with their models

Summary: Fourth Grade

During their work on this task, students moved from forming categories on an intuitive basis to refining their language of description for what they found in each grade-level set to, finally, producing dimensional models. After some experience with various external audiences to spur revision, children began to

think about how to communicate most efficiently. At this point, the "graph" structure emerged. Using the table structure encouraged students to make judgments about the most useful and important features to include versus those that were considered not that informative. These considerations included thinking about how to combine categories and, in some cases, explicitly identifying the proportions of cases that fit into a category. In addition to these improvements in the models, children's communication improved notably. Thinking in a group improved, not only within small groups, but also in the whole group. Especially important was students' tendency to listen more carefully to one another as they took part in what proved to be productive conversations.

At the end of the task, students were asked to reflect about what they had learned and how useful it would be. Students recalled that they had originally expected the task to be a cinch but were surprised at the complexity of thinking involved. For example, one child wrote, "It was harder than we thought . . . one fifth-grader looked like a third-grader!" A common theme in the reflections was students' awareness that it is more difficult to interpret models made by other students than models they themselves had developed.

Figure 9.7. Students' model showing the use of descriptive phrases (e.g., 1 out of 3) to describe attributes observed in a given age group.

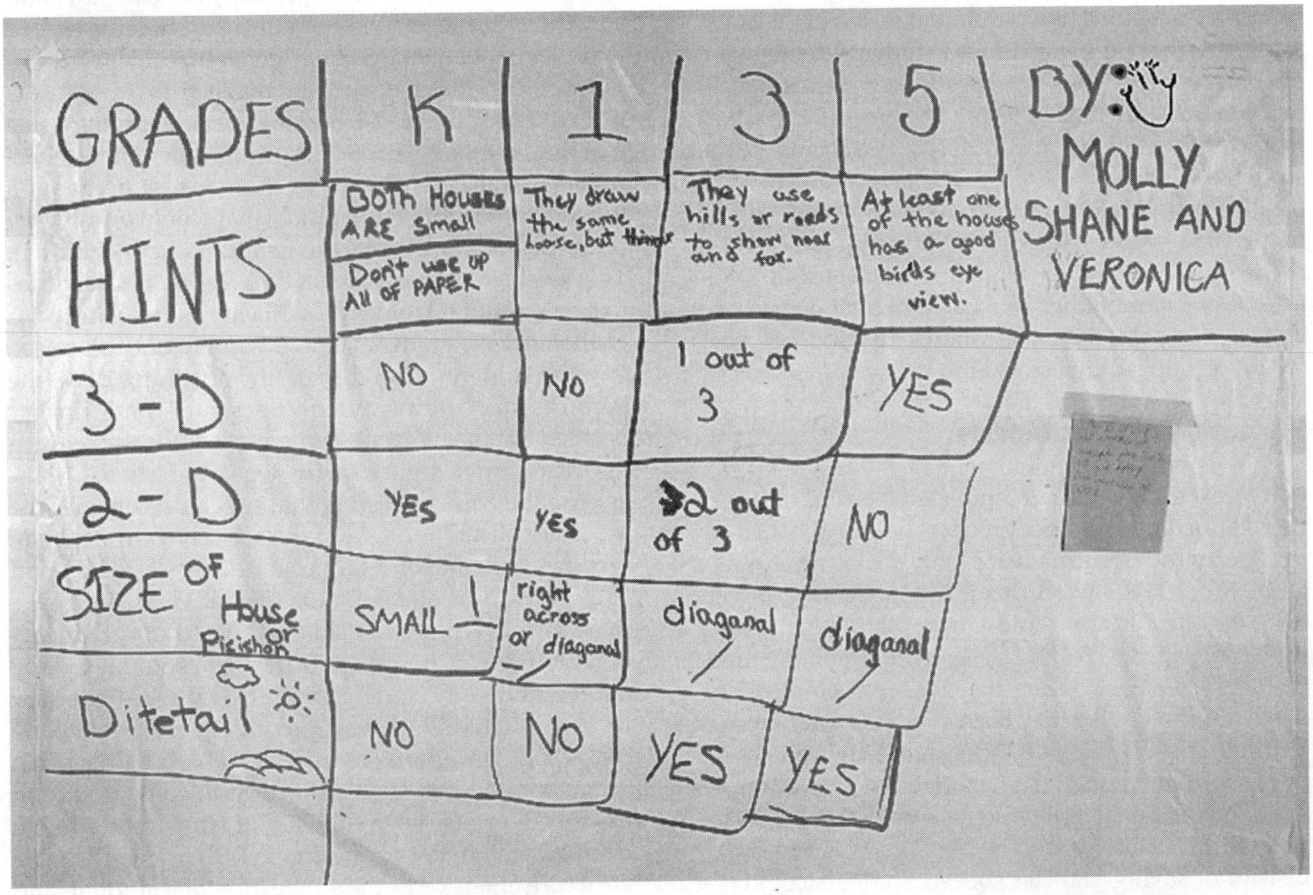

GRADES	K	1	3	5	BY: MOLLY SHANE AND VERONICA
HINTS	BOTH HOUSES ARE Small / Don't use up All of PAPER	They draw the same house, but things	They use hills or roads to show near and far.	At least one of the houses has a good birds eye view.	
3-D	NO	NO	1 out of 3	YES	
2-D	YES	yes	2 out of 3	NO	
SIZE of House or Picishon	SMALL	right across or diagonal	diagonal	diagonal	
Ditetail	NO	NO	YES	YES	

FIFTH GRADE

In the fifth grade, Mark started out by telling his class that they would be designing a model that would predict what grade a student was in by the way the student drew a self-portrait. Mark then proceeded to tell the students what the "end product" of the lesson would look like. He said, "You will get a set of drawings. You should be able to look at the first drawing, then look at your model. Your model should be able to tell you what grade the person is in who drew the picture. Next, you will flip to new drawings and use your model to identify the grade level of the student who drew it, and so on, until you have identified the grade levels of all the artists."

Mark then told his class that the artists came from kindergarten and first, third, and fifth grades. He split the class into groups of three to work on their models, telling the groups to spread out their 12 drawings and look them over to try first to classify them into grade-alike groups simply by using their intuition. He emphasized, however, that they needed to be able to explain why they classified the pictures the way that they did.

Identifying Attributes

Before children began their sorting, Mark introduced the word *attributes*. The class then proceeded to identify the attributes of a chair, including "has four metal legs and a plastic seat," "not living," "it slides on the floor," "has a backrest," and "is blue." Then Mark held up another, slightly different chair and asked if the attributes of the first chair matched those of the second. Students readily seemed to realize that they could fine-tune attributes to be too specific—the chosen attributes could describe only a particular case rather than a class. The discussion then turned to whether the students could develop a model that would apply to all chairs. Children proposed attributes such as "If you look at it from the side the seat forms an L-shape" and "They have legs."

At that point, the students were given a data recording sheet to help them classify the self-portraits. As in the fourth grade, the sheet separated the recording space for each grade onto a different region of the paper, a strategy that perhaps fed into students' tendency to overlook comparisons from grade to grade. Some students started off simply listing the attributes for each grade level (see Figure 9.8a). There was no evidence that students tried to come up with a common set of attributes that would carry across all grades. An exception is Figure 9.8b. Although attributes are not written in the same order for each grade, this sheet shows considerable commonality in what was included. As we will explain below, these attributes served as the basis for this group's dimensional model.

Evaluation of First Models

Once the students had completed the attribute sheet, they handed it to another group, who were challenged to classify the portraits using only the attributes as a guide. The class agreed that if the models were good ones, the other group would end up placing the pictures in the same grades as the group who originally made the attribute sheet. When the class reassembled, students discussed what they liked about the other group's attribute sheet and how they thought that group could improve their model. They suggested, for example, avoiding relational terms such as *sometimes*, *bigger than*, *better than*, *not always*, and *fancier*. They suggested that instead of saying "fancier shoes," students could say "shoes with shoelaces."

These discussions (and Mark's "encouragement") inspired the students to revise their models. The small-print additions to Figure 9.8b show some of the revisions these students made to their model. After revising, students learned the actual grade of the artists who created the self-portraits. They were then asked to check their model and evaluate how well it had performed.

Structure of Models

By the beginning of the 3rd day of instruction, the students seemed to assume that they were done and that the task had been satisfactorily accomplished. However, Mark asked if there might be a better way to organize or display the data so pictures could be placed into the correct grade level more quickly. Students appeared to take that question as a query about the kind of information included in the model, rather than as a question about the form of the model. For example, one student suggested simply copying each picture and then putting the grade level next to each copied picture. Mark agreed that this strategy would certainly guarantee exhaustive and correct classification of each picture, but

he asked students what would happen if a new set of pictures were introduced. This failed to faze one student, who said, "You would just copy those pictures and add them to the list!" Eventually, the students agreed that the model would not be "generalizeable." The important shift that the students made at that point was from thinking of the task literally (i.e., identifying a rule that would guarantee correct classification of *these* pictures) to thinking of it as a general question about a model (i.e., formulating a model that would classify *any* set of pictures drawn by elementary school children). This shift from after-the-fact description of categories to a rule set that would allow them to form categories challenged the students in every grade of this project.

One student noticed that "the attributes of all the pictures are pretty much the same" and further pointed out that they all seemed to include things such as "head, stick figures with legs, and stuff." Mark asked if he was suggesting that we could consider the attribute "head" and, "Maybe we have a first-grade type of head, maybe a kindergarten, first-, third-, and fifth-grade type of head?" On the board, Mark drew a table format with "head" at the top and the grade levels listed down the side in order. The student readily agreed and went on to explain that it was necessary to "put what kind of head" at each grade level, along with "legs, compare [whether] stick, [whether] first grade colored in," and so on. Hence, compared with the fourth grade (where the table structure needed to be prompted by an adult), in the fifth grade, the table structure emerged at the suggestion of a student, and after only 2 days of instruction.

Mark suggested that students select the attributes that they thought were important and carry them across the four grade levels, using a model that "we will call a table graph." Figure 9.9a shows the "table graph" that one group of students made based on their attribute lists. Notice that they switched from a text representation to a drawing representation, possibly to distinguish the differences in "heads," "arms," "legs," and so on, at each grade level. Similar to what occurred in the fourth grade, once the table model emerged, all the students in the class immediately adopted it. From this point on, no more box models were developed.

One group, however, did simply lift their attributes out of the box structure suggested by the recording notation and stick them into a tablelike format, which listed attributes grade by grade but did not always carry each attribute across grades. In a whole-class discussion, the group considered the relative disadvantages of such an approach and compared this strategy to an idealized model provided by the teacher. Another group of students developed a model, shown in Figure 9.9b, in which the columns (headed by attributes) were very salient, but the rows (organized by grade

Figure 9.8. Examples of student data recording sheets. Although students tended to overlook comparisons across grades, one group's data sheet (b) showed considerable commonality across grades.

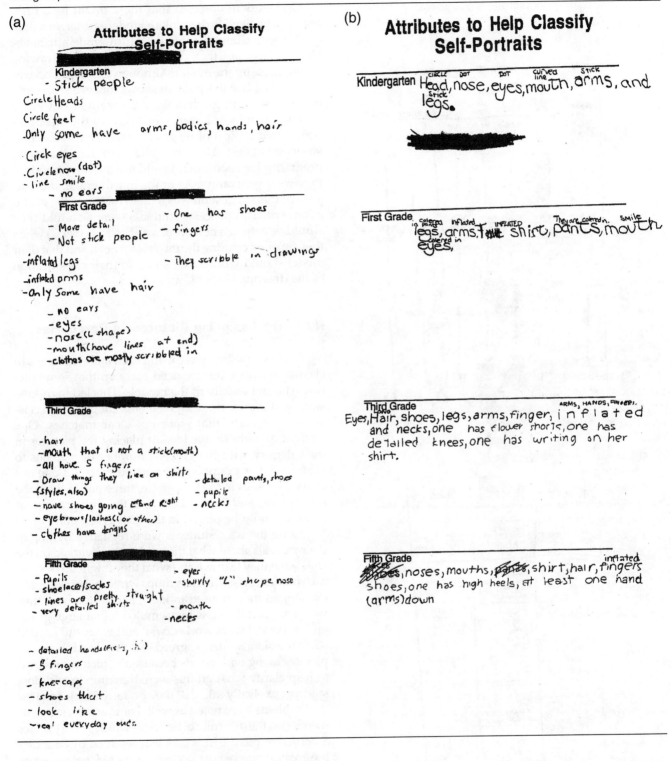

(a)

Attributes to Help Classify Self-Portraits

Kindergarten
- Stick people

Circle Heads
Circle feet
Only some have arms, bodies, hands, hair

Circle eyes
Circle nose (dot)
- line smile
    - no ears

First Grade
- More detail
- Not stick people
- One has shoes
- fingers

-inflated legs
-inflated arms
-only some have hair
- They scribble in drawings

    - no ears
    - eyes
    - nose (L shape)
    - mouth (have lines at end)
    - clothes are mostly scribbled in

Third Grade
-hair
-mouth that is not a stick(mouth)
-all have 5 fingers
- Draw things they like on shirts
  (styles, also)
- have shoes going left and right
- eyebrows/lashes (i or other)
- clothes have designs
- detailed pants, shoes
- pupils
- necks

Fifth Grade
- Pupils
- shoelace/socks
- lines are pretty straight
- very detailed shirts
- eyes
- swirly "L" shape nose
- mouth
- necks

- detailed hands (fists, etc.)
- 5 fingers
- kneecaps
- shoes that
- look like
- real everyday ones

(b)

Attributes to Help Classify Self-Portraits

Kindergarten Head, nose, eyes, mouth, arms, and legs.

First Grade legs, arms, shirt, pants, mouth eyes,

Third Grade Eyes, Hair, shoes, legs, arms, finger, inflated and necks, one has flower shorts, one has detailed knees, one has writing on her shirt.

Fifth Grade noses, mouths, shirt, hair, fingers shoes, one has high heels, at least one hand (arms) down

Figure 9.9. Example of students' "table graphs" (based on their attribute lists). Note how in (b) the unevenness of rows complicates comparison across grade levels.

(a)

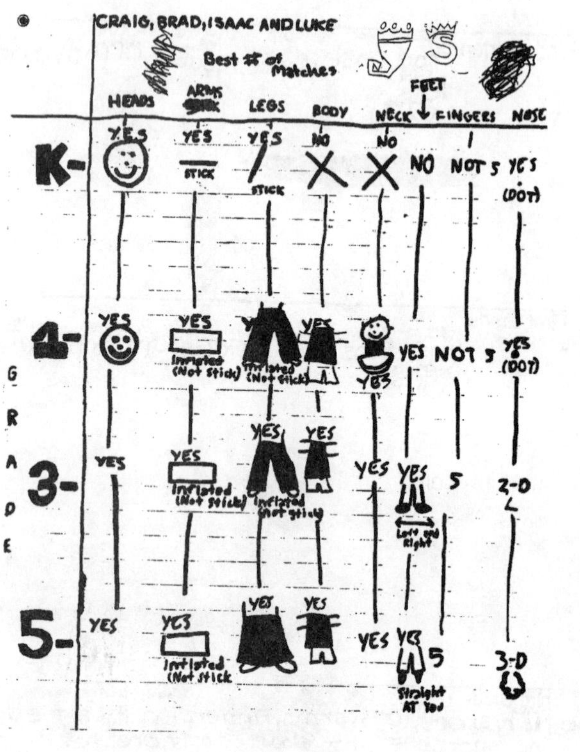

(b)

level) were very difficult to see. Although this model worked, it was difficult to compare grade levels with it.

One student objected that there might be a fifth-grader who liked to draw like a kindergartner, or a first-grader who drew pictures with fifth-grade attributes. He was arguing that these variabilities in drawing would mess up the model. Although this objection was not dealt with at this point, it shows that even this early in the task, fifth-graders were aware that not every drawing would necessarily embody all the attributes considered typical of its grade level. The researcher-observer suggested that the students pretend they were programming robots that would use the rules (models) they were generating. As in the fourth grade, the purpose of this suggestion was to help motivate the evaluation/criticism process. Students were also told they would be getting a new set of self-portraits (Set C) when they finished creating the models for Set B and that their model should work successfully in their classification of the drawings in Set C as well.

Rules for Assigning Pictures to Categories

Because children were using each other's models to classify pictures, they noticed early on that some pictures did not exactly fit the models. This led to discussions and even some disagreements about how to classify the pictures that were not clear matches. One student brought up the idea of placing the pictures in the category with the greatest number of matches to attributes. For example, if a portrait matched one out of six attributes in the first grade, three out of six in the third grade, and four out of six in the fifth grade, that portrait would be placed in the fifth-grade pile.

Along the way, students were regularly writing in their journals about what they did as they worked on the task, what they learned, and what they might do next. At each model-revision cycle, groups wrote in their journals, exchanged their revised models, and tested how they worked. Then the class reassembled into a large group and discussed what worked well and what still needed some revision. Students agreed that they liked the use of pictures along with words because the pictures seemed to help clarify what groups were thinking. In addition, students explicitly said that they preferred table models.

Problems were noted as well. For example, students mentioned the difficulty of deciding which grade to place a particular picture in, a problem resolved by counting the greatest number of matches, and noted that occasionally they came across portraits that did not fit any of the grade-level models. Wording was also questioned (e.g., "a basic head shape"). Some groups continued to use relative words such as *some, mostly,* or *not always.* The students considered it a problem that some groups drew pictures with no words to explain them, claiming that it was not always clear what the pictures were meant to represent. Students noticed that the attributes for the third and fifth grades were very similar, making it difficult to distinguish between these grades.

The third and final evolution of one group's model clearly shows the increasing levels of abstraction that children were mastering as they continued with the cycles of application and revision (see Figure 9.10). This final model relies less on pictures (which students judged "too specific") and more on text (which captured in more general language the dimensions that students considered important).

The Emergence of "Big Ideas" in Modeling

Toward the end of instruction on this project, Mark and the researcher-observer had a discussion after class in which they considered the "big ideas" that students might be acquiring at this point in the task. The following points were raised in that discussion:

1. Children's idea of a model had changed. Instead of simply classifying pictures, they were focusing on generating a description of what their eyes were telling them.
2. No longer were children trying to find *the* distinguishing attribute for each grade. Instead, they were concerned with "fitting" *lists* of attributes.
3. Children were developing strategies for combining information. One way was to ignore information that would lead to competing conclusions, but the predominant solution was to count matches.
4. Children were moving away from *particular* examples to *typical* examples.

Figure 9.10. One group's final model (third revision) of data collected on self-portraits across grade levels.

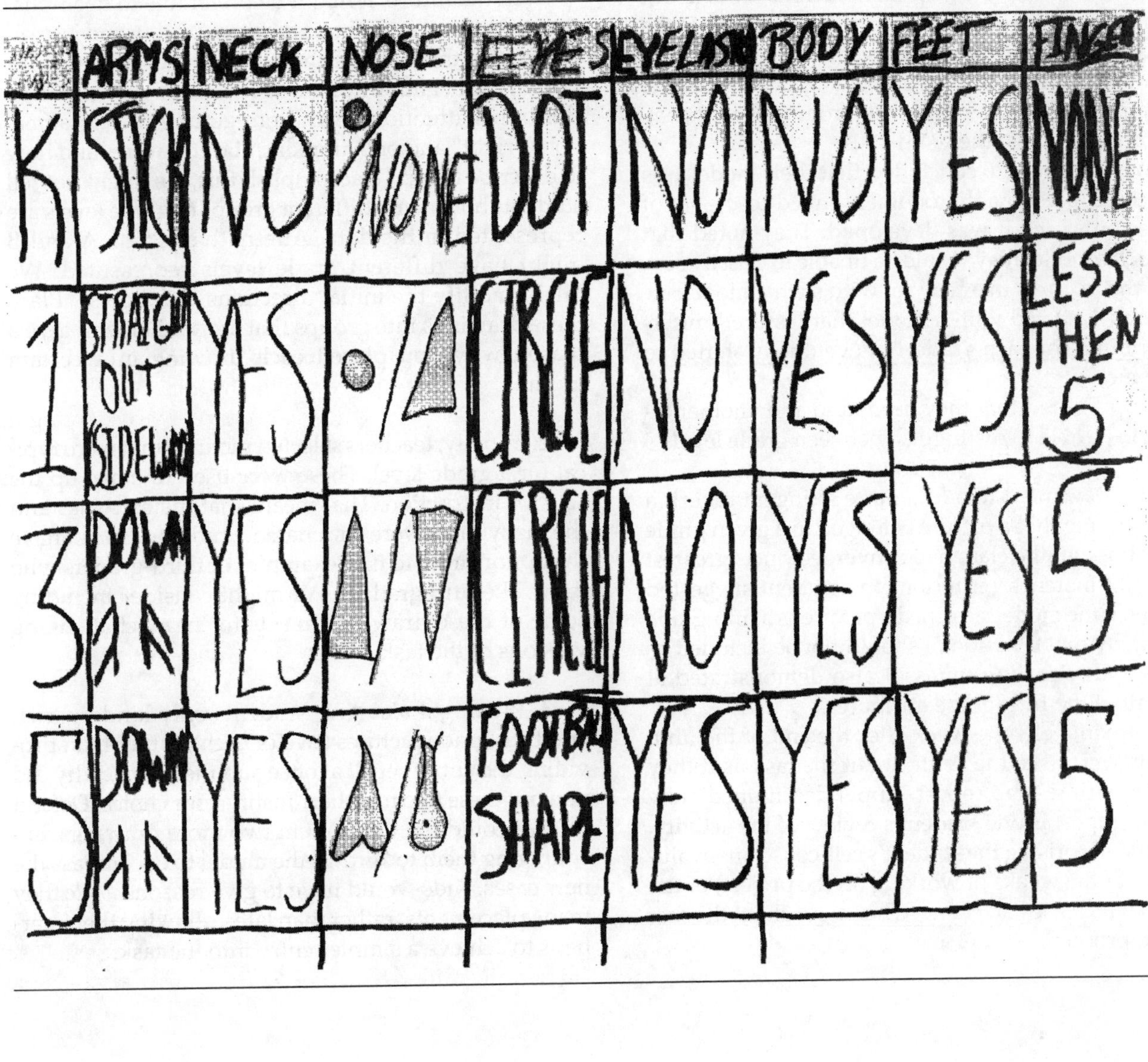

	ARMS	NECK	NOSE	EYES	EYELASH	BODY	FEET	FINGERS
K	STICK	NO	%/NONE	DOT	NO	NO	YES	NONE
1	STRAIGHT OUT SIDEWAYS	YES	•/△	CIRCLE	NO	YES	YES	LESS THEN 5
3	DOWN ↓↑	YES	△/▽	CIRCLE	NO	YES	YES	5
5	DOWN ↓↑	YES	△/▽	FOOTBALL SHAPE	YES	YES	YES	5

In sum, the following big ideas were considered central to this task: data structure, tables and what they are good for, the idea of a model, the concept of combining information, and the concept of typicality.

In the final days of the unit, Mark brought in some real-life examples of data-classification models. One model summarized the criteria (based on their effects) for classifying earthquakes on the Richter scale. The second was a table for comparing the features of several different computer programs designed to achieve similar functions. Students talked through the features and functions of these models and agreed that their own models had similar purposes.

Model Testing

As a final challenge, Mark asked the students to test their newly revised models on a new set of pictures, Set C. Each group independently classified the pictures into grade levels and then recorded the results. These final classifications motivated a final evaluation session, in which students summed up their current ideas about their models. Here are some of the final comments the groups made about their models:

Group 1 noted that they had changed the attribute descriptor under "first-grade feet" from "one with feet, two without" to just the word "yes."

Groups 2, 3, and 6 concluded that their model was too specific, presumably too finely tuned to the set of pictures on which it was developed. They noted that with such a model they would be unable to classify several of the pictures in a new set with such a model.

Group 4 started with a model that featured different attributes for each grade, but eventually shifted to a table model.

Group 5 noted that they needed to add another attribute to be able to distinguish between grade levels 3 and 5.

Group 6 wanted to add a more stringent criterion for concluding that a picture belonged to a given grade level. Although the class had converged on a "greatest number of matches" criterion, one student suggested that even if the model classified a picture as a fifth-grade drawing by that criterion, it should not be included as a fifth-grade drawing unless it also demonstrated at least half of the fifth-grade attributes.

Approximately one week after the end of the unit, students were asked to write about the task as if they were preparing a lab report. Appended immediately after this report is one student's review of the activity. We found surprising the student's self-conscious evaluation (over the weeks of working on the project) of the ways in which she had changed her mind about the best ways to proceed.

Summary: Fifth Grade

Over the three rounds of revision, the fifth-graders shifted from simply thinking of and listing attributes that they found in each grade to developing structures that were progressively more model-like. This process involved greater abstraction of the data, probably based on the need to justify to other groups what they had selected for inclusion in the model, and why. Students began by relying on uninformative phrases such as "good hair" and "bigger than" and progressed to two-dimensional models organized as tables. Over successive cycles of revision, the table models became more diagnostic, as students eliminated descriptors that did not do "any work" and settled on criteria both for combining information and deciding into which of several alternative classifications a picture would fit.

POSSIBLE MODIFICATIONS TO THE TASK

1. In the future, it might be preferable to deemphasize grade level as the basis for classification and instead emphasize the features shared by sets of drawings, at least at the beginning of the task. This might help focus children's attention away from getting the classifications "right" and onto thinking about features and how to describe them. To accomplish this, we might not tell students how many different groups or grade levels are represented in the data. Alternatively, Sets A and B might have different grade levels represented. We might modify the initial directions as follows: "Place these drawings into groups that are similar, and give a reason why you placed each drawing in a certain group."

2. Initially, teachers selected pictures that were typical for a grade level. These were used to make up the sets for instruction. That meant that the extremes and the fuzzy cases were eliminated. Students did not have the opportunity to find examples of third-graders who drew like fifth-graders. We might consider including some of these drawings in sets for more challenging versions of the task.

3. We might also give students only kindergarten and fifth-grade pictures (two of each), rather than providing the entire set all at once and then ask, "Why did you put these two together? Justify your choice. Defend it." We could then give them two more drawings, encouraging them to "grow" the model to encompass the new cases. Kids would have to give reasons *while* they made placements, rather than later, allowing them perhaps to achieve a simpler entry into the task.

4. It might be possible to use Venn diagrams to make the categorization more explicit. For example, within the kindergarten drawings, we might classify features as "No Hair," "No Neck," and "No Clothes" (see Figure 9.11a). If we considered these classes together, we might get the intersecting set shown in Figure 9.11b. If a drawing could be placed into overlapping areas on the Venn diagrams, it would more likely be a kindergarten drawing. If it "belonged" in the centermost area (the area where all three circles overlap), the drawing would almost certainly be one drawn by a kindergartner.

The criterion that the older groups devised for placement was that a drawing fit in the category with the "most number of matches." This is a difficult idea for younger children. They may be helped by a visual

model (e.g., a Venn diagram). They might also need to be reminded that each drawing needs to be tested for every grade level.

5. It might be interesting to let the students have more time to explore some of their original ideas that do not directly lead to the idea of a dimensional model. For example, some kids had a strong feeling that the "level of detail" might be a good predictor of grade level. We never really let them go very far with that. The following are additional interesting questions that might be investigated as well:

- Why don't first-graders draw details? Do they notice them?
- If we ask younger children to evaluate the drawings of older children, do the drawings of the younger children then begin to incorporate some of the features that they noticed in the older children's drawings?
- The last question might be investigated further by avoiding the necessity that younger children actually do the drawings by hand. For example, do their drawings show more sophistication if they use computer drawing programs (which do not require sophisticated motor skills and that modularize some of the difficult features for them)?

Figure 9.11. Using Venn Diagrams to make categorization of self-portraits more explicit: (a) categories considered separately; (b) categories/classes considered together.

6. It would be interesting to see what notations children themselves invent for recording attributes of the drawings. We suspect that the notational systems we provided influenced the way they thought about the task. Of course, time is always limited, but in the future it might be interesting to see how they generate, evaluate, and agree on solutions to this problem.

7. For younger children, it might be preferable to start with a three-part model, including younger, middle, and older grades rather than all four grades, as in the current task. (Older grades may find this version too easy).

(a)

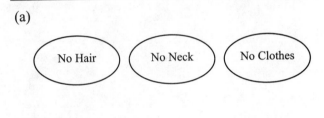

(b)

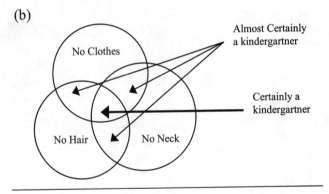

Appendix

Sample Student Report Written on a Computer

Introduction

Hi! My name is Katie Foster, and today I'd like to talk about my project on classification and models (charts). Actually, my whole class is working on this project. We have a bunch of drawings made by kids in kindergarten, first grade, third grade, and fifth grade. Each picture shows a house that is near and a house that's far away. The question that I would like to answer is as follows: Can you make a model that can classify each house picture according to the grade of its artist? I got in a group with two other girls and we decided to find out. I think that when another group tries to use our model to classify the pictures they will get about 7 out of 12 correct. Of course, that's just a guess, and I have no way to tell if I'm right or not. Read on to find out how I answer my question.

Procedure

First of all, to answer my question my group made a model that shows the different attributes that each grade displays in their drawings (The drawings' attributes are the characteristics they show.). To make our chart we needed pencils, an eraser, a large sheet of paper, markers, the drawings, and our minds. We received the pictures and sorted them according to their grade level using our eyes. Then we were told the real grade that each drawing came from. Before we started our chart we listed all the attributes that each grade's drawings showed. For example, we listed "no background," "one small detail (window, door, etc.)," and a few other things under "kindergarten." We decided to make our model be a list of attributes in a table format. There would be different picture attributes shown for each grade. I remembered from a previous discus-

sion our class had that a model that showed different attributes for each grade worked pretty well. We had been doing something similar to this except we were using self-portraits instead of house drawings.

Next, we drew in the graph on the big paper (after some discussion about how many columns to make). Down the side of our model we wrote "K" for kindergarten, "1" for first grade, "3" for third grade, and "5" for fifth grade. Across the top we wrote "Attribute 1," "Attribute 2," and so on, all the way to "Attribute 6." Then we copied down our list of attributes into the boxes of our chart. We had to think of a few more attributes for some of the grades.

We collected our data by switching models with another group. Using the new models, each group had to try to classify, or group, the drawings according to the grade that the model said they were in.

After a while we shared as a class how well each model worked. The group that had our model said that our model was pretty good, but it took along time to use. They said that because you have to read through everything, it took a while. Since the group with our model didn't finish using it, we only know that of the pictures they sorted they got three correct. After the discussion we got a chance to revise our model. My group didn't really know what to do. The other group simply told us that our model was too slow. They didn't tell us any other things that we could improve on. So we just changed a little of the wording on our model. Next, we sorted the pictures again, but this time we used our own model and there was a new set of drawings. Each of us would take a picture and figure out what grade it's from and take another picture. When we were done, we counted up the number we got right (the correct grades of the pictures were on the chalkboard). Our model got 14 out of 20 pictures right.

Results

My results told me that I couldn't make a perfect model. Although 14 out of 20 is pretty good. Our model did a bit better than I expected it to. When I compared 7/12, my guess, with 7/10 (14/20 in lowest terms), I could see that we got more right than I had guessed.

New Directions

There are some things that we could change about our model to make it more accurate. For one thing we had a lot of words in the model. I've found that the more words and details you put in your model the more specific to one set of drawings it will be. Another thing we could do is to make sure we don't have any words that might be confusing (I know we have a few of those in our model.). Words that can be confusing are ones like "usually" or "some." For example, "some" could be confusing because it can mean a lot, a little, or anything in between. If a model uses that kind of words, it can be hard to understand and use.

There are also some new experiments we could do with models. For one thing we could add drawings from second- and fourth-grade artists. Another thing we could do is have more pictures to work with. Then it would be more of a challenge to find attributes that fit all of the drawings.

There are some things that we should have done in this experiment. I think it would have been better if both sets of drawings had the same number of pictures in them. Then it would have been easier to compare my guess to my results. We also should have had one more chance to revise and test our models. I think we could make a better chart. I'm sure many other things could be done with models as well.

Acknowledgments

I would like to thank Mr. Rohlfing and Mr. Lehrer for telling me how to do the project. I would also like to thank Angela and Cathy, the girls in my group. Without these people I couldn't have done this project.

Index

About the Editors and the Contributors

Richard Lehrer, Professor of Educational Psychology at the University of Wisconsin-Madison, regards education as a design science, in which the design of learning environments and the study of student learning are pursued in close coordination. Rich is particularly interested in the long-term development of children's mathematical reasoning when the terrain of mathematics is expanded to include measurement, geometry, and data modeling throughout the elementary grades. His research with Leona Schauble focuses on how children learn to participate in, and appreciate the differences between, mathematical and scientific practices. He currently co-leads a coalition of mathematicians and educators who are developing a national research agenda on children's understanding of data and statistics.

Leona Schauble, Professor of Educational Psychology at the University of Wisconsin-Madison, has studied learning in schools and in informal learning environments, such as museums and broadcast television. A particular interest is the long-term development of scientific reasoning. For the past 8 years, Leona has been working with Richard Lehrer on classroom investigations of model-based reasoning, trying to understand the resources and challenges that young children bring to the table as they attempt to appropriate disciplinary forms of thinking and reasoning.

Jennie Clement has been teaching in the Verona School District since 1988. She has been working with colleagues and researchers since 1992 to explore how young children develop understanding of space and geometry and more recently as a member of the Modeling in Mathematics and Science Collaborative.

Carmen Curtis has taught second and third graders in Verona, Wisconsin since 1986. For more than 10 years she has collaborated with colleagues and researchers to explore how young children develop ways of thinking about shape, measurement, and data. She has served as a teacher coordinator for the Modeling in Mathematics and Science Program for much of the past 5 years

Erin DiPerna taught second and third grade for 5 years while participating in the Modeling in Math and Science Project. During that time, she received her Masters in Cognitive Psychology. Erin is now living in Pennsylvania and stays home full-time with her two children.

Jean Gavin began her teaching career in 1990 and has taught at grade levels 1–5, including multiage, since that time. She entered the Modeling in Math and Science Project at its inception and continues to pursue her interest in mathematics education.

Nancy D. Giles is a project assistant at the Waisman Center at the University of Wisconsin-Madison and a dissertator in the human development area of the Department of Educational Psychology at UW. She has taught human development courses at UW-Madison and at the University of West Florida. Her research interests span cognitive development and teaching, learning, and motivation. Her dissertation focuses on teachers' efforts to both assist and challenge students' learning and on the interplay of teacher and student knowledge, strategies, and dispositions. She received a B.A. in journalism from the University of North Texas and an M.A. in psychology from UWF.

Sally Hanner has taught several grades at Country View Elementary School in Verona, WI and has a strong interest in the growth and development of student reasoning in mathematics and science.

Eric James teaches a multi-age first- and second-grade class at Country View Elementary School and has worked with the Modeling in Mathematics and Science Collaborative since its inception.

Deborah Lucas teaches sixth-grade math, science, social studies, and language arts in an urban school in Madison, WI. Her 16 years have included both elementary and middle school experiences. She is interested in helping students develop and appreciate distinctions among literacies in language, mathematics, and science.

Angie Putz has been a primary elementary teacher challenging children's thinking for the past 17 years in Wisconsin and Minnesota. She has a strong interest in broadening the scope of children's mathematics education to

include data, space, and geometry. She earned her masters degree in educational psychology at the University of Wisconsin-Madison while participating in the Modeling in Mathematics and Science Collaborative.

Mark Rohlfing has been teaching grades four, five, and six since 1988. He is currently teaching sixth grade in Verona, Wisconsin, specializing in math, science, and technology integration.

Susan Wainwright has been teaching elementary children for 28 years. She was involved in the Modeling in Mathematics and Science Program for educators for 5 years. Her masters degree is in Curriculum and Instruction from the University of Wisconsin-Madison.